D1558990

Northwest Vista College
Learning Resource Center
3535 North Ellison Drive
San Antonio, Texas 78251

New Deal Theater

New Deal Theater

The Vernacular Tradition in American Political Theater

Ilka Saal

NEW DEAL THEATER

First published in 2007 by
PALGRAVE MACMILLAN™
175 Fifth Avenue, New York, N.Y. 10010 and
Houndmills, Basingstoke, Hampshire, England RG21 6XS
Companies and representatives throughout the world.

PALGRAVE MACMILLAN is the global academic imprint of the Palgrave Macmillan division of St. Martin's Press, LLC and of Palgrave Macmillan Ltd. Macmillan® is a registered trademark in the United States, United Kingdom and other countries. Palgrave is a registered trademark in the European Union and other countries.

ISBN-13: 978–1–4039–7801–1
ISBN-10: 1–4039–7801–8

Library of Congress Cataloging-in-Publication Data is available from the Library of Congress.

A catalogue record for this book is available from the British Library.

Design by Newgen Imaging Systems (P) Ltd., Chennai, India.

First edition: November 2007

10 9 8 7 6 5 4 3 2 1

Printed in the United States of America.

Für Annegret und Peter Saal

Contents

Acknowledgments

There are several individuals and institutions that helped this book come to fruition. I would like to acknowledge the generous research support of the University of Richmond and the German Academic Exchange Service (DAAD). I would, furthermore, like to thank the faculty at the John F. Kennedy Institute for North American Studies at the Freie Universität Berlin and, in particular, the library staff of the institute for providing me with an academic home during my research in Berlin. I am also much indebted to Elke Pfeil of the Brecht Archive at the Akademie der Künste Berlin, to the staff of the Performing Arts Reading Room at the Library of Congress and of the Theatre Collection at the New York Public Library, and to Jeri Townley of Interlibrary Loan Services at the Boatwright Library of the University of Richmond.

Reingard Nethersole, John Marx, Drew Eisenhauer, Matthew Allen, Thomas Claviez, Stefan Brandt, Gerhard Wolf, and Ori Belkind have read parts of the manuscript at various stages of the project. Their astute comments and provocative questions have greatly contributed to giving this book its final shape—my warmest thanks to all of you! Special thanks also to Bernhard Malkmus for his enduring support and good cheer as well as to my friend Johanna Hofer for designing a wonderful cover image for this book.

Finally, my deepest gratitude goes to my friends in Richmond, Atlanta, New York, Toronto, Leipzig, and Berlin as well as to my family for supporting me in a myriad of ways throughout this endeavor.

Portions of chapters one and two have appeared in the essay "Vernacularizing Brecht: The Political Theater of the New Deal," in *Interrogating America through Theatre and Performance*, ed. William Demastes. New York and London: Palgrave Macmillan, 2006.

Prologue

When in the fall of 1935 Bertolt Brecht attempted to transfer his concept of political theater to the United States, he was faced with two dilemmas: his American colleagues had no idea what epic theater was, and, more importantly, they had no interest in it. Brecht's encounter with the professional leftist stage ended in a spectacular scandal: Theatre Union, New York's foremost proletarian theater of the time, which had agreed to a production of his epic play *The Mother*, kicked him and co-author Hanns Eisler out of rehearsals. With this drastic gesture weeks of mutual recriminations came to a halt, weeks during which Theatre Union had become increasingly annoyed with Brecht's and Eisler's insistence on principles of epic theater, while the two authors had likewise renounced all efforts to adapt the play for American audiences with colorful German invectives. Although Theatre Union proceeded unperturbed by further interventions, the final production flopped. All attempts of translating the play for American audiences, notwithstanding, the critics resisted precisely the few remaining alienation effects, dismissing the play as simply "too German in form and spirit."[1] Not surprisingly, the general public failed to carry the production, thereby shutting down the first attempt of staging epic theater in the United States.

Theater scholars have given little thought to what might have prompted the fall-out between Brecht, Eisler, and Theatre Union. Morgan Himmelstein laconically remarked, "He had had two chances. [. . .] So much for Brecht."[2]—So much for Brecht? Given the fact that by 1935 Brecht had already secured his reputation as Weimar's leading young playwright, such quick dismissal seems rash at best. Moreover, considering the liberal climate of Roosevelt's New Deal and the increasing visibility and influence of committed art in the public sphere at the time, it is rather surprising that a play that only three years earlier had captured audiences in Berlin should now fail in New York. Theatre Union's political agenda was, furthermore, not that dissimilar from Brecht's, aiming to represent "deep-going social conflicts, the economic, emotional and cultural problems that confront the majority of people."[3] So what went wrong with Brecht on Broadway?

A closer reading of the production reveals that the fall-out between Brecht and Theatre Union had little to do with personal disagreement but with a profound discrepancy in the aesthetic conception of political theater. While Brecht insisted that critical thinking and political agency could be brought about only by *alienating* the spectator from the stage, Theatre Union believed that *empathy* was indispensable to the successful political education of the audience. What was at stake then in the argument over the New York *Mother* is precisely the question of what form is most expedient to the political mobilization of a broad public. Brecht and Theatre Union offered very different, even antithetical solutions to this question: one anchored in European modernism, the other in American mass culture. Their encounter therefore presents us with a compelling case study in political theater, for it succinctly poses what Fredric Jameson describes as "the dilemma of form and public—shared and faced by both modernism and mass culture, but 'solved' in antithetical ways."[4]

While the modernist approach to political theater is fairly well known, the mass cultural approach has seen little investigation to date.[5] And yet, it was just this alternative tradition of political theater which upstaged Brecht in 1935 as well as one year later his colleague Erwin Piscator.[6] In the ensuing discussion, I shall examine the aesthetics and politics of the American political theater of the time. I will show that the leftist stages of the New Deal solved the dilemma of form and public by persistently *vernacularizing* the political issues at hand—that is, by translating them into a language commensurate with the cultural experience of a broad public steeped in mass culture. With this, the New Deal theater took a distinctly different aesthetic turn than its modernist counterpart in Europe: emphasizing absorption over alienation, verisimilitude over abstraction. Whereas modernist directors insisted on the sharp break with existing traditions, conventions, and institutions of bourgeois art, the proponents of a vernacular praxis of political theater worked with those very conventions and venues that the former so vehemently rejected.

Although such vernacularization might be easily dismissed as at best politically naïve and at worst inherently reactionary by the dominant, Frankfurt School–inflected analysis of political theater, it nevertheless proved to be effective in the context of the American left's attempt of building a broad Popular Front in support of Roosevelt's New Deal and against fascism and war—a success that cannot be assessed through a merely Brechtian or Adornian reading of its aesthetics. The failure of Brecht on Broadway thus not only points to the cultural contingency of models of political theater, but it also reveals the existence of a vital alternative tradition of political art, one that has so far largely been ignored in theater histories.

This revision of political theater is long overdue in Theater Studies, where political theater is conventionally assessed in modernist terms and the vernacular model is largely effaced from theater histories due to its lack of a contentious aesthetics. American Studies, by contrast, has discussed New Deal theater in a number of publications, most of them dating from the 1960s. Daniel Aaron's *Writers on the Left* (1961), Gerald Rabkin's *Drama and Commitment* (1964), Eberhard Brüning's *Das amerikanische Drama der dreißiger Jahre* (1966), and Malcolm Goldstein's *The Political Stage* (1974) were groundbreaking in mapping New Deal culture. Their focus of analysis, however, lies squarely on content, investigating political theater merely to the extent to which it reflects the widespread social commitment of the period. These studies fail to examine the function of form in political theater, let alone to differentiate between modernist and vernacular approaches. Ira Levine's study *Left-Wing Dramatic Theory in the American Theatre* (1980), by contrast, represents a first attempt at analyzing the aesthetics of American political theater against the background of ongoing political and cultural change.[7]

In the 1990s, there have been two fresh approaches to the leftist culture of the New Deal: Barbara Foley's *Radical Representations* (1993) breaks up the established dichotomy of realism versus modernism by showing that although realism informed much of the cultural productions of the time, it was not a rigidly defined doctrine but remained open to innovation and experimentation. Michael Denning's seminal study *The Cultural Front* (1997) shows how leftist culture of the 1930s emerged out of the collaborative effort of various forces: immigrant workers and European émigrés, modernist artists and union organizers, labor organizations, private enterprise, and government institutions alike. Together they created a vibrant leftist culture that amalgamated the high and the low, the modern and the traditional, the auratic and the mass produced—a culture that helped to consolidate plebeians and patricians into a strong Popular Front. While Foley's work focuses on fiction and Denning's on cultural production in general (using some theater performances for examples), both studies open up a space for theorizing vernacular political theater outside the dominant modernist paradigm of the Frankfurt School— that is, by examining the period from the point of view of popular agency in the production and reception of performances.[8]

My book builds on the works of Levine, Foley, and Denning. It sketches out the various cultural vectors that promoted the emergence of a vibrant vernacular political theater tradition in the United States in the 1930s and shows not only to what extent these vectors determined the aesthetic theory and praxis of political theater but also how the vernacular theater effectively used these aesthetics in the consolidation of a heterogeneous public against capitalist exploitation, racism, fascism, and war. I also explain why an exclusively modernist approach (like that of Brecht) was doomed to fail in this particular cultural moment.

On the New Deal stage, the vernacular approach had two clear advantages over a modernist one. First, in appropriating the aesthetics of the middlebrow—the new cultural force that in merging the high and the low, art and commerce, collapsed long-entrenched cultural distinctions—the vernacular theater straddled barriers of taste, education, and class alike, in this manner reaching out to a wide and diverse public. Moreover, the middlebrow emphasis on accessibility, absorption, and visceral gratification enabled vernacular political theater to tease out the moment of pleasure in the political, which it deemed crucial for facilitating the identification of audiences with the political issues at hand. In seeking to make the political pleasurable and palatable, the vernacular theater of the New Deal often appealed to its spectators above all as consumers (sublimating class distinctions in the ideal of a shared consumer identity). I will show that in emulating the aesthetics of the middlebrow, leftist theaters of the New Deal struck a precarious alliance with the culture industry, which was not always beneficial to leftist politics. At the same time, the vernacular approach to political theater allowed New Deal theaters to emphasize and rehearse the cult of the common person, which has marked American literature and culture since its inception. Employing the trope of the common man, New Deal theater reaffirmed the revolutionary heritage of the country and professed its faith in the perfectibility of American capitalism through the joined effort of the common people. This cultural nationalism was intimately tied to the consumer aesthetics of the middlebrow.

In the subsequent chapters, I shall examine the cultural context, aesthetic strategies, political effects, and historical trajectory of the vernacular tradition in American political theater as well as its relevance for contemporary theater praxis. As we approach this study of New Deal theater, we should remember that leftist culture during the 1930s was also mass culture, which means that at its time of production, vernacular political theater was far from being marginalized. Its peripheral status was retroactively bestowed by generations of scholars convinced that it did not merit the attention of European modernist performance. If my book takes on the appearance of a salvage operation, then it does so in the context of a critical heritage that has made necessary the paradoxical effort of recovering work that in its day significantly shaped American culture.

Brecht's experience on Broadway was symptomatic for the period since it so succinctly reveals the profound discrepancy at the heart of political theater. As such, I treat it as a point of departure for reconsidering political theater in the New Deal era as a whole. In chapter one, I will show how Theatre Union systematically vernacularized Brecht's epic drama *Mother* by retranslating it into the very conventions of bourgeois drama (stage illusionism, empathy, catharsis), which Brecht had sought to undermine in his sparse "non-Aristotelian" version. I will show how the shift from epic to naturalist dramaturgy had profound political implications. Brecht's encounter with the American leftist theater thus not only presents us with a crucial aesthetic disjunction at the heart of political theater, but it also challenges us to reconsider our definition of the political in political theater.

In chapter two, I propose a genealogy of political theater that can help us explain its two different, and largely antithetical, strands—that is, the emergence of a modernist and a vernacular praxis. I argue that due to the lack of a formative historical avant-garde movement on the American stage, the hegemony of realism and naturalism and with it the intrinsic commodity character of the American theater had by the 1930s never been systematically challenged. New Deal theater hence lacked the strong suspicion of and vehement opposition to bourgeois commodity culture typical of its modernist colleague. Rather, it abundantly employed forms of popular and mass culture in an effort of reaching out to diverse audiences. In the United States, this vernacular praxis was further enhanced by the revival of a strong discourse of cultural nationalism during the New Deal. Insisting on the experience of the common man, leftist theaters evoked the democratic traditions of American nationhood and nation-building, asserting their faith that political change can be effected through the electoral process. We shall see that the vernacular theater of the New Deal was therefore mostly reformatory rather than revolutionary in its politics, upholding a firm belief in the perfectibility of capitalism in the interest of the common consumer.

Chapter three traces the influence of the amateur workers' theater movement of the early 1930s on the professional theaters that shaped leftist culture in the second half of the decade. Using the example of the Group Theatre's landmark production of Clifford Odets's *Waiting for Lefty*, I argue that while the professional theater absorbed some of the agitprop techniques of the amateur troupes, it shrewdly integrated them with the realist conventions of bourgeois theater. Such amalgamation enabled a play like *Waiting for Lefty* to be successful with working- and middle-class audiences alike. The shift toward realism in the portrayal of characters and situations became more and more pronounced during the second half of the 1930s, especially with the endorsement of the doctrine of "revolutionary realism" at the American Writers' Congress in April 1935. *Waiting for Lefty* anticipated this shift in aesthetics by incorporating it in its very form. The shift toward realism, moreover, went hand in hand with a shift in audience. Underneath its proletarian rhetoric and call for revolution, *Waiting for Lefty* was profoundly petit bourgeois, addressing the anxieties of an impoverished middle class for whom the economic recession had brought about a profound crisis of political identity.

Chapter four returns to a more extensive discussion of the aesthetics and politics of Theatre Union, America's foremost workers' theater of the period. As Brecht's epic drama failed, its own proletarian melodramas—*Peace on Earth* (1933), *Stevedore* (1934), and *Black Pit* (1935)—were very successful. The genre of melodrama proved to be particularly useful for developing a populist leftist aesthetics that would appeal to organized and unorganized workers as well as middle-class audiences alike, since it allowed for combining a clear political argumentation with the emotional fervor and visceral appeal that would arouse even the more conservative spectators. Theatre Union coped with such inherent genre limitation as the formulaic return to a previous social order by combining the promise of revolutionary change with the affirmation of the country's revolutionary legacy, thereby also translating class struggle into democratic continuity. Yet, in the process of developing the genre of proletarian melodrama, the theater also began to shift its emphasis from emotive speech and action-driven plot to the photo-mimetic realism of character and situation.

Theatre Union's rapprochement with bourgeois realism was indicative of the general cultural reorientation of the American left in mid decade. At the First American Writers' Congress in April 1935, the gradual "popular turn" of the American left in aesthetics and politics became most evident. As it replaced capitalism with fascism as its political opponent, and as the Communist Party transformed its battle cry from "Towards a Communist America!" to "Communism is 20th century Americanism," the political theater increasingly turned to the conventions of bourgeois drama. Concurrently, it replaced collective class struggle as the dominant paradigm of social conflict with the worker's individual struggle of securing decent living conditions and protecting his family. As the subsequent congress of 1937 showed most clearly, the general thrust of leftist cultural critique was no longer the dismantling of an exploitative capitalist system but the defense of liberal democracy against the looming threat of fascism.

Chapter five deals with three late examples of New Deal theater: Marc Blitzstein's proletarian opera *The Cradle Will Rock* (1937), the Living Newspaper of the Federal Theatre Project (1936–1938), and the labor revue *Pins and Needles* (1937). While engaging in some modernist experimentation, all three productions nonetheless remained firmly embedded in a vernacular aesthetics with regards to their audience approach. They appealed to a broad Popular Front and particularly middle-class audience. *The Cradle Will Rock* effectively combined the metaphoric evocation of strike and unionism with middle-class satire and sentimental lament by way of urging the middle class to a political realignment with the working class in support of industrial unionism and in defense against fascist tendencies at home. With issues like *One Third of a Nation* (1938), the Living Newspaper likewise endorsed a liberal ideology. Targeting the American common man—who incidentally is also the common consumer—the Living Newspaper appealed to its spectators' national democratic as well as liberal consumer consciousness, aiming to elicit their support for government reforms. *Pins and Needles* similarly spoke to the consumer identity of its spectators when it presented its moderate political satire as a spectacle of consumption. Imitating the grand Broadway follies of the 1920s, the labor revue suggested that consumption itself was the solution to the economic crisis, that the aches of capitalism could be remedied in the affirmation of such essential characteristics as drive, optimism, and abundance. However, as the show became increasingly commodified for Broadway, it lost its amateur origins along with its progressive labor stance. In that regard, *Pins and Needles* also points up the limits of a vernacular praxis of political theater.

Chapter six, finally, traces the evolution of vernacular and modernist political theater to the contemporary period. I here focus chiefly on the 1960s, arguing that during this cultural moment the amalgamation and transformation of the two older traditions finally became possible. Not only did the period witness the renaissance of political theater, but in their attempt to break with the hegemony of Broadway realism and to unsettle the cultural and political status quo, artists turned to their modernist predecessors of the 1920s and 1930s: they discovered the ritual force of Artaud's theater of cruelty, and they began to study Brecht's theories of alienation. Epic theater, along with other models of modernist interventions, was no longer considered a foreign irritant but a source of inspiration and potential renewal. In this regard, the sixties avant-garde took a very different approach to the dilemma of public and form than its New Deal predecessor. As political theater artists revived a modernist praxis, they sought to bring it into a productive alliance with mass culture—the second main source of inspiration for sixties artists. In the example of El Teatro Campesino and the Bread and Puppet Theater, I will show how the two theater groups effected such alliance, and how, in the process, they transformed our previous understanding of both a modernist and a vernacular praxis of political theater. In fact, so I argue, in the political theater of the 1960s the great divide of modernism and mass culture disappeared. Its disappearance paved the way for the emergence of a postmodernist praxis of political theater.

Chapter One

Brecht on Broadway: Reconsidering Political Theater

Bertolt Brecht's encounter with the American political theater in 1935 points us to a profound aesthetic discrepancy at the heart of political theater by revealing the existence of a vital, non-modernist tradition of articulating a leftist cultural critique. Theatre Union's adaptation of his epic drama *The Mother* evinces the characteristics that were typical for many New Deal productions and can therefore be considered emblematic of the predominant leftist aesthetics of the time. The visible clash of its vernacular aesthetic with Brecht's inherent modernist approach in the final production of *Mother*, moreover, triggered ardent debates among leftist critics over the form and function of political art in the United States—discussions that were to shape other New Deal productions as well. For these reasons, I deem Brecht's experience with leftist Broadway crucial to understanding the praxis of New Deal theater as a whole as well as the cultural logic of its time. In what follows, I shall examine the aesthetics and politics of Theatre Union's production of Brecht's play more closely. Besides playing out the conflict between the two conceptions of political theater, I will also consider what kind of questions this encounter poses for our understanding of political theater as such.

Vernacularizing Brecht

The Mother: The Life of the Revolutionary Pelagea Vlassova of Tver (1932), an adaptation of Maxim Gorky's celebrated *Bildungsroman* of 1906, represents Brecht's first full-length epic drama and as such a significant step in his formulation of a non-Aristotelian dramaturgy.[1] With this, Brecht meant to launch a frontal attack against what he perceived to be the pillars of bourgeois theater: identification and absorption. These, so he held, essentially seduced the spectator into complicity with the ruling ideology, effectively preempting critical thinking and political action. To rid the theater of this attitude,

Brecht proposed drastic measures: if theater was to provide its audience with what he liked to call "a workable picture of the world" ("ein praktikables Weltbild"), then empathy had to be given up.[2] "Once illusion is sacrificed to free discussion, and once the spectator, instead of being enabled to have an experience, is forced as it were to cast his vote," Brecht insisted, "then a change has been launched which goes far beyond formal matters and begins for the first time to affect the theatre's social function."[3]

Brecht's solution to the task of moving the audience from empathy to discussion was *Verfremdung* (alienation). Here, it is important to remember that for Brecht *Verfremdung* represented not just an innovative aesthetic effect in the spirit of modernist experimentation but entailed an entire political program. Besides considering it his main strategy of shutting down empathy, Brecht also saw in it a means of creating a distance between actor and character as well as stage and audience (distantiation), of defamiliarizing or estranging the ordinary and familiar (in the spirit of the Formalist concept of *ostranenie*), and, finally, of depicting characters and situations in their historical contingency and thus as subject to change (historicization).[4] As Fredric Jameson emphasizes, the purpose of *Verfremdung* is an entirely political one; it is "to make you aware that the objects and institutions you thought to be natural were really only historical, the result of change, they themselves henceforth become changeable."[5] In short, alienation is the crucial aesthetic function in Brecht's epic dramaturgy, which is to perform a specific political role, namely "to hand the world over to [the workers'] minds and hearts, for them to change as they think fit."[6] It is in the context of this aesthetic *and* political program that we have to read Brecht's adaptation of Gorky's novel. Designing *Die Mutter* as "a piece of anti-metaphysical, materialistic, non-Aristotelian drama," Brecht had stripped the Gorky original of its naturalist and sentimental overtones and purposely reduced it to what Walter Benjamin called "a sociological experiment concerning the revolutionizing of a mother."[7]

Theatre Union, however, had little interest in presenting its audience with a detached scientific experiment. Their enthusiasm was primarily for Gorky, who had been widely hailed as the father of Soviet literature and whose novel was considered to be the paradigmatic work of socialist realism.[8] What they wanted was a play in the "Western, Ibsen tradition," "a simple story, very human, very warm," and with this goal in mind the theater asked translator Paul Peters to adapt the play for American audiences.[9] Naturally, Peters was disturbed by the fragmentary character of Brecht's text, its "abrupt changes of mood and style and its insufficient dramatization of personal scenes."[10] He began to smooth out scene transitions, to integrate Eisler's songs with the dramatic action, to flesh out dialogues, and to develop the psychology of the protagonists—all with the purpose of getting closer to the Gorky original and of "striving for some kind of identification of prospective audience and stage characters."[11]

In transforming moments of alienation into moments of identification, Peters, of course, went against the very grain of epic theater. Brecht called attention to such profound distortion of his political intention in a series of protest letters to Theatre Union as well as to the American Communist Party (CPUSA), to whom he turned for mediation. "[I]n this matter I cannot give in," he insisted. "The political content of the play cannot be fully expressed in any other form; had I thought differently, I myself would have chosen a different form."[12] He continued to point out that while the New York public was naturally different from the Berlin public, "the adaptation you have sent me, strikes me not as particularly American but as particularly naturalist. [. . .] I am simply sick of the old naturalist play. That works with kerosene lamps but not with electric light."[13] From the start, Brecht and Theatre Union were thus embroiled in profound disagreement—notably, however, not over the militant content of the play but over the form of its American adaptation.

The fundamental aesthetic disjunction between Brecht's and Theatre Union's concept of political theater is most apparent in the two different opening scenes. Peters chooses a classic naturalist opening:

(It is early morning in the kitchen and living room of Pelagea Vlassova. The Mother is cooking soup for her son. Pavel enters from the little adjacent room, buttoning his shirt collar. He carries a book in his hand.)

Pavel: Good morning, mother.
Mother: But, Pavel, it's only five o'clock.
Pavel: I know, mother. I got up early this morning. I've got some work to do.

(He sits down and starts lacing his shoes, meanwhile reading in the book, which he has placed on the table.)

Mother: (looking at him, troubled; then shaking her head.) Work to do! (She goes back to the stove and stirs the soup.) Pavel.
Pavel: (without looking up from his book.) Yes, mother.
Mother: I'm almost ashamed to give you this soup for dinner; it's so thin. But I haven't anything to put in it, Pavel; not a thing in the house. That penny an hour they cut you on your wages last

week: that makes such a difference, Pavel. I skimp and I save, but somehow I just can't make it up. [. . .] Yes, yes, you'll leave one of these days. (She sits down, fretting.) What am I to do, Pavel, what am I to do? I stretch every kopek as far as it will go. I scrape on wood and I skimp on light. I patch and I darn and I save. But it doesn't do any good, Pavel. It doesn't do any good. I don't know what to do.

(Pavel is still reading his book. The Mother gets up and starts to clean the room. She brushes his coat; she dusts the furniture and sweeps the floor.)[14]

Compare this to Brecht's sparse epic beginning:

(Pelagea Vlassova's room in Tver).

Vlassova: I am quite ashamed to offer this soup to my son. But I've no dripping left to put in it, not even half a spoonful. Only last week they cut a kopeck an hour off his wages, and I can't make that up however hard I try. I know how heavy his job is, and how badly he needs feeding up. It is bad that I cannot offer my son better soup; he's young and has barely stopped growing. [. . .] And so he is getting more and more discontented. [. . .] Presently he'll leave me. What am I to do, Pelagea Vlassova, forty-two, a worker's widow and a worker's mother? I count the pennies over and over again. I try it this way and I try it that. One day I skimp on firewood, another day on clothing. But I can't manage. I don't see any answer.

(Her son Pavel has picked up his cap and his container, and left. The Mother tidies the room).[15]

Two crucial differences stand out: First, where Brecht immediately pre-empts all stage illusionism in the direct address of the audience and the radical dismantling of the fourth wall, Peters attempts to secure that very illusion by translating Vlassova's apostrophe into dialogue, dramatic action, and stage setting. Rather than being presented up front as in Brecht, the economic predicament of the family emerges slowly through much maternal fussing. Redirecting the dramatic focus from interaction with the audience to the interaction between characters on stage, Peters effectively eliminates our presence as spectators, banishing us to the keyhole of the little hut in Tver. The aim of such Diderotian relegation to the role of the hidden voyeur is to maximize our absorption in the dramatic action along with our *emotional* investment in it—all this in marked contrast to the *critical* reflection that Brecht seeks to elicit.

Second, the discrepancy between an epic and a naturalist approach to political theater is also apparent in the depiction of the protagonist,

Pelagea Vlassova. Brecht purposely introduces her as a political subject and agent in her own rights ("Pelagea Vlassova, forty-two, a worker's widow and a worker's mother"). Peters, by contrast, portrays her first and foremost as a social type, the apprehensive mother whose agency consists entirely of the constant fretting and fussing over her son. In the end, Vlassova's political maturation will appear to result less from a series of conscious decisions or from growing political awareness than from constant maternal worries. Her final choice to join the proletarian revolution is presented here as the "natural" consequence of working-class motherhood. Without doubt, these dramaturgical decisions largely pre-empt the political lesson at the heart of Brecht's parable by naturalizing and universalizing what Brecht wanted to portray as historical and particular. However, just as Brecht's lesson becomes effaced, another lesson is enabled: dissociated from the politics of concrete socio-economic circumstances, the question of the revolution can now be restated in terms of sentimental family politics.

This brief example already illustrates that the formal shift from epic to naturalist dramaturgy has not merely profound aesthetic but also political consequences. Brecht aims at creating the distance he deems necessary for a primarily rational evaluation of the protagonists' actions. He has in mind an audience of experts who take a partisan yet critical interest in the performance of their actors (preferably cigar in hand), and it is their critical expertise that can forge a bond between stage and audience as well as among spectators, which would ideally endure beyond the walls of the theater and provide a common basis for political action. *Verfremdung* becomes the primary means of encouraging such judicious attitude in the spectator. Theatre Union, by contrast, presumes an audience whose members might not share the same partisan interest in the performance. In order to overcome social and political differences in the audience, it falls back on the sentimental strategy of building up the human appeal of a story ("very human, very warm"). Its dramaturgy is primarily aimed at enlisting the spectators' emotional support for a mother (and not a worker), of involving them in the politics of the play through empathy for her sufferings and struggles. In this manner, it seeks to facilitate access for those spectators to whom the characters and situation might otherwise be entirely foreign, such as spectators of non-proletarian background. A common platform for potential political action rests here completely on the supposition of empathy with the fate of a mother and her family—presumably universal values that transcend class allegiances and ideological viewpoints. In shifting from ideological to emotional argumentation, Peters effectively sentimentalizes the political. This strategic move, however, also suggests an entirely different conception of participatory democracy and political struggle, namely one in which alliances are built primarily on the basis of emotional identification rather than cognitive effort.

Peters's strategic sentimentalization of the political is most evident at the dramatic climax of the play. Pavel's death, for Brecht an important but minor episode in Vlassova's political maturation, becomes for Peters the moment of dramatic and political catharsis. In Brecht, Pavel is shot off-stage, and the chorus of workers reports the incident in its usual matter-of-fact tone: "Comrade Vlassova, your son has been shot."[16] Peters deems it more effective to have Pavel shot and die *on* stage shortly before the end of the play. For this, he devices an entirely new scene, including a brief chase sequence. As the police deposit Pavel's corpse at the mother's feet, the following dialogue unfolds among the neighbors:

> *First Woman*: He spoke the truth, so they killed him.
> *Second Woman*: They shot him because he was for the workers. He was for peace.
> *Third Woman*: Such a fine young man!
> *Second Woman*: What he did was good. It was good! The whole rotten autocracy should be overthrown! (A murmur of assent from everyone.)
> *First Woman*: Don't worry, Pavel. We'll get revenge for you, Pavel. (Cries of assent from everyone.)
> *Inspector*: (returning to the hall with the two police, and closing the door behind him.) Go on back to your holes, you people. Now go on. Get out of here.
> (Low angry murmurs from the crowd as the police start pushing them back. The light dims out in the hallway, as the voice of the first woman rises above the murmur:)
> *First Woman*: It won't be long, Pavel. It won't be long!
> (Within the study the Mother stands looking at her son.)
> *Mother*: (quietly) You hear! What you did was good, Pavel. The workers will revenge you, Pavel. They won't forget. It won't be long now, Pavel. It won't be long. (Blackout.)[17]

Here, Peters falls back on a classic trope of sentimental literature by way of prompting the final conversion of Vlassova and her neighbors: the death of the child.[18] This device allows him once again to plead the case of the Vlassov family on a highly emotional basis. Where Brecht purposely disallows empathy and identification in this scene, Peters builds up its inherent visceral appeal and channels maternal feelings into political commitment. As the mother mourns her son, the chorus of neighbors spells out the moral lesson of Pavel's martyrdom, leaving no doubt as to what ought to be done. Brecht's sparse, sociological experiment in the "revolutionizing of a mother" is here translated into a viscerally stimulating revolutionary melodrama.

In sum, the logic of Peters's sentimental dramaturgy is to secure verisimilitude in the presentation of characters and action by systematically setting up and preserving the illusion of the fourth wall, to facilitate audience identification with the protagonists by sentimentalizing the mother-son relationship, and, finally, to build up dramatic suspense toward an emotional climax finding its release in a moment of revolutionary pathos on and ideally also off-stage. All this is geared toward eliciting the empathy of a broad audience (regardless of social status) for the mother and, by implication, the revolution.

Brecht himself keenly discerned the logic of this approach when he wrote to his American colleagues: "Instead of admiration / You strive for sympathy with the mother when she loses her son. / The son's death / You slyly put at the end. That, you think, is how to make the spectator / Keep up his interest till the curtain falls."[19] Perhaps he even understood that Peters's dramaturgical decisions were less a sign of immaturity or ignorance than of a consistent cultural logic that was deeply embedded in the economic and political processes of the American 1930s.

The sentimental dramaturgy of Theatre Union reflected the awareness of leftist theaters in the United States that they too were dependent on the box office and had to take into account the conditioning of its audiences by the hegemony of naturalism on the commercial stage as well as the consumerist demand that moral/political education be combined with visceral entertainment. In the following chapters, we shall see that Theatre Union's adaptation was, in fact, quite typical for the praxis of leftist professional theaters of the time and in line with larger discussions over the form and public of political art. In the mid-1930s, the radical left, in an effort to build a broad Popular Front, relinquished its former sectarian stance for a more inclusive platform, one that also appealed to the middle classes. Concurrently, we also note an increasing tendency to politicize the spectators by using more conventional forms of representation, which would secure mass appeal.

The conflict between Theatre Union and Brecht over the aesthetics of political theater, already immanent in Peters's textual adaptation, finally erupted during rehearsals. Both Brecht and Eisler considered the staging, directing, and performance of the play a "dilettantish distortion" of their aesthetics and a severe violation of their principal goal of influencing "the working masses politically."[20] Dissatisfied with the strong naturalist inflection of script and production, they continued to demand to be given the opportunity "to shape our play into the political and artistic form it deserves."[21] Their protests were to no avail; if anything they only further alienated the troupe from an epic aesthetics. Theater member George Sklar describes the situation: "In all fairness to Brecht, I must admit that we were impatient with his 'epic theatre' themes. For one thing we were soon so embroiled in differences that we never could sit down and hear him out."[22]

From this and similar comments, it becomes clear that the troupe had only rudimentary knowledge of and, above all, little interest in Brecht's approach to political theater.[23] For them, epic theater boiled down to "non-involvement," and, as Sklar made clear, "Theatre Union wanted a responsive audience, not a frustrated one."[24] In other words, the theater firmly believed that the best way of mobilizing the public was by appealing to their empathy and by revealing the universal human issues at the heart of the political.

In accordance with this logic, it set out to stage the play according to Broadway conventions. Director Victor Wolfson cast the play with Method-trained actors, thereby seeking to tease out the "inner lives" of characters that were simply not conceived along psychological lines.[25] In addition, he insisted on integrating Eisler's song with the dramatic action of the play in the manner of the American musical style. Instead of addressing the audience directly, the chorus was to present its songs to the characters, thereby aiming for a more diegetic and heightened emotional effect. Eisler tried to correct this mistake by explaining patiently to the theater board that epic music did not "express a state of the soul but [was] meant to force the interpreters into a certain attitude, a certain gesture."[26] It therefore had to be presented as an independent part of the production and clearly separated from the action. But it was precisely alienation effects such as these that Wolfson and his team sought to eliminate. As announced in various advertisements by Theatre Union, *Mother* was to be "A Stirring Play with Music."[27]

The result was an odd hybrid of styles, a blend of naturalism and epic theater with a dash of musical and agitprop. The critics noted as much during opening night on 19 November 1935. J. M. Olgin of the communist *Daily Worker* detected "a struggle of two styles," with the realism of Theatre Union often getting into the way of the "special realism required by Brecht."[28] The conservative *New York American* likewise pointed out that the production "divided against itself could not stand."[29] While the emotional acting and naturalist setting invited close audience involvement, the episodic plot as well as alienation effects such as songs and slides persistently kept the audience at a distance.

The majority of critics, however, did not object so much to the unsuccessful blending of two different styles as to the few remaining epic elements. Burns Mantle simply felt cheated "out of a thrill."[30] Wilella Waldorf similarly suggested that the play might be much better off without Eisler's songs, which kept interrupting "a story which was, however you look at it, interesting and often very touching."[31] Arthur Pollock, finally, wondered how far propaganda could spread if the audience was "given nothing at all for their emotions to take hold of."[32] Curiously enough, there seemed to be consensus among bourgeois critics that it was the very task of political theater to sway the political opinion of conservatives like themselves and to do so precisely on the basis of emotional agitation. "It is not the workers who stand in need of conversion," a frustrated Mantle exclaimed, but "it is the likes of you and me the Theatre Union should reach."[33]

Debates on the left, by contrast, showed little concern for the question of who exactly stood most in need of agitation. Instead, leftist reviewers focused their discussion on the question whether Brecht's "special realism" was at all suitable for American audiences. Olgin vehemently objected to the lack of individualization in characters other than the mother, insisting that proletarian drama needed to portray workers and capitalists as "living human beings, men and women of flesh and blood."[34] John Gassner of the workers' journal *New Theatre* complained about the insufficient development of "the dramatic portion—that is, the mother's story."[35] Michael Gold, one of the leading leftist cultural authorities of the time, conceded that *Mother* might be worth seeing "as an example of a stylistic experiment of Germany's most illustrious playwright" but dismissed the play as utterly unsuitable for American audiences.[36] According to him, the American political theater needed more plays of a "dynamic socialist realism, applied to the American scene."[37] Even James T. Farrell of the pro-modernist *Partisan Review* found that Brecht's play evinced "unnecessary revolutionary snobbery."[38]

Such concerns with the alleged lack of realism and Americanism in Brecht's play echoed larger concerns on the American left with the formulation of a native theory of political art. Debates over the form and public of leftist political theater had recently come to a head at the American Writers' Congress in April 1935. As I shall show in greater detail in chapter four, in the course of 1935 the left had begun to adapt its cultural politics to international developments (such as the rise of fascism abroad, the war in Spain, and the directives of the Seventh Congress of the Comintern) by abandoning the militant anti-capitalist stance of the early 1930s for a more inclusive appeal to all liberal and democratic forces. The new goal was to consolidate a broad and heterogeneous public in a united Popular Front. The delegates of the First American Writers' Congress concurred that this goal could best be achieved by creating an easily accessible and viscerally stimulating "revolutionary realism" anchored in American themes and symbols.

Brecht's epic drama, however, still very much reflected the militant spirit of the Weimar Republic (as well as of early New Deal agitprop). It was written under the sign of the impeding proletarian revolution, resolutely calling the workers to armed resistance against an oppressive capitalist system. Yet, by 1935, the revolution was no longer on the agenda of the American left. Instead, it now sought to implement the gradual transformation of capitalism into socialism and to consolidate a Popular Front against fascism and war. By the summer of 1936, even CPUSA insisted that the "life needs of the majority of workers, farmers and middle classes" could be realized "even under the present capitalist system."[39] Given this context, it is not surprising that in the final revolutionary tableau of *Mother*, Theatre Union refused to arm the workers as had been the case in the Berlin production of 1932.

Moreover, in the spirit of Earl Browder's new election campaign ("Communism is 20th century Americanism"), Theatre Union supplemented Brecht's choice of a Marx quote for the proscenium banner ("The history of all hitherto existing society is the history of class struggle") with a quote by Jefferson: "All authority belongs to the people." In this manner, it not only shrewdly Americanized the concept of the revolution, but it also transformed the revolution to come into one that had already taken place, the bourgeois revolution of 1776. With such measures, Theatre Union strove to present itself as a "United Front theatre organized to produce plays that all honest militant workers and middle class sympathizers can support."[40]

Yet, as pointed out earlier, such attempts at mitigating the militant content of the play notwithstanding, the play's main offense remained, as Gorelik put it, "its strange approach in script and form."[41] Its sparse, non-Aristotelian form (regardless of all attempts of naturalizing and Americanizing it) failed to "emotionally overpower" the onlooker and "remain[ed] too distant from his periphery of feeling," as one reviewer succinctly remarked.[42] He added, "After all, at least in this country, we are still instinctively individualistic, rather than collectivistic, and we prefer, subconsciously, our drama in terms of individual strife and conflict and clash."[43] Given this public reception, it is not surprising that the New York production of *Mother* folded prematurely—after only thirty-six performances. Already in early December of 1935, the board informed "Comrade Brecht" of the closing of the play. It explained that while the subscribers of workers' organizations seemed to have liked the play well enough, there had been very little box office sale.[44] Some critics even contend that the flop of *Mother* might have been the decisive factor in the premature closing of Theatre Union in 1937.[45]

Due to his ill-starred encounter with America's leading proletarian theater, Brecht lost much sympathy with the American left. With the notable exceptions of set designer Mordecai Gorelik and agitprop director John Bonn, Brecht was left with few admirers in New York. He subsequently forewarned his German friend and colleague Erwin Piscator "to stay away from the so-called leftist theaters," for they "have the worst 'producer manners' of Broadway, albeit without the latter's know-how."[46] While Brecht stayed away from Broadway, he shortly after had to cope with the producer manners of Hollywood. His collaboration with John Wexley on the script of Fritz Lang's *Hangmen also Die* (1942) evinced similar tensions between his epic principles and the vernacular demands of the American film industry.[47]

Brecht conceded in hindsight that "although wavering in its principles, there was sufficiently left in the New York *Mother* production to qualify it as epic."[48] But, as we have seen, it was precisely this epic quality that prompted it to fail on the American stage. When three months later Piscator's epic drama *Case of Clyde Griffiths* flopped for similar reasons, it was clear that these productions represented more than just botched American debuts—namely the failure of epic theater as such on the New Deal stage. As Clifford Odets, member of the Group Theatre that produced Piscator's play, concluded, "America is not going in Piscator's direction."[49] What he meant was that America was not going in the epic direction—at least not for the time being.

Reconsidering Political Theater

Brecht's encounter with Theatre Union is important not only in that it is symptomatic of the aesthetics of leftist New Deal theaters as well as of larger cultural debates of the period but also in that it allows us to distinguish between two vibrant and competing aesthetic traditions seeking to resolve Jameson's "dilemma of form and public" in antithetical ways: one anchored in European modernism, the other in American mass culture.[50] I am here referring to them as the *modernist* and the *vernacular* praxes of political theater. The conflict of these two traditions, which is so clearly evident in the New York production of *Mother*, raises a number of relevant issues about the aesthetics and function of political theater as such.

First, the competing modernist and vernacular tendencies at play in the New York *Mother* reveal an incompatible understanding of what role distance and absorption, alienation and empathy, *ratio* and *emotio* ought to perform in political theater—a question that continues to occupy theater and cultural studies. These aesthetic differences are also indicative of fundamentally different conceptions of the audience. Like many other New Deal stages, Theatre Union trusted above all in the emotional competence of its spectators. It therefore favored such vernacular forms of theater as naturalism and melodrama, which allowed it to maximize the emotional involvement of its audiences. Through *emotio*, it sought to bridge discrepancies in educational and cultural background as well as political differences and to create a common platform for political action on the basis of empathy. Brecht, like many other European modernists, by contrast, had great faith in the cognitive abilities of the masses. For him, a worker was just as capable of understanding abstraction as an intellectual as long as it provided her with a "workable picture of the world." The key to such pragmatic concept of mimesis was *Verfremdung*. For Brecht, then, it was precisely the shared distance to the dramatic representation and the shared interest in the assessment of its usefulness and practicability that would serve as the basis for the formation of political consciousness and, later, political action.

Related to these considerations is the question of how each theater practice defined the character and purpose of mimesis. Both Brecht and Theatre Union held on to the *imitatio* principle of art, subscribing to some concept of realism that remains anchored in, what Jameson calls, "a form of aesthetic experience which yet lays claim to a binding relationship to the real itself."[51] But at the same time the conflict between Brecht and Theatre Union also evinces a different understanding of the function of realism, even of mimesis as such. For Brecht, realism was never a question of verisimilitude or of proven mimetic principles but of praxis and utility. Any stylistic means, including fragmentation and abstraction, could be used toward realistic ends. As he declared in response to Georg Lukács's attack on the modernist technique of montage, "Art does not become unrealistic by changing the proportions, but by changing them in such a way that if the audience took its representations as a practical guide to insights and impulses it would go astray in real life."[52] For him, realism therefore meant depicting reality in such a manner that it enabled audiences to analyze reality critically. Above all, a work of art became realistic when it was capable of unmasking "the prevailing view of things as the view of those who are in power" and when it expressed the standpoint of the class that could offer the broadest solutions to the problems of humanity.[53]

Theatre Union's attempt of adapting *Mother* in "the Western, Ibsen tradition," however, reveals a very different understanding of realism. In its emphasis on principles of construction and on accessibility to the broad masses, it is very much akin to Lukács's concept of realism. As Lukács made clear in the famous "realism debate" of 1938, he considered realism the only truly progressive and avant-gardistic form of mimesis since it allowed for integrating the artist's subjective experience of reality with a so-called objective social totality in a form that was easily accessible to the reader "without the need for external commentary" and that was readily recognizable as "reality as it truly is."[54] For Lukács, realism was primarily a formal principal of literary production, the blueprint of which he found in nineteenth century bourgeois literature, especially in its signature features of a spontaneous unity of the particular and the general and of the artistic mediation of a sense of immediacy. These very characteristics were also endorsed by the American left, when at the Writers' Congress of 1935 communist playwright John Howard Lawson urged his fellow writers to return to the tradition of the well-made play, to technique "in its most conservative and classical sense."[55]

It is in the spirit of such Lukácsian understanding of realism that we have to read Theatre Union's various attempts of erasing the episodic character of Brecht's text and of integrating Eisler's songs with the dramatic action. Like Lukács, it believed that the organic unity of the final product would increase the accessibility of the play for a large number of spectators by facilitating the translation of the issues presented into the language of the spectator's own experience. Brecht and Eisler, by contrast, never bothered with such formal questions of accessibility assuming that the broad masses would recognize and appropriate that which was useful to them. Hence where Theatre Union's insistence on organic unity emphasized the finished product, Brecht and Eisler stressed the productive process. For them, the final image/word/*Gestus* had to retain the traces of its production so that the alternative to what was presented could be inferred by the spectator.[56] In this manner, Brecht substituted the contemplative pleasure that Lukács's or Theatre Union's ordinary reader/spectator would take in the artistic concealment of contradiction with the cognitive challenge of finding solutions in real life to the contradictions presented on stage.

We thus encounter two very different conceptions of realism along with two incongruent notions of how art can intervene in the social. While for Brecht political struggle is intimately linked to the cognitive struggle stimulated by the heterogeneous character of a work of art, Theatre Union unwittingly endorsed the Lukácsian position that it was the aesthetic pleasure in the organic unity of a finished product that would make the spectator receptive to its political message. It remains to be seen what kind of political struggle can ensue from such different aesthetic foundations. As Lukács makes clear, for him the primary function of realism in the mid-1930s was to make "the soul of the masses" receptive to "the new type of revolutionary democracy that is represented by the Popular Front"[57]—a position that Theatre Union supported as well.

Finally, I want to point out one other problem that arises from the conflict between Brecht and Theatre Union: the question of how to assess these different concepts of political theater. Arguably, the disjunction in the aesthetic conception of political theater is reproduced in the theories we use to assess them. Theater scholars have tended to evaluate the efficacy of political theater in exclusively modernist and Frankfurt School–inflected terms, measuring political value precisely by the degree to which a play attempts to resist what Brecht describes as the culinary principle ("das Kulinarische") and Theodor W. Adorno as the commodity structure at the heart of the bourgeois culture industry. The commodity, however, tends to promote conformity with rather than resistance to the dominant culture. Erika Fischer-Lichte, for example, focuses her recent study of twentieth-century theater (*Die Entdeckung des Zuschauers*, 1997) on the various ways in which modern theater has broken with the conventional paradigms of reception and perception by way of shaking the spectator out of their alleged passivity and complicity with a hegemonic cultural apparatus. Not surprisingly, her discussion of political theater centers on the iconoclastic work of Erwin Piscator in the early 1920s and not on the New Deal theater of the 1930s.[58]

Does that mean that American political theater directors were less interested in the spectator than their Weimar colleagues? Or does it even mean that by foregoing iconoclastic experimentation New Deal theater was less political? Without doubt, an approach like Fischer-Lichte's is invaluable to an analysis of the politics of form in modern theater (as they either undermine or comply with a given culture industry). However, it does not allow us to locate any positive value in forms of political theater that choose to cooperate with the dominant cultural apparatus using its very conventions, traditions, and venues.

In this regard, the modernist/Frankfurt School–inflected focus also tends to overlook the various expressions of popular agency involved in the production and reception of a work of art. It can thus also not account for the failure of Brecht on Broadway.

The more recent methods of cultural studies, which originated at the Centre for Contemporary Cultural Studies in Birmingham and have quickly spread to the United States, attempt to correct this over-sight. Stuart Hall's groundbreaking essay "Notes on Deconstructing the Popular" (1981) has opened up the field for a more affirmative study of forms of popular and consumer culture. He warns us against a reductive reading of the popular as either the site of resistance or containment. According to him, popular culture is neither the site of heroic resistance to reform and educational processes handed down from above, nor is it the various forms superimposed on the people by the dominant cultural apparatus. Rather, it is a double movement of both these impulses, turning the cultural field into a constant battle-field "where no once-for-all victories are obtained but where there are always strategic points to be won and lost."[59] Hall thus highlights the moment of agency inherent in the production and reception of culture. The popular becomes the principle of the active expropriation of tra-ditions, practices, and forms. His definition of the popular as agency and of popular culture as the site of ongoing transformations and negotiations between culture industries and mass audiences has enabled new ways of thinking about mass culture.

It was particularly Michael Denning's seminal study of 1930s popular culture, *The Cultural Front* (1997), that opened up the possibility for rethinking political theater along those lines. In the spirit of Hall, Denning demonstrates that the American cultural front of the 1930s was shaped from both below and above, emerging out of the joined efforts of workers and intellectuals, unions, culture industries, and state institutions. Focusing on the agency cultural workers of the New Deal asserted in the production and expropriation of cultural forms, Denning is able to show how a popular and commercial Broadway success such as the labor revue *Pins and Needles* could contribute to the overall "laboring" of American culture.[60] With this term, Denning refers to the increased visibility and influence of working-class culture under the New Deal, which left its mark on the politics of that period as well as on American culture as a whole. Seen from this angle, the most political show of the period turns out to be, not Brecht's militant epic drama *Mother*, but the colorful *Pins and Needles* that sang and danced itself into the hearts of millions of Americans, including the president and his wife.

In chapter five, I will show in more detail how exactly this revue, which originated in the drama workshops of the International Ladies' Garment Workers' Union (ILGWU), succeeded in asserting proletarian agency within modern consumer culture and in establishing working-class identity on Broadway. I will also show the ways in which the increasing commodification of the show for commercial purposes points up the limitations of vernacular aesthetics. As *Pins and Needles* became polished for Broadway audiences, it increasingly lost its amateur origins along with its progressive ethnic labor stance—a point that Denning does not account for. Here a careful analysis of the politics of form can indeed provide a much needed corrective in the assessment of the political efficacy of the vernacular theater.

Depending on whether we focus our analysis on the question of agency in the production and reception of forms of political theater or whether we investigate how a consumer aesthetics can also induce complicity with the dominant culture industry, we can arrive at very different, even antithetical evaluations of the efficacy of political theater. What we need then is a methodology that does not entirely forego the concerns of the Frankfurt School and their conceptual tools but that at the same time resists their impulse to assimilate all forms of popular and mass culture to the general principle of reification. As Hall reminds us, the forms provided by commercial culture are rarely purely manipulative, for "alongside the false appeals [. . .] there are also elements of recognition and identification, something approaching a recreation of recognizable experiences and attitudes, to which people are responding."[61] In the following chapters, I attempt to offer such a fresh approach to political theater, one that considers both the politics of form along with those of popular agency, one that teases out the problems of commodification while also paying attention to the various ways in which working-class people have made use of popular and mass culture.

Brecht's encounter with the leftist theater of the New Deal succinctly poses such important questions about our understanding of the nature of political theater as well as about our methods of assessing its political efficacy. These questions challenge us to reconsider our existing canon of political theater and, above all, the very notion of the political in political theater.

Chapter Two

Disjunctive Aesthetics: A Genealogy of Political Theater

What Is Political Theater?

"Politics in a work of literature is like a pistol-shot in the middle of a concert, something loud and vulgar, and yet a thing to which it is not possible to refuse one's attention."[1] Stendhal's offhand remark has often been interpreted as endorsing a strict opposition between two antithetical spheres: the realm of the aesthetic on the one hand and the realm of the social on the other—art versus politics, and never the twain shall meet. In this view, the very concept of political art seems paradoxical, if not entirely impossible. As such, it has been treated by a number of critics. Irving Howe, for instance, insists that a "political novel" is a contradiction in terms, which can be overcome only if the novel manages to evoke "a moral order beyond ideology."[2] Such Kantian understanding of art as the realm of disinterested pleasure that sublates the necessity of the everyday in the freedom of the aesthetic entails not only the negation of concrete and pressing social concerns but also the devaluation of a vast body of art that for centuries has sought to integrate the two. So what if we read Stendhal differently—that is, under the contention that all art is always political? Might we then not so much be appalled but thrilled by the explicitness of a pistol shot in the middle of a concert? Might we not applaud its effectiveness, the way it undeniably attracts our attention? Might we perhaps even consider it part of the performance?

It is precisely the blunt manifestations of the political in art that compel this study of New Deal theater. At a time of economic depression and intense labor conflict, the pistol shots of social struggle rang out frequently on the American stage, metaphorically invoked in the eruption of the "International" during amateur street performances, in Clifford Odets's rallying cry for "Strike!" at the end of *Waiting for Lefty* as well as in the Living Newspaper's appeal for government intervention: "Can you hear us, Washington?" Although these calls to action were not always subtle and artistically refined, they were, without doubt, effective, startling their spectators into an awareness of political problems at hand and compelling them to take a stand. For the American workers of the period a play such as *Waiting for Lefty* functioned like "a kind of light machine gun that you wheeled in to use whenever there was any kind of strike trouble," as Odets explains.[3]

This study then understands political theater as a praxis that seeks to mobilize its audiences by providing them with a public forum for the discussion of current political issues, for the elucidation of their underlying socio-economic structures and the drawing up of solutions. According to this concept, political theater functions not simply as commentary on the social but as an active intervention in it. Although political effect is often achieved at the cost of bluntness of content and crudeness of form, the "machine gun aesthetics" of political theater are nevertheless not without artistic value, as has been commonly argued. On the contrary, they often distinguish themselves by an intense visceral appeal. The aesthetic is, however, always an explicit function of the political. As theater scholar Klaus Gleber maintains, "Political theater is a stage praxis that becomes political not only in the process of reception, but that understands itself to be anchored in politics already in its very intention, its thematic objective, and the functional use of aesthetic techniques; it is an aesthetics aiming at political effect."[4]

It is precisely for this reason that it is so important to understand the profound aesthetic disjunction at the heart of political theater, which was so poignantly revealed in Brecht's encounter with the theater of the New Deal. This disjunction succinctly captures what Fredric Jameson has described as the "dilemma of form and public—shared by both modernism and mass culture."[5] In what follows, I shall unravel the two different aesthetic trajectories that led to such antithetical solutions and analyze to what extent the difference in aesthetics is also linked to a difference in politics. For now, however, what needs to be asserted is that the two models of political theater share a profound commitment to social change on behalf of the underprivileged, marginalized, and oppressed.

In general, when we speak of political theater we typically mean the political theater of the left. While the right certainly also has its literary bards, it is the literature of commitment to social equality and justice that has been the most radical. "It is a literature of protest, not approval, of outrage, not tribute," Eric Bentley asserts.[6] Walter Rideout similarly defines radical literature as "one which demonstrates, either explicitly or implicitly, that its author objects to the human suffering imposed by some socio-economic system and advocates that the system be fundamentally changed."[7] The same general definition can be applied to the political theater analyzed here.

The political theater of the left has a vivid tradition, emerging most distinctly in the 1920s and 1930s in Europe and the United States. In fact, it was in this period that the term "political theater" was coined. In the wake of World War I and under the impact of the ensuing revolutionary upheavals in Germany and Russia, a great number of artists began to conceptualize theater as a political tool, a means for transforming reality according to a leftist worldview. "Political" was now no longer a mere descriptive attribute used by theater critics in reference to "socially committed" art but became a declaration, a manifesto of theater makers. In other words, the political no longer emerged in the reception process alone but became an integral part of the production process itself. Authors, directors, designers, technicians, actors, and stagehands alike rigorously began to subordinate subject matter and form to the overall goal of mobilizing the audience to social change on behalf of the subjugated and marginalized. Moreover, political theater was to be a way of thinking and living. It was to have a radical impact on the audience and through the audience on reality itself.

Due to its revolutionary background in the great political and artistic upheavals of the early twentieth century, this praxis of political theater has commonly been defined in the context of European modernism. *Modernist* political theater stands for provocative anti-bourgeois politics and bold formal experimentation. Thanks to its formal iconoclasm and revolutionary spirit it has gained a prominent place in theater histories—so prominent, in fact, that it has often stood in metonymically for political theater as such. Yet, our preoccupation with this kind of political theater has also effectively effaced another form of political theater, which not only coexisted with the modernist one but has as rich a tradition and has played as active a role in society: *vernacular* political theater. The latter was particularly influential on the stages of New Deal America. Rather than insisting on the complete rupture with previous aesthetic traditions and on bold formal experimentation, this theater chose to convey its political message primarily through conventional modes (realism, naturalism) and popular forms (melodrama, vaudeville, musical). Yet, while it might seem less innovative and radical than its modernist cousin, its lack of iconoclasm did not make the vernacular political theater less outspoken or successful. Rather, with the modernist and vernacular model of theater we encounter two different cultural and political objectives and, concurrently, two different ways of realizing them.

In what follows, I shall delineate the various aesthetic traditions and cultural vectors that determined the emergence of modernist and vernacular political theater in the first half of the twentieth century. It will become evident that the two have in fact common roots in the bourgeois tradition of melodrama and naturalism but parted precisely at the moment of the appearance of modernism in theater. From this point on, one strand of political theater, the modernist one, rigorously pursued an oppositional praxis that insisted on radical breaks with previous (bourgeois) traditions and established (bourgeois) institutions. The other strand pragmatically merged in *bricolage*-like fashion conventions and traditions irreverent of their previous social function, integrating and adapting whatever seemed most useful for its purposes. This selection process was determined by a confluence of various cultural factors. The aesthetic disjunction at the heart of political theater is thus also mirrored in two distinct formation processes: a series of ruptures and dialectic sublations on the one hand and a *bricolage* of established conventions shaped by various cultural contingencies on the other.

Modernist Political Theater

The story of modernist political theater is well known today. It is the story of Bertolt Brecht and Erwin Piscator, Vsevolod Meyerhold and Sergey Eisenstein, to name some of the most illustrious names. In fact, theater scholars have almost exclusively focused on the work of these artists, turning their story into a kind of master narrative of political theater, thereby largely effacing alternative practices. This master narrative usually situates the work of the leading political directors of the first half of the twentieth century within the context of European modernism, representing it as part of a general avant-garde movement.[8]

However, such conflation of modernism, avant-garde, and political theater is problematic. It cannot go beyond conceptualizing political theater as part of an overall departure from traditions and conventions in the modern theater. Thus, it can account only for such basic characteristics as iconoclastic experimentation, provocative anti-bourgeois declarations, and the overarching goal of inciting an audience response. These characteristics are, however, also typical for other modernist movements such as symbolism, expressionism, futurism, Dadaism, and surrealism—all of which have been considered avant-gardist at some point. It cannot tell us what the position of political theater is within modernism and how it relates to the various other modernist strands.

If we are to understand the emergence of modernist political theater properly, we need to distinguish carefully between the various moments of modernism and particularly between the terms modernism and avant-garde. Only then will we be able to relate political theater to other modernist practices and get clear on what ultimately distinguishes a modernist political theater praxis.

Peter Bürger's influential study *Theory of the Avant-Garde* (1974), which to date is still the most comprehensive and convincing attempt at theorizing the avant-garde, is particularly useful here. Bürger carefully historicizes the avant-garde as a specific moment and function *within* European modernism; namely the moment when bourgeois art is first able to recognize and criticize its own status and function in bourgeois society without, however, being able to transcend it. What Bürger calls the historical avant-garde is thus not simply synonymous with European modernism but represents a crucial moment within it: the moment of crisis.[9]

This crisis was, according to Bürger, brought about by art's persistent drive toward autonomy. The increasing accumulation of specialized knowledge along with the concurrent differentiation of the various social spheres in bourgeois culture enabled art to gain an ever-greater degree of autonomy from the social, persistently moving it from a stage of semi-autonomy in the eighteenth century to a stage of almost complete autonomy in the aestheticism of the turn of the nineteenth century. As Bürger emphasizes, it is precisely at this moment of aesthetic apotheosis that the flip side of the persistent drive toward autonomy became fully visible: "Only after art, in nineteenth-century Aestheticism, has altogether detached itself from the praxis of life can the aesthetic develop 'purely'. But the other side of autonomy, art's lack of social impact, also becomes recognizable."[10] Now that art wanted to be nothing but art, the consequences of its previous evolution became most evident: its complete dissociation from life praxis and its utter lack of social effect ("gesellschaftliche Folgenlosigkeit").

Enter the historical avant-garde of the 1910s and 1920s, with which bourgeois art for the first time became critical of itself. According to Bürger, the futurists, Dadaists, and surrealists recognized the chasm that had opened up between art and the social, and in launching an attack against the very institution of art in bourgeois society, they attempted to reintegrate the two. Notably they did so not by calling for socially significant art but by boldly proclaiming the aestheticization of life—a declaration that found its most emblematic expression in Marcel Duchamp's *Fountain* (1917). Putting his signature "R. Mutt" on an ordinary, mass-manufactured urinal, Duchamp provocatively renounced all claims to what Benjamin calls "the auratic," thereby seeking to enforce an integration of art and life. For Bürger, such aestheticization of life, however, presents at best a false sublation of art's autonomy. Duchamp's *Fountain* might have blurred the distinction between art and life, but it did not change the status of art in bourgeois society, nor did it retranslate art into life. What it did, however, was address the chasm between the two. For the first time art succeeded in revealing "the nexus between autonomy and the absence of any consequences."[11] Precisely this is the historical function and achievement of the historical avant-garde.

Bürger's trajectory stops at this crucial moment. He cannot conceptualize a post-avant-garde precisely because he cannot conceptualize the evolution of art in terms other than those of a dialectics of autonomy within bourgeois society. Hence, Bürger's argument cannot account for the phenomenon of political art—an art praxis that never conceived of itself in terms of autonomy (or its negation) but always as an integral function of the social.[12] Jochen Schulte-Sasse underscores this shortcoming in his critical foreword to Bürger's theory: "Only when confronted with the potential of post-avant-garde art does Bürger apparently fail to pursue the logical conclusions of his own analysis and relate it to a body of texts that has begun exploring this potential"—such as the work of Brecht.[13]

Bürger's *Theory of the Avant-Garde* is, nonetheless, useful for developing a theory of modernist political theater. First, by theorizing the historical avant-garde as the moment of crisis in bourgeois art, Bürger unwittingly sets the stage for the emergence of political art. As Erwin Piscator explains with regard to the pioneering role of Dada, "These iconoclasts cleared the decks, abandoned the bourgeois position they had grown up in, and returned to the point of departure from which the proletariat must approach art."[14] In other words, the existence of a historical avant-garde (as well as its failure) was in many regards the prerequisite for the emergence of a *modernist* praxis of political theater. The revolutionary aesthetics of Europe's leading political directors were, in fact, deeply indebted to the iconoclasm of the historical avant-garde, among them Brecht and Piscator's epic theater, Meyerhold's constructivism, and Eisenstein's "Theater of Eccentricity." Traces of the birth of modernist political theater out of the spirit of the avant-garde are evident in some of its most fundamental characteristics: its vehement opposition to bourgeois institution art as well as its insistence on the radical rupture with all bourgeois traditions.

Bürger's theory is also useful in that it explains the emergence of the historical avant-garde as a series of sublations of previous modes of cultural production—that is, as both negation and continuation (*Aufhebung*). For example, while the historical avant-garde rejected the formal solipsism of aestheticism, it nevertheless clung to the idea that aestheticization was the way of overcoming an adversary social totality. But where aestheticism had retreated into the complete aestheticization of form, the avant-garde now ventured into the aestheticization of life. By extending Bürger's dialectical view of the evolution of modern art to modernist political theater, we are thus able to understand a crucial contradiction at the heart of its praxis. While Brecht and Piscator defined their work in vehement opposition to bourgeois institution art, they also inherited one of its most profound characteristics: the Schillerian vision of art as a source and means of enlightenment and education.[15] Modernist political theater is therefore marked not only by ruptures with previous traditions but also by their continuation. This conflicted relationship is part and parcel of its aesthetic and political program and as such evident in its high degree of self-reflexivity as well as the constant referencing and critiquing of previous modes of cultural production. On the basis of these two crucial emphases in Bürger's theory, we can now devise the following genealogy of political theater.

Arguably, the roots of modern political theater extend as far back as the melodramas of the French Revolution, Denis Diderot's bourgeois domestic tragedy, and Gotthold Ephraim Lessing's enlightenment *Trauerspiel*. But it was only with the naturalist movement of the late nineteenth century that the political mission of modern theater was enunciated most clearly. Naturalism most rigorously adhered to George Brandes's dictum that it was the very function of art in bourgeois society to submit social problems for debate.[16] It was the first movement to systematically elucidate the social and economic structures of society as well as the first to put the working class on stage.

Up to this point, modernist and vernacular political theater share common roots and beginnings. But it is precisely with regard to their naturalist legacy that the two strands of modern political theater begin to diverge. As we have seen in the example of Theatre Union's production of Brecht's *Mother*, vernacular political theater continues to maintain a rather unproblematic relationship to its bourgeois heritage, frequently falling back onto a classic naturalist dramaturgy and mise-en-scène by way of facilitating the emotional absorption and identification of its spectators with the characters on stage. In naturalism we have, after all, the closest realization of Diderot's emphatic belief that the most stirring and true-to-life plays could emerge only when the audience was under the impression that it was completely shut out from the action on stage and when the actors were entirely unaware of its presence.[17]

Modernist political theater, by contrast, has a rather conflicted relationship with naturalism. While it endorses its social agenda, it vehemently opposes its aesthetics, particularly its fixation on photographic mimesis and empathy.[18] According to Brecht, the naturalist preoccupation with the minute reproduction of "a slice of life" all too often resulted in "the creation of such an impression of naturalness that one can no longer interpose one's judgment, imagination and reactions, and must simply conform by sharing the experience and becoming one of 'nature's' objects."[19] Moreover, the focus on eliciting empathy with the oppressed, so Brecht surmised, tended to prevent the audience from interpolating their own critical judgment, and above all, from realizing that oppression was not a natural condition of life. More often than not, empathy thus ended up legitimizing rather than changing existing conditions.[20] Last but not least, to the mind of its modernist detractors, the naturalist stage most clearly articulated the separateness of art from life since the naturalist goal of absorbing its spectators completely in the dramatic experience could only be sustained by banishing them behind an invisible fourth wall. Despite its commitment to relating art to life by reproducing the latter as accurately as possible on stage, naturalism thus paradoxically found itself furthest removed from the reality of the beholder and, arguably, from the very praxis of life.[21] For all these reasons, a new generation of artists began to part with the naturalist tenets of illusionism, absorption, and empathy—thereby also instigating a split in the genealogy of modern political theater. For now, let us follow the modernist strand further and examine how the trajectory of its emergence impacted its aesthetics and politics.

While naturalism presented the culmination of bourgeois illusionist theater, it also already contained the seeds of its undoing. The "great free air of reality" that Émile Zola had let in through the backcloth in order to "give a shiver of real life to the painted trees" ended up stifling actors and spectators alike.[22] Around 1900 we notice a decisive break with the dominant naturalist theater praxis as artists increasingly resisted and critiqued it for "naturalizing" the theater experience and for failing to challenge the perception of the audience. In order to denaturalize the theatrical experience, to tear down the fourth wall, and to reach out to the audience again, an emerging art theater movement (*Kunsttheaterbewegung*) began to device various non-mimetic forms of representation. The ensuing rupture manifested itself most clearly in the relationship between Konstantin Stanislavsky and his disciple Vsevolod Meyerhold. The latter opposed the excessive mimetic realism of his teacher, arguing that Stanislavsky's brilliant, yet minute recreations of life on stage, denied the spectators any imaginative participation in the theatrical event. For Meyerhold, however, the spectator was the fourth creator in the theater, whose imagination ought to be challenged with a high degree of artifice and stylization.[23]

Around the time that Meyerhold began to experiment with forms of "Stylized Theater," numerous other theater artists also began to explore the use of space, movement, light, music, set, and design.[24] Some of the most emblematic innovations took place in stage architecture as theater artists deliberately manipulated the distance between stage and auditorium. The fourth wall of the bourgeois deep stage (fittingly called *Guckkastenbühne* in German for its narrow peephole vision) was torn down, the apron abolished, and the orchestra pit bridged.[25] Foremost among these experiments was Walter Gropius's plan for a *Totaltheater*. It represented the most radical departure from the static bourgeois stage. Designed for Piscator's political multimedia spectacles, this highly versatile "theater instrument" could be converted (even during a single performance) into any classical stage design, including deep stage, proscenium stage, and arena stage.[26] With the help of an extensive system of spotlights, loudspeakers, film projectors, and project screens installed along the walls and ceilings of the entire theater, it could, moreover, "catapult the spectator in the midst of the dramatic action, [. . .] integrate him spatially into the spectacle, rather than allowing him to escape behind the curtain," as Gropius explained his vision.[27]

Art theater experimentations took various directions and degrees and were, in fact, much too heterogeneous to constitute an actual "movement" united by a single agenda. When theater historians nevertheless refer to this phase in Western theater as a movement, they highlight the one objective linking these various experiments: to reestablish contact with the audience by *retheatricalizing* the stage. Breaking with conventional modes of representation and perception, they prompted their spectators to participate creatively in the theatrical event, thereby bringing them back into the presence of the actors.[28] The experiments of Meyerhold, Adolphe Appia, Georg Fuchs, Jacques Copeau, and Max Reinhardt were unthinkable without their audiences. The two defining objectives of the art theaters therefore are, as Fischer-Lichte suggests, the rediscovery of the spectator and the concurrent shift from internal communication on stage to the external communication with the audience.[29] The modernist political theater was to take up both of these objectives along with a preference for stylization and abstraction over verisimilitude and photographic realism.

The art theaters' rebellion against naturalism was also an attack against a bourgeois society, in which art and life seemed so widely separated. But while their theatrical innovations represented an important step toward a fundamental reconceptualization of the relationship of art to life, they fell short of an actual reintegration of the two spheres precisely because they were not yet aware of their own precarious position within bourgeois society. A form of self-critique was still absent. Instead, art theaters mainly chose to resist and negate bourgeois art and life through radical aesthetic experimentation.

As Bürger reminds us, this self-reflexivity, that is, the awareness that bourgeois art was part of the very social totality that produced and reinforced the autonomy of art, became possible only with the arrival of the historical avant-garde. The futurists in Italy and Russia, the Dadaists in Zürich and Berlin, and the surrealists in Paris were clearly offsprings of the art theaters, but at the same time they also radically differed from their predecessors—a difference that is simply erased when both movements are subsumed under the popular umbrella term "theater avant-garde." Surely, the Russian futurists' determination to throw "Pushkin, Dostoeyvsky, Tolstoy, etc. etc. [. . .] overboard from the Steamboat of Modernity" was of an entirely different order than, let us say, Vassily Kandinsky's goal to achieve "a certain complex of vibrations" in art through the synaesthesia of sound, color, and words.[30] The former demanded not simply the retheatricalization of theater but the abolition of all known forms of theater. In their place, the futurists postulated the radical New. This avant-gardist "New" was new not simply by virtue of innovation but, above all, by virtue of its complete opposition to all prevailing values, as Renato Poggioli has pointed out.[31] Most significantly, their "affection for radical thought, rhetoric, and action in opposition to accepted values" was, as Richard Schechner underscores, at the heart not only of their politics but also of their bohemian lifestyle.[32] In other words, their rebellions spread from the stage to life itself. In the end, however, this all-inclusive rebellion against bourgeois art and life remained rather ill defined, exhausting itself in a host of polemical declarations, proclamations, and manifestoes.

At the same time that the historical avant-garde rebelled against its predecessors, it also continued some of its aesthetic projects; above all, the art theaters' intended emancipation of the spectator. No longer content with stimulating the imaginative participation of the audience (as Meyerhold had postulated), it sought to shock and provoke them, to elicit verbal protest and physical action. The Russian futurists, for example, provocatively entitled their manifesto *A Slap in the Face of*

Public Taste (1912). Italian futurist Filippo Tommaso Marinetti, on the other hand, quite seriously presented a whole catalogue of suggestions on how to cause laughter, commotion, and fighting in the audience by smearing seats with glue, selling the same seat twice, or sprinkling it with itching powder. Eisenstein similarly considered enhancing his "Theater of Attractions" by setting off firecrackers under the spectators' seats (a quite literal rendition of Stendhal's pistol shot).[33] The provocation of the audience represented another important step in the direction of political theater. The historical avant-garde managed to shake the audience from its presumed passivity, provoking critical as well as physical participation. What their concept of audience mobilization however lacked was a purposeful pedagogy. Once they had aroused their spectators, they failed to guide their newly acquired activism. Thus, while the historical avant-garde effectively demonstrated the inconsequentiality of the bourgeois stage, it remained incapable of transcending it. Vladimir Mayakovsky's notorious bright yellow tie signaled a general sense of departure at futurist happenings, but for the time being this departure dead-ended in the complete aestheticization of his own life praxis. It was, however, at this moment of heightened self-critique and absolute iconoclasm that political theater could emerge.

I have given this detailed account of the emergence of modernist political theater out of previous modernist movements in order to show the extent to which it is heir to these previous traditions in bourgeois theater in a dialectical sense, both negating and maintaining them. On the one hand, modernist political theater defined itself in strict opposition to its bourgeois predecessors, for none of them had succeeded in reintegrating art and life. Piscator, who had been affiliated with Berlin Dada, realized as much when he prefaced his work in political theater with the declaration: "Away with art, make an end of it!"[34] He insisted that in political theater "art was only a means to an end. A political means. A propagandistic means. A pedagogical means."[35] This new understanding of art, however, went hand in hand with a new understanding of social totality. As Brecht made clear, the call for a new theater, which so radically refunctioned art on behalf of life, and more specifically in the interests of the oppressed, was nothing less than the call for a new social formation.[36] On the other hand, however, political theater was also very much heir to all preceding bourgeois modernist traditions. From the naturalist stage, it took over the social agenda; from the art theaters, it learned the value of formal innovation and inherited the lesson that the retheatricalization of the stage was imperative to the emancipation of the spectator; and finally, from the historical avant-garde it acquired its taste for *épater les bourgeois* along with the vehement rejection of the bourgeois cultural apparatus.

The trajectory also explains some of the most prominent character-istics of the aesthetics of modernist political theater: its insistence on radical ruptures with the conventions of bourgeois theater, its empha-sis on innovation and abstraction, and its high degree of self-reflexivity. Yet, along with these characteristics, it also inherited the modernist suspicion of the commodity form and of mass culture. While mod-ernist political theater sought to represent the interests of the masses and intervene in the social on their behalf, while it even abundantly employed popular forms by way of shocking the middle classes and reaching out to the working classes, it nevertheless understood itself in strict opposition to mass culture, rejecting it for its complicity with a bourgeois culture industry. In this last point, modernist political theater differed decisively from its vernacular cousin.

Vernacular Political Theater

In contrast to modernist political theater, the story of vernacular polit-ical theater has been told very little. We still lack a terminology and theory to describe its emergence and to analyze its characteristics and function. So far, we can only surmise that the modernist trajectory of political theater described above would serve us ill in trying to concep-tualize Theatre Union's adaptation of Brecht for American audiences or any other form of New Deal theater. In what follows, I will attempt to develop such a terminology and theory. If my methodology differs from that of the preceding section, then it is due to the *bricolage* nature of this particular praxis of political theater.

To begin with, it should be evident from our discussion in the previ-ous chapter that the aesthetics of Theatre Union (to the degree that they were evident in the New York *Mother* production) have little in com-mon with the aesthetics of modernist political theater delineated above. Rather than insisting on radical innovation, it went back to the proven tradition of realist dramaturgy and naturalist staging. Nor did it evince a deep suspicion of bourgeois institution art or of commodity structures. When Theatre Union translated Brecht's epic drama into the commer-cial language of David Belasco's melodramatic realism, it did so with the explicit goal of catering to the expectations of its audience. As one the-ater member put it, it wanted "a responsive audience, not a frustrated one."[37] In other words, it used the familiar forms of an established culture industry by way of "selling" its political agenda to the public.

It is because of such deliberate deployment of the commodity form as a vehicle for mobilizing a broad audience that I refer to this praxis of political theater as *vernacular*. I here borrow the term from Jameson, whose characterization of postmodern architecture also captures the essence of vernacular political theater. Postmodern buildings, he writes, "no longer attempt, as did the masterworks and monuments of high modernism, to insert a different, a distinct, an elevated, a new Utopian language into the tawdry and commercial sign system of the surrounding city, but rather they seek to speak that very language, using its lexicon and syntax."[38] I likewise understand vernacularity in political theater as the capacity to speak the language of a proven, that is, commercially successful, sign system. With this, we already have a first, crucial building block for a definition of vernacular political theater and for an understanding of its emergence as a result of various cultural vectors in the American 1930s.

The practice of deploying the language of an established culture industry was typical for the majority of professional leftist theaters of the 1930s. It is evident in the strike songs of Clifford Odets, the labor union revue *Pins and Needles*, Marc Blitzstein's proletarian opera *The Cradle Will Rock*, and even the Living Newspapers of the Federal Theatre Project. Despite great differences in form and despite the occasional use of modernist techniques, in the end these diverse expressions of political theater all approached Jameson's "dilemma of form and public" in a similar manner. Drawing on the vernacular of American theater, they fell back onto a customary lexicon of entertainment (melodrama, naturalism, revue, musical) and a conventional syntax of empathy, identification, and absorption. Above all, they shared a similar attitude toward form and audience: to reach out toward a broad and heterogeneous public by appealing to them as consumers.

In addition to Jameson's understanding of vernacularity as the expression of an intrinsic commodity character, I also want to recuperate another definition of vernacularity. As Sieglinde Lemke has shown in a recent essay, the term has been used in the name of various identity politics over the course of the past century.[39] I here want to take up its deployment by the first generation of scholars of American culture. Critics such as Constance Rourke, Leo Marx, and Henry Nash Smith have used the term "vernacular" to designate an indigenous mode of cultural production, which in drawing on the colloquial language of the "common man" was profoundly non-elitist, democratic, and populist in form and politics. In fact, in the American vernacular form and politics were inseparable. This is also the case in the later deployment of the term in African American and Postcolonial

Studies, which, too, stress the inherent oppositional force of the vernacular in its aesthetics and politics. Here, however, the emphasis shifts from asserting a politics of commonality to asserting a subaltern politics of difference—a usage that will become important again in the 1960s.[40] Since the political theater of the 1930s foregrounded *common* denominators such as national, democratic, and economic identity in its rhetoric, I will primarily use the earlier definition of the term. Yet, my usage also differs from that of the early Americanists in that it does not treat the vernacular as simply synonymous with some kind of authentic folk or popular culture that resisted the dominant European forms. Rather, in my understanding the vernacular draws on forms and expressions of popular culture in order to reach out to as broad and diverse an audience as possible. Like Jameson, I therefore see a process of commodification inherent in the deployment of vernacular forms.

It ought to be pointed out here that in this regard the vernacular has a decisively different relation to the popular than the modernist. While modernist practices certainly also make ample use of popular forms and expressions, they use them primarily as means of alienation (*Verfremdung*) and not of commodification—that is, in order to break with dominant and common paradigms of production and perception (rather than enhancing them). The vernacular aims to achieve precisely the opposite: to facilitate communication with a mass audience, to endorse the culinary appeal of its products by tapping into the popular, the familiar, the conventional, and to allow for easy identification, absorption, and empathy.

Let us add a third definition of the vernacular, which can further illuminate the idiosyncratic aesthetics of New Deal theater. In his recent study of black public thinkers, Grant Farred argues that vernacularity is key to political efficaciousness. "Vernacularize," Farred writes,

> [a]lways explore and explicate the links between the popular and the political. Never underestimate the capacity of the popular to elucidate the ideological, to animate the political, never overlook the vernacular as a means of producing a subaltern or postcolonial voice that resists, subverts, disrupts, reconfigures, or impacts the dominant discourse. For disempowered constituencies, resistance against the domination is extremely difficult without a vernacular component.[41]

In other words, Farred understands the vernacular as a highly effective strategy of linking the political to the popular, of teasing out those elements of popular purchase in the political issue at hand that can elicit popular agency. For him, it is "that mode in which the political and the popular conjoin identificatory pleasure with ideological resistance."[42] While Farred defines the vernacular here foremost as a means of production, it can also be read as a strategy of decoding the political in such a way that the political becomes pleasurable and that pleasure is channeled into political activism.

It is important to note that for Farred the popular is synonymous with "the common" rather than with "the folk." It is that which has popular purchase or mass appeal. Yet, just as for Stuart Hall, this definition designates the popular neither as the site of passive acceptance of forms superimposed on it nor as the unadulterated, heroic resistance against them, but as a field of constant negotiations between producer and recipient, which in triggering interest and eliciting pleasure has transformative potential.[43] The vernacular, then, is a means of enabling this negotiation by way of translating the political into a popular language and of provoking that kind of intense "identificatory pleasure" that can lead to political action. Without the latter, so Farred insists, the political would not only be tedious but perhaps also entirely unsuccessful. It is in the vernacular that the political becomes animated and pleasurable—and precisely here lies its greatest political potential. As Farred reminds us, the political might not always be pleasurable, "but the pleasurable is always potentially political."[44]

Farred's theory of vernacularity supplements Jameson's in a useful way: vernacularity is now not only the capacity to speak the language of an established, commercial sign system but also the capacity to speak in a language resonant with the experience of subjugated communities—or, in Farred's words, "the discourse that is almost invariably, despite or because of itself, imprinted with the mark of the politically subjugated: the immigrant, the working class, the black or ethnic community."[45] The link between the two is evident in American consumer culture: With the advent of consumer culture in the interwar period, the experience of subjugated communities began to be increasingly shaped by commercial sign systems. This transformation was not necessarily a negative one. As cultural critics Lizabeth Cohen and Michael Denning have shown, the experience of mass culture provided disparate ethnic and social communities with a common basis for political action.[46]

From Jameson, Farred, and the early Americanists' concepts of vernacularity, we can now derive a working definition of vernacularity in political theater: Vernacular political theater seeks to stimulate political action by eliciting the audience's identificatory pleasure in the political. It teases out this moment of pleasure with the help of the culinary appeal and visceral affect of forms of popular and commodity culture, which it utilizes for elucidating, animating, and transmitting the political. This strategy implies a radically democratic approach to form and public. Trying to reach as broad and diverse an audience as possible (an audience of common men and women), vernacular political theater does not discriminate in its formal choices. It often takes up the language of the established theater industry, drawing on classical and popular forms of representation alike. It employs a wide array of cultural expressions, ranging from realism and naturalism to melodrama and musical revue—regardless of their previous role and function on the bourgeois stage. Moreover, in doing so, it effectively collapses the distinction between high and low, innovative and traditional, elitist and mass culture—distinctions that modernism so strongly relies on. In this regard, the vernacular is intrinsically related to the middlebrow, with which it shares similar aesthetic and political objectives—a point to which I shall return. Precisely because it falls back on an already established sign system, the vernacular does not, in principal, reject the conventional venues of the dominant culture industry but attempts to refunction them for its own purposes. Notably, vernacular political theater is thus not so much an effort at replacing bourgeois art and life praxis with an alternative (proletarian) culture, as it is an effort to expropriate and transform it.

By now, it is apparent that the emergence of vernacular political theater cannot be explained, unlike that of its modernist cousin, in terms of a series of ruptures and dialectic sublations. Rather, it needs to be theorized as the result of a confluence of various cultural vectors. In what follows, I shall examine those vectors that influenced the American theater of the 1930s and analyze how they interlinked in the formation of strong vernacular praxis of political theater. This will enable us to comprehend why the American political theater so clearly privileged the vernacular approach over the modernist one at the time.

To begin with, let me return to the work of early scholars of American culture, who regard the vernacular as an inherent trait of American national culture. Leo Marx, father of American Studies, theorizes vernacularity as an *Ur*-American impulse, which manifests itself most prominently in a series of literary techniques designed to invent an American national character that is independent of and different from Europe.[47] Not surprisingly, the vernacular strategy in American literature—which Marx considers to be most prominent in Mark Twain and Walt Whitman—evinces a fervent patriotism (at times chauvinistic though never uncritical) and a radically republican stance. "There can be no question that Whitman celebrates America at the expense of Europe and the past," Marx writes, namely by dispensing with "the stylistic elegance" that was widely deemed to be the literary counterpart of European political oppression at the time.[48] This is precisely where Marx detects "the aggressive moment" that so often underlies the American vernacular, "its urge to defy what pretends to be a superior culture."[49] The mark of this defiance of a dominating European culture is, so Marx, an "unremitting anti-intellectualism" and its concurrent highlighting of the immediacy of the experience of the common man (often rendered via vivid descriptions of the quotidian, detailed accounts of labor processes, and first-person narratives). The American hero is by definition the common, the vernacular hero. He is Huck Finn, who by following his heart and common sense rather than the established racial mores of society commits a radical act of defiance and rebellion. "Here [on the raft] is the core of the vernacular," Marx writes in a later version of his essay. "It is not simply a style but a style with a politics in view"—one committed to a radical sense of egalitarianism.[50] From the start, the vernacular has therefore been more than a literary technique in American culture; namely "an ideal vision of the nation's destiny."[51] While Marx's concept of the vernacular is intimately linked to that of cultural nationalism, he is, however, far from being uncritically acceptant of American nationhood. Rather, for Marx, the vernacular is fueled by an egalitarian faith and utopian standard "that we can scarcely imagine nowadays." "The political ideal is freedom," he explains, "freedom from the oppression of society, and freedom to establish the egalitarian community."[52]

Marx's analysis of the vernacular tradition in American literature accomplishes two things. It suggests that the aesthetics and politics of the vernacular are inseparable from a sense of cultural and political independence from European domination, and it concurrently sets up some of its key paradigms: its plebeian origins and profound anti-intellectualism, its emphasis on the immediacy of experience of the common man, and the underlying cultural nationalism of its approach—all of these traits we will encounter again in modified form on the New Deal stage, where Marx's vernacular cultural nationalism experienced a significant renaissance.[53]

As the country struggled to recover from the economic crisis of 1929 and as it sought to rally all liberal forces into a strong Popular Front against war and fascism and in the defense of civil liberties, the New Deal government along with the country's cultural front deliberately reactivated the trope of the common man. James Agee's and Walker Evans's *Fortune* magazine-sponsored documentary of Southern shareholders *Let Us Now Praise Famous Men* (1936–1941) and Paul Robeson's rendition of Earl Robinson's Popular Front anthem "Ballad

for Americans" (1939) are only two of the many prominent examples
of the decade's deliberate revival of a vernacular American identity. It
was to culminate in Henry Wallace's proclamation of the "Century of
the Common Man" in May 1942 (the government response to Henry
Luce's "American Century"). Even CPUSA succumbed to such prevalent Americanism when adopting the populist slogan "Communism is
20th century Americanism" for its election campaign of 1936. The
invocation of the "American people," so Kenneth Burke convincingly
argued in his contribution to the American Writers' Congress of 1935,
was after all the most effective trope of the second half of the 1930s.[54]

In addition to the prominent revival of cultural nationalism, I want
to suggest three other crucial cultural developments that shaped the
vernacular character of New Deal theater. First, in contrast to Europe,
the United States lacked a strong, transformative historical avant-
garde, which explains not only the rather artless attitude of leftist theaters to the question of reification but also the persisting hegemony of
realism and naturalism on the American stage. In the debate over
whether or not America produced an indigenous theater avant-garde
during the first half of the twentieth century, I here share the position
that despite the existence of an important and vibrant Little Theater
movement in the 1910s and 1920s and a few other serious attempts at
épater les bourgeois (such as by the New Playwrights), one cannot
speak of a significant historical avant-garde movement on the
American stage.[55] As Andreas Huyssen explains, in the United States
"the iconoclastic rebellion against a bourgeois cultural heritage would
have made neither artistic nor political sense," since "the literary and
artistic heritage never played as central a role in legitimizing bourgeois
domination as it did in Europe."[56] Bert Cardullo's and Robert Knopf's
anthology *Theater of the Avant-Garde 1890–1950* (2001) and Arnold
Aronson's *American Avant-Garde Theatre* (2000) reinforce this view;
the former focuses almost entirely on French, German, Italian, Russian
avant-gardists (except for an honorary tribute to Gertrude Stein), while
the latter begins the history of the American avant-garde only after
World War II.[57] Aronson acknowledges that American playwrights of
the 1910s and 1920s were certainly influenced by the European avant-
garde, even adopting some of its strategies, but he also points out that
they continued to use these elements within "a basically realistic framework and psychological character structure," thereby foregoing a
wholesale rejection of bourgeois institution art.[58] I agree with him in
that the iconoclastic experiments of the Provincetown Players (e.g.,
Susan Glaspell, Alfred Kreymborg) and the New Playwrights (e.g., John
Howard Lawson, John Dos Passos) did not amount to more than acts

of individual protest against the status quo. Therefore, they did not signify a fundamental crisis of bourgeois institution art and, in that regard, did not have the same transformative effect on the future development of theater as did the historical avant-garde in Europe. The absence of a powerful theater avant-garde in the first half of the twentieth century is, arguably, one of the main factors for the unquestioned and persisting hegemony of realism and naturalism on the American stage.

Second, the American theater, including its leftist stages, has always been a commercial enterprise. While the European theater tended to maintain a great number of federally or municipally subsidized stages (precisely because here theater functioned as a means of legitimizing the hegemony of bourgeois culture and ideology), American theater was from the start in the hands of private entrepreneurship rather than public education. As German playwright Friedrich Wolf conceded upon his arrival in New York, "We Europeans have to try to forget our concept of theater, as an institution with a tradition. [. . .] Theater here is the producer, that is, the entrepreneur, who raises the money for a production and seeks out a director."[59] As its own producer, or even when backed up by an individual, a theater would normally try to seek to ensure the profit of the play beforehand. This meant, as one Broadway critic put it, "not to present a play that the audience might want to see, but to present one that it already wants to see, and has probably seen, in varying guises, many times before."[60] The prevalent habit of judging a play by its potential box office success thus determined not only the selection and production of the play but also its public reception by critics and audiences. Within such a thoroughly commercialized theater culture it was, of course, much more difficult to launch a radical aesthetic, let alone political protest, against bourgeois institution art. After all, to ensure that the public was going to carry the production meant to fill not only the balconies but also the orchestra seats.

While leftist stages such as Theatre Union tried to work with a democratic price scale and to build subscription services with various workers' organizations, they still needed the more affluent middle class for financial support. "The most radical playwrights have been weakened by the circumstance that if their plays are to be acted at all, they must conform to standards made on Broadway and not in heaven," *New Masses* critic Robert Forsythe dryly commented.[61] In fact, only the government-sponsored Federal Theatre remained entirely independent of the box office and was thus able not only to maintain a thoroughly low price scale but also to engage in theatrical experiments—albeit for a short-lived period only.[62] The aesthetic license of most other professional leftist theaters was, without doubt, severely curbed by the demands of the box office, anchoring them in the cultural mainstream. This tendency was most likely further exacerbated precisely by the aforesaid lack of a sweeping avant-garde movement, which arguably enabled leftist theaters to continue to assume a rather artless attitude toward the commercialism of Broadway and toward their own commodity character.

Finally, probably the most decisive factor in the emergence of a strong vernacular theater tradition on the American stage is the unprecedented explosion of consumer culture in the interwar period and the concomitant emergence and ascent of a new cultural force: the middlebrow (again, in sharp contrast to Europe where consumerism did not arrive till the 1950s).[63] The mass manufacturing of everyday commodities as well as their standardized distribution enabled American workers to participate in mass consumption and to transform themselves quickly from producers into consumers. As the American economy shifted to a consumer industry, the nation experienced an unparalleled diffusion of high culture. The public began to acquire culture in the same vein that it had previously acquired industrial commodities. Ben Blake comments, "The middle class particularly [. . .] strove for culture as much as it had striven for material goods. It could afford the best."[64] Several cultural institutions (publishing houses, theaters, universities, public lecture systems) picked up on this trend, supplying the middle classes with what had previously been considered artifacts of high culture.

The landmark event in the new commercial distribution of high culture was, as Janice Radway astutely observes, the emergence of the Book-of-the-Month-Club in 1926, which began to cater specifically to an aspiring middle class. When Book Club founder Harry Sherman marketed Shakespeare's poetry along with a box of chocolates, he held out the dual promise of the acquisition of cultural status along with that of immediate sensual gratification. With this compelling gesture he, however, also brazenly blurred and collapsed revered distinctions between high and low, sacred and profane, art and commerce— distinctions that had been solidly entrenched in American culture since the late nineteenth century. They now suddenly gave way to a "disturbing new nebula," a new permeable space: the middlebrow.[65]

With the emergence of the middlebrow, the cultural hegemony of an older Brahmin elite was suddenly called into question. Their anxiety over this new cultural miscegenation was, however, not so much prompted by aesthetic affront, nor by fear of the close proximity of the middlebrow to the lowbrow, but by "a highly concrete political fear of rival cultural authorities," as Radway argues.[66] The "scandal of the middlebrow" pointed to the masses striving for cultural participation and thus brought into sharp relief "the problem of the mass audience in the twentieth century and [. . .] the various attempts by the intellectual elite to deny its existence, to address it, to assemble it for political work."[67]

The new arbiters of the middlebrow managed to assemble this mass audience with what Radway terms a "sentimental education"[68]—that is, by combining the intellectual and moral edification of high culture with the immediate visceral appeal of low culture. Not surprisingly, the sentimental education of the middlebrow relied on such familiar culinary paradigms as immediacy, absorption, and identification—the very paradigms modernism so vehemently rejected. Sherman's offer of Shakespeare along with a box of chocolates provided an ingenious solution to the dilemma of form and public—a solution that was, as David Savran has shown, eagerly adapted by the American theater of the 1920 and 1930s, turning it into the most emblematic of middlebrow arts.[69] We find the same impulse at work in the vernacular praxis of leftist theaters: they too shrewdly combined the promise of political education with emotional satisfaction, thus effectively absorbing the aesthetics of the middlebrow, which, lest we forget, is also the aesthetics of consumerism.

In sum, the four cultural vectors that determined the emergence of a vibrant vernacular tradition in American political theater— the renaissance of a vernacular cultural nationalism, the lack of a transformative historical avant-garde, the intrinsic commercialism of American theater, and, above all, the spread of consumer culture and the concomitant ascent of middlebrow aesthetics—enabled the emergence of a vernacular praxis of political theater on the New Deal stage (over a modernist one). They also contributed to the formation of its idiosyncratic characteristics, such as its emphasis on immediacy, identification, and absorption (over alienation and abstraction), its insistence on empathy as the largest common denominator of a broad and heterogeneous group of people, and its overall allegiance to established traditions and proven forms of mass culture. We now also begin to understand the cultural contingency of the American solution to the "dilemma of form and public."

New Deal Theater, Its Public and Politics

After the preceding discussion of the formal aspects of the dilemma of form and public, a few more words about the public of New Deal theater seem to be in order. John Howard Lawson once called the American theater of the 1930s "an expression of a middle class mind."[70] With this, he referred to the general middle-class sensibility permeating American audiences regardless of class affiliations. Even though leftist theaters such as Theatre Union explicitly defined themselves as "proletarian," their audiences often lacked the high degree of class consciousness and political organization suggested by this attribute. How can we make sense of this allegedly "middle class mind" of the American theater public?

In a study entitled *Why Is There No Socialism in the United States?* sociologist Werner Sombart suggested as early as 1906 that the relative affluence of the American working class and the existence of greater opportunities for upward mobility in American society, compared to European societies, led to the rapid *embourgeoisement* of American workers.[71] Some thirty years later, literary critic V. F. Calverton likewise insisted that "the American proletariat [was] the last class to identify itself as proletarian" and most likely to seek its alliance with the middle class.[72] As a consequence, class struggle in the United States rarely manifested itself between proletariat and bourgeoisie but rather "between two bourgeoisies, the big bourgeoisie and the little (or petit) bourgeoisie, with the workers identifying their interests throughout our political history with the little bourgeoisie."[73] Dissociating class struggle from its technical Marxist definition, Sombart and Calverton suggest that in the United States social conflict articulates itself primarily as the opposition between "petit" and "big" bourgeoisie, or more precisely between the common man and corporate interests. Such definition of social conflict, however, stands in marked contrast to the politics of European modernist political theater where opposition is always expressed precisely along Marxist class lines.

According to another argument, the significance of class as the crucial category of social analysis has been further undermined in the United States by a preoccupation with the category of race. In his compelling study *The Wages of Whiteness* (1991), David Roediger shows how especially among Irish and Eastern European immigrant workers the desire not to be identified as "black" by WASP middle-class Americans and to be assimilated as quickly as possible into this dominant group led to an increasing racialization of class conflict and rarely to its direct articulation in class struggle. Particularly the crude racism of minstrel shows functioned as an effective means of masking class tensions and ethnic discrimination by projecting "a common, respectable and increasingly smug whiteness under the blackface," aimed at transforming class and ethnic conflict into a shared antagonism to African Americans.[74]

In the wake of the Depression, the rapid proletarianization of large sections of the middle class, ironically, further contributed to the dissolution of the Marxist category of class. Although many members of the middle class were now, from an economic point of view, working class (their identity no longer tied to the question of property but to that of employment), they nevertheless continued to cling to a notion of superior caste, which manifested itself above all in an adherence to middle-class tastes and values. As critic Lewis Corey explains in his study *The Crisis of the Middle Class* (1935), the demise of the fragmented and impoverished middle class consisted precisely in their refusal to acknowledge their changed role in the economy. Instead, they tended to hold on to the very identity that had brought about their crisis and that now prevented them from engaging in political activism, such as unionization and strike.[75]

In short, these various factors—the rapid *embourgeoisement* of workers in the United States, the confounding of class struggle with racial conflict, the sudden fall of the middle class into labor, and we might want to add the rise of consumerism—contributed to the overlaying of class identification (worker) with other, more complex, social identifications (non-black, petit bourgeois, consumer), thereby preempting a radical opposition between working and middle classes—which was so characteristic of political theaters in Europe at the time.

In the United States, it was this heterogeneous audience of working men and women of various cultural and social backgrounds, identifications, and allegiances that the professional leftist theaters of the 1930s sought to address and to assemble for political work. The sentimental education of the middlebrow proved to be particularly suitable for this purpose since it addressed its audience primarily as consumers, a category that replaced and subsumed all other identifications. The middlebrow did not distinguish between the carriage trade of Broadway and the audiences of music halls, between patrons of book clubs or those of dime store literature, but in providing an easily accessible and pleasurable education of sorts, it appealed to all. With its emphasis on the immediacy of experience (that "true-to-life-ring") and the visceral stimulation of its readers, the middlebrow closely assimilated both the well-established traditions of bourgeois entertainment (appealing to an aspiring as well as fallen middle class) and to the more sensational aesthetics operating in working-class culture.

Let me add a few words about the perception and reception of vernacular and modernist aesthetics by working men and women at the time. Studies of the period show that for many readers and critics, the pulps turned out to be the real proletarian literature of the "Red Decade." A survey conducted by the proletarian *Pen & Hammer Bulletin* revealed that the pulps enjoyed much wider circulation and greater influence than all major proletarian newspapers taken together. The Marxist authors of the survey were, of course, quick to conclude that their findings once again attested to the pernicious influence of mass culture on the American working class, which was "kept esthetically and ideologically illiterate by the capitalist class and is so oppressed in its daily life that it is driven to accept the literature of escape and distraction offered it by the pulps and shinies."[76] Yet, as cultural critic Erin Smith suggests, the popularity of lowbrow fiction among workers also reflected their active engagement with consumer capitalism.[77] The popular detective stories of the 1930s and 1940s, for example, taught their male readers (by inviting them to identify with the hard-boiled detective heroes) how to navigate urban culture, how to actively shape their lives and careers, and how to feel at home in commodity culture. Something similar can be asserted about the readership of pulp romances.[78]

The proletarian novel, by contrast, particularly when using modernist techniques, did not fare well at all. At the American Writers' Congress of 1935, Henry Hart lamented the pitiful sales of proletarian fiction and warned his comrades that publishers might begin to refuse their writing altogether: "I have heard it already said, proletarian and revolutionary novels don't sell."[79] One reason why proletarian novels did not sell was, as Louis Adamic deduced from a private survey, that the majority of workers felt baffled and intimated by the detached rational argumentation and "queer writing" of their authors.[80] A Pittsburgh worker, for example, commented on William Rollins's *The Shadow Before* and John Dos Passos's *1919*:

I didn't finish it, I couldn't. It's full of queer spelling, queer paragraphing, italics, and words in big type and all jumbled up in places, like parts of John Dos Passos's books. And Dos Passos, by the way, why does he write so queer? I read *1919*, which everybody seemed to rave about when it came out, and man, it was like solving puzzles from start to finish. Some of the things I solved were interesting and true, I don't say they weren't; but why should a writer want to turn reading into a game? Why should I spend a week or two puzzling over a book? Why shouldn't they write so a fellow who isn't altogether dumb could understand things right away? Do they want to make me feel stupid and humble before their genius, or is that art?[81]

Concluding from this and similar comments that the workers disliked any "mannerism and tricks," Adamic appealed to his fellow proletarian writers to steer away from "queer" (i.e., modernist) writing and produce "truthful" and "well-written" texts.[82] Most importantly, so Adamic insisted, in "scope and emotional appeal, [they] should appeal to any American, regardless of class and instigate them to social change."[83] With this, Adamic voiced a rather conservative but nevertheless widespread sentiment of the time. If socially committed art was to be more than a hothouse creation, it had to reach out both to the readers of pulp fiction and the readers of the book-of-the-month clubs. This meant that it could not afford to be sectarian, neither in its politics nor in its aesthetics. This view, although highly debated, informed much of the discussion over political art at the time, as I will show in more detail in chapter four.

It is precisely here that the strength of New Deal theaters stands out most clearly vis-à-vis the more experimental proletarian novel. Insisting on a "non-queer"—that is, vernacular dramaturgy, professional leftist theaters succeeded in attracting the audience that the modernist political novel sought in vain. Emulating the consumer aesthetics of the middlebrow, they recognized that political education had to be made palatable in order to be effective. This strategy, however, was not without ideological consequences—which leads us to a last crucial distinction of vernacular political theater.

While with the advent of consumer culture, the sudden equal access to commodities did not automatically erase class distinctions, as Lizabeth Cohen has convincingly shown in her essay "The Class Experience of Mass Consumption" (1993), it certainly encouraged a sense of egalitarianism and faith in the market economy among working-class consumers. The utopia of a shared consumer identity overcoming all class tensions was actively promoted by the mass media presenting consumerism as twentieth-century egalitarianism. Cohen insists that despite such official rhetoric "mass" never replaced "class" in American working-class culture and that the ideal of the liberal consumer model, in which a depoliticized working class identified fully with the middle class, did not emerge in practice.[84] But she also concedes that it nevertheless persisted as an ideology, which most likely affected the political and aesthetic choices of the working class. As Cohen points out, in general American workers were not opposed to capitalism itself, as long as it operated according to certain standards of fairness and morality. In contrast to European workers, who tended to be more anti-capitalist, so Cohen argues elsewhere, American workers of the 1930s sought to improve their living and working conditions

> neither through anticapitalist and extragovernmental [*sic*] revolutionary uprisings nor through perpetuation of the status quo of welfare capitalism but rather through their growing investment in two institutions they felt would make capitalism more moral and fair—an activist welfare state concerned with equalizing wealth and privilege and a national union movement of factory workers committed to keeping a check on self-interested employers.[85]

Putting their weight behind Roosevelt's New Deal and supporting a strong union movement, these workers became, on the one hand, "more aware of their distinctive class interests," but, on the other hand, they also "became tied more than ever intended to the status quo," Cohen concludes.[86] In other words, one could argue that the common experience of mass culture not only provided workers with a common basis for building a class-based institution like the Congress of Industrial Organizations (CIO) but that it also fostered a widespread conviction that capitalism must be and could be made fair.

The vernacular political theater of the New Deal reflected and promoted this ideology in appealing, first and foremost, to the consumer identity of its working- and middle-class spectators and providing them with spectacles of consumption—again all in marked distinction to the modernist praxis of political theater. The labor revue *Pins and Needles*, which was staged by the International Ladies' Garment Workers' Union (ILGWU), dressed its political satires in the language of the great Broadway follies of the 1920s, using catchy tunes, elaborate dance routines, and lavish sets and costumes. While in content the show insisted that the rampant *laissez faire* capitalism of giant corporations needed to be curbed and that the interest of the common man needed to be reasserted through government intervention, its visual display of the aesthetics of consumerism rarely called capitalism itself into question. Similarly, the Living Newspaper of the Federal Theatre Project would remind their audience that underneath all class differences they were all "common consumers" and that by supporting the New Deal government in taking control of such essential consumer products as electricity and public housing, this capitalist society could work to the benefit of all. In general, when a leftist production ended in the call for "Strike!" (*Waiting for Lefty*), the affirmation of the democratic identity of "We, the People" (*Peace on Earth*), or the appeal for government intervention "Can you hear us, Washington?" (*One Third of a Nation*), it was rarely a call for revolution but rather a plea for reform and an affirmation of the country's democratic legacy.

We can thus add another distinctive feature to our list of characteristics: the vernacular political theater of the New Deal tends to be reformist rather than revolutionary in its political agenda. As Daniel Aaron pointedly remarked on the myth of a "Red Decade," in the 1930s "the American writer's running quarrel with his society [. . .] may have sprung as much or more from his identity with that society than from his alienation."[87] This takes us back to our initial consideration of vernacularity as a sign of a deeply embedded cultural nationalism, asserting itself in a vehement anti-intellectual stance and the concurrent emphasis on identification with the immediacy of experience of the common man. Again, the consumer aesthetics of the middlebrow with its emphasis of precisely those characteristics valued by the American vernacular proved to be the ideal vehicle for the promotion of such cultural nationalism. It is therefore not surprising that in the political theater of the New Deal the battle cry "We, the People!" is also intimately linked to the assertion "We, the Consumers!"

Chapter Three

Strike Songs: Working- and Middle-Class Revolutionaries

Looking Left: Broadway and the Workers' Theaters

When the stock marked crashed in October 1929, the professional theaters did not respond. With the fading out of the Little Theater movement of the early 1920s, Broadway had resigned itself to general musings about the metaphysical longing of man. It had no significant comment to offer on the current crisis. What is more, the typical Broadway audience, the carriage trade, had long been conditioned not to expect anything relevant from the stage. Mordecai Gorelik mockingly commented, "The playgoer is asked to check his reasoning powers at the door. [. . .] What he sees on the stage does not, apparently, matter very much; it is important that it be a story whipped up in excitement and bathed in dreamlike nostalgia."[1] As early as 1928, with prosperity still at its height, the professional theater was largely considered dead. During the Depression, Broadway simply watched its audiences shrink away as fewer and fewer members of the middle class could afford Broadway prices and as more and more wandered off to the movie theaters.[2] Moreover, it had nothing to say to the ones who stayed. As usual, it kept offering distraction and entertainment, deliberately refraining from reflecting on the national crisis. As observers of the time remarked, Broadway had become "completely superfluous" to those who were interested in what was happening all around them.[3]

At the same time, there existed a broad public that took a keen interest in contemporary events, demanding plays that discussed the economic and social crisis. It was a public of working- and lower-middle-class people eager to share their experience and opinions in a public forum like the theater. While Broadway stagnated, this demanding public developed a lively drama on the amateur stages of its immigrant communities, at strike, rallies, and in union halls. This vibrant workers' theater movement was to be crucial to the development of professional leftist theaters of the New Deal as well. In what follows, I shall give a brief overview of its history and aesthetics in order to trace its influence on the emergence of a vernacular praxis of political theater.

The new public first announced its presence on Broadway in December 1931, at the opening of Claire and Paul Sifton's play *1931*.[4] "Seldom has a bad play stunned an audience quite so completely," a bewildered Brooks Atkinson declared.[5] The play was a rather crude exercise in expressionism but startled its audiences and critics by sheer virtue of topicality. For the first time one of the most pressing social concerns was addressed on the commercial stage: mass unemployment. In the parable of Everyman Adam undergoing the turmoil of the recent economic recession, the Siftons had created a modern morality play that vividly depicted how long-term unemployment affected the American people emotionally, psychologically, and socially. For the Broadway carriage trade, such topical verve was so surprising that upon leaving the theater, Percy Hammond of the *New York Herald Tribune* felt compelled to reassure himself that surely life was not as bleak and cruel in the streets as portrayed on stage. Looking at the men and women in line for the movies, he was relieved to see that "none of them was cold or hungry. They were warmly clothed and had the price of admission."[6] Hammond's incredulity and deliberate ignorance of the thirteen million unemployed on the other side of Broadway was not atypical for the patrons of the Great White Way.[7] In the end, their general disinterest shut down the Siftons' play after only nine performances. But during those nine evenings, Hammond along with the fur-coated and jewelried public in the orchestra seats were forced to acknowledge the presence of a lively "new" audience—the spectators in the galleries who enthusiastically applauded each performance.[8]

"The theatre being born in America today is a theatre of workers," Hallie Flanagan observed that very same year. "Admittedly a weapon in the class struggle, this theatre is being forged in the factories and mines."[9] The workers' theater drew its inspiration and vitality from a variety of sources. One source was the numerous immigrant theater groups, who cultivated within their ethnic communities both the classic humanist tradition of the European People's Theatre (e.g., the Ukrainian Dramatic Circle, the Yiddish Art Theatre, the Hungarian Dramatic Circle) as well as the iconoclastic experiments of German agitprop and Russian constructivism (e.g., the German Proletbühne, the Jewish Artef, the Hungarian Uj Elöre).[10]

At the same time, intellectuals and theater professionals became increasingly interested in and involved with the amateur workers' theater, as for instance evident in their collaboration on the Paterson Strike Pageant of 1913. In the 1920s, as more and more intellectuals rallied to the support of the workers' movement, various professional leftist theaters emerged.[11] Foremost among them was the Workers' Drama League (founded by John Howard Lawson, Michael Gold, Jasper Deeter, and Ida Rauh in 1926), which committed itself to dramatizing the lives of workers for a working-class audience. Although the troupe fell apart within two years, it led to the establishment of another professional "workers'" theater a year later—the New Playwrights' Theatre of Lawson, Gold, Francis Farragoh, Em Jo Basshe, and John Dos Passos. The New Playwrights too insisted that theirs was a workers' "theater of social protest"—even though their theater was heavily endowed by banker Otto Kahn.[12] Their provocative, iconoclastic productions earned them the title "the revolting playwrights"; yet, aside from a vehement anti-bourgeois stance, it remained unclear what exactly the group's politics were. It dissolved after three seasons but not without having stirred up considerable attention in professional circles. Despite their general evanescence, all these experiments by intellectuals and artists were important in that they marked the distinctive leftward turn of the American intelligentsia at the end of the 1920s, its increasing commitment to social change, particularly in the wake of the Sacco/Vanzetti trial of 1927 and the Black Thursday of 1929.

Above all, it was the labor movement that recognized the urgent need for a public discussion of all aspects of the crisis and supported the formation of numerous amateur theater groups within trade unions, farm leagues, social and athletic clubs, student and foreign language organizations throughout the country. Leading among them were the German-speaking Proletbühne (1925) and the English-speaking Workers Laboratory Theatre (WLT, 1928); both were militant street theater troupes that played at rallies and meetings and specialized in mass chants and other agitprop techniques.[13] In April 1932, a dozen of these amateur troupes convened in New York for the First National Workers' Theatre Spartakiade and Conference. The convention culminated in the founding of a national umbrella organization, the League of Workers Theatres (LOWT). Over the next decade, LOWT established itself as the backbone of the American proletarian theater movement. With the help of its monthly magazine *Workers Theatre* (launched the previous year by WLT and Proletbühne) it managed to reach out to hundreds of amateur organizations, providing them with dramatic scripts and theoretical foundations, helping them to organize and share their ideas. By 1934, it supported over 400 amateur theaters across the country—a third of them foreign language troupes. Its magazine achieved a circulation of over 10,000 copies in 1934, reaching 18,000 in 1938. In 1933, the League launched its first professional English-speaking workers' theater, the Theatre Union. In short, the organized labor movement played an invaluable role in redefining the function of theater in American society, reaching out to broad sections of the population and insisting on the contemporary relevance of artistic productions. The stimuli it sent out extended far beyond the proletarian theater movement proper, influencing the emergence of a dynamic leftist culture in the United States, both amateur and professional. They extended as far as the government.

In the mid-1930s, Washington also discovered the significance of this lively new theater and its public when it set up among its various Works Progress Administration (WPA) programs the Federal Theatre Project (FTP). FTP was to serve two primary functions: to provide work for thousands of unemployed theater workers and to create a theater of entertainment and education for the American people. In doing so, it heavily relied on the resources and talents of the workers' theaters. At the same time, FTP also contributed to the latter's efforts of using the arts as a forum for the discussion of ongoing problems. As FTP director Hallie Flanagan wrote, "It is time that the theatre is brought face to face with the great economic problems of the day, of which unemployment is one."[14] Aside from that, FTP was to "stimulate theatergoing" in general and, in this manner, to contribute to the revival of the commercial stage as well.[15]

The American theater was thus helped along by amateurs and professionals, labor, intelligentsia, and government alike. Targeting an audience of lower-salaried employees, farmers, and workers, the new theater groups helped to break up the popular conception of dramatic arts as a prerogative of the Broadway carriage trade, opening it up to millions of people across the United States. At the time, this vibrant new theater culture was widely hailed as "the living theater."[16] By 1935, even the conservative press had to acknowledge its existence. The London *Times Literary Supplement* dedicated an entire front page to the progressive swing in American drama, proclaiming "American Writers Look Left."[17] The *New York Times* likewise conceded that "the commercial theatre's custodians have lifted their eyes from the ledgers and discovered pretty close to their doorstep a lustily kicking youngster, well shed of its swaddling clothes."[18] Broadway could now no longer bar its stages to socially committed drama, and in turn it was to receive a new lease on life.

American Agitprop

The influence of the amateur theater movement on professional leftist drama in the United States cannot be stressed enough. It made "hundreds of thousands of workers theater-conscious," and by linking up labor organizations with the theater, it laid the basis for the subscription system that supported the work of professional leftist theaters such as Theatre Union.[19] Its aesthetic influence was evident in the most important productions of the period: Clifford Odets's *Waiting for Lefty*, Theatre Union's proletarian melodramas, Marc Blitzstein's opera *The Cradle Will Rock*, and the government-sponsored Living Newspaper—all of which will be the subject of subsequent chapters.

Just like in Soviet Russia and the Weimar Republic, the work of these amateur and semi-professional theater groups was often marked by the overt theatricality of agitprop. Agitprop was the dominant style of American political theater from about the late 1920s (the time of the inception of the first amateur workers' theaters) to about 1935 (the time of the emergence of the first professional workers' theaters)—a period roughly corresponding to the most militant phase of American class struggle. As early as 1932, we begin to notice a decisive shift in the work of these political theater groups toward a more classic realist approach. This shift was to lead to the eventual abandonment of radical proletarianism and the formulation of a native theory of revolutionary realism at the First American Writers' Congress of 1935. This aesthetic transition from a more radical to a more conservative aesthetics closely follows international political developments, particularly the new alliance of communism with liberal bourgeois forces and its official adaptation of a united front platform. As critic Ira Levine observes, "[W]ith this policy, the international communist movement suspended its insurgent activity against capitalism and, in the face of growing fascist power, adopted a program of accommodation with liberalism and the democratic bourgeois governments of Europe and America."[20]

However, the concomitant change in aesthetics was far from being drastic or surprising. Rather, as I will show in this chapter, in the United States agitprop and realism were not considered to be incommensurable, as they were in Europe. On the contrary, American leftist theaters often regarded and used agitprop techniques not as means of alienation and distantiation but as means of heightening the verisimilitude of the performance and of maximizing audience identification with the play. Such counter-intuitive conception of agitprop had, as we will see, little to do with European modernist aesthetics but was, on the contrary, very much embedded in a vernacular understanding of political theater. The switch toward realism around the year 1935 therefore signified above all a gradual shift of emphasis, rather than a radical transition, in the approach of New Deal theaters to the question of form and public. A closer look at the concept and function of agitprop in the United States will be useful in explaining this unproblematic transition.

The first phase of workers' theaters (late 1920s–early 1930s) was marked by the street work of numerous amateur troupes, taking their performances directly to the mines and factories, to union meetings and picket lines. Their skits were, due to the rudimentary training of the troupes, their extreme mobility and flexibility, and the brevity of their performances (mostly lasting only fifteen minutes) often "crude in plot and characterization and full of revolutionary clichés," as observer Ben Blake described them.[21] At the same time, they also revealed "a hard-hitting directness of statement that would often strike off flaming sparks of emotion in the beholder."[22]

In *Scottsboro* (1931), one of the most popular Proletbühnen pieces, players clad in black would encircle the spectators from all sides, reciting their lines (at times with the help of megaphones) in a fast-paced staccato rhythm:

> *1st player*: Attention!
> *2nd player*: Attention, workers!
> *3rd player*: Friends!
> *4th player*: Fellow workers!
> *5th player*: Comrades!
> *All six*: ATTENTION!
> *1st player*: Hear the story—of the nine Negro boys—in Scottsboro, Alabama.[23]

As Blake recollects, "The players would crouch forward, and in a half-whisper that conveyed all the horrors and pathos of the plight of the victims, would chant in unison the refrain that kept recurring throughout the piece": "In Scottsboro / In Scottsboro / Murder stalks the streets / In Scottsboro / In Scottsboro / Death haunts the cells."[24] These mass chants had a distinctive style, which Flanagan described as "a direct, terse, hard hitting phraseology, a machine gun repetition, a sharp, type analysis with no individual characterization and a climax often ending in a mass demonstration."[25]

In general, it was not so much the militant content of a skit but the sheer viscerality of its presentation that carried the performance and aroused its audience, often prompting them to a spontaneous display of solidarity. "The audience is taken by surprise," Michael Gold explains, "workers like themselves rise to shout passionate slogans or to storm the platform. The audience is swept more and more into the excitement all around them; they become one with the actors, a real mass; before the recitation is over, everyone in the hall should be shouting: Strike! Strike!"[26] The strong affect of such technique is most apparent in the fact that the skits of the German Proletbühne managed to electrify even the non-German-speaking spectators.

In the early 1930s, troupes such as Proletbühne began to mushroom all over the country: the Rebel Players of Los Angeles, the Red Dust Players of Oklahoma, the Blue Blouses of Chicago, the Solidarity Players of Boston, to name only a few. Most prominent among them was the Shock Troupe of the Workers Laboratory Theatre—a small mobile collective that was "available on a few hours' notice for emergency performances at strikers' meetings and other labor events [. . .] to entertain, educate and maintain the morale of the workers."[27] The influence of agitprop also quickly extended beyond the amateur theater movement proper, affecting professional drama as well. The Siftons' *1931*, for instance, extensively borrowed from the fast-paced rhythm of the mass chant and the montage technique of agitprop. Rapidly crosscutting the individual fate of the protagonist with the collective fate of the unemployed masses, the authors accentuated the pace of the action and heightened the dramatic suspense. The most spectacular appearance of agitprop on Broadway, however, came with Clifford Odets's *Waiting for Lefty* in 1935, to which I shall return shortly.

Without doubt, the aesthetics of American workers' theaters owed much to the influence of the Russian Blue Blouses and German Arbeiter-Sprechchöre, whose work had been introduced to the United States by immigrants, travelers to Europe, and publications in theater magazines. But the American troupes nevertheless sought to adjust this style to the needs and experiences of American workers. What stands out in this endeavor is the emphasis on mass appeal and complete identification of the spectators with the performers. "The play must be written in the dialogue of the masses, about situations that the masses are familiar with, about types that they can quickly recognize," Albert Prentis of WLT insists.[28] Only if the audience was able to identify easily and completely with the actors in the play could the goal of awakening class consciousness and of prompting labor organization be realized.

Although American agitprop performers defined their work, just like their European colleagues, as "anti-realist"—that is, in opposition to the naturalist aesthetics of bourgeois stages—they nevertheless retained their faith in the emphatic force of such classic concepts as identification and verisimilitude. Unlike the modernist understanding of agitprop as an alienation technique, as a means of exposing the theatricality of a performance, they considered agitprop a tool of enhancing the impression that what was unfolding in front of the spectators was, in fact, life itself. Such diegetic deployment of theatricality was far from being a contradiction in terms. As Jake Shapiro explained, the amateur theaters' use of agitprop had nothing to do with modernist attempts of breaking with the illusionism of the bourgeois stage, which according to him had resulted "in the bizarre only."[29] On the contrary, in the workers' theater the problem of the separation of stage and audience never existed to begin with. "Our actors are workers," Shapiro insisted, "[t]hey carry no halo. They are part of the masses and the message of the play is their message."[30] According to this logic, the hard-hitting directness of agitprop would greatly enhance the impression of immediacy and verisimilitude of a performance. "Our actors can walk off into the audience or rise from the audience without danger of being bizarre. They are working men and women and walking off among their comrades."[31] Precisely by remaining completely themselves, the worker-actors would emphasize their kinship with the worker-spectators rather than create some kind of intellectual distance. Hence, even though anti-realism remained one of the cardinal rules of American agitprop (alongside with collectivism, simplicity, and mobility), it was here theorized as the style most *realistic* to a working-class audience. In this understanding, militant agitprop became ironically one and the same with Diderot's call for absolute verisimilitude of place and situation and complete identification of spectator, actor, and character—the very key tenets of bourgeois sentimental drama.

Given such vernacular conception of agitprop as a means of enhancing the immediacy of dramatic experience and concurrently of audience identification, the shift toward realism and accommodation with the bourgeois stage in mid decade was far from abrupt. As Levine stresses, it had very little to do with the proclamation of the doctrine of socialist realism at the Soviet Writers' Congress of 1934, as has been widely assumed but was "an indigenous American development" that was already well under way by the time the Soviet doctrine reached America.[32] Indeed, John Bonn of Proletbühne had urged his fellow worker-actors as early as 1932 to take a more "active attitude towards the bourgeois theater"—that is, to begin to adopt certain classic techniques from the commercial stage and to establish their own stationary theaters.[33]

Bonn deemed such professionalization necessary for primarily two reasons: on the one hand, it would allow proletarian theaters to draw the workers away from the bourgeois stage, and on the other hand, it would enable the theater troupes to reach out to bourgeois audiences as well. According to him, this could best be achieved through stationary theaters since they allowed for the use of more elaborate technical means and thus offered greater possibilities for affecting the audience emotionally. Ideally, the workers' theater could then operate on two fronts, by using "the flashlight effect of the mobile up-to-date agitprop theatre as well as the impetus of the slower but broad attack of the more complicated stationary theatre."[34] While Bonn still stressed the need for both models, leftist theater practitioners and critics began to weigh in more and more on behalf of the latter. The success of Theatre Union, which within its first two seasons drew an audience of half a million, inspired the establishment of similar professional stationary enterprises in Philadelphia, Chicago, Davenport, New Orleans, Los Angeles, and San Francisco. While agitprop street theater continued its work till about 1935, landing a last grand hit with the WLT one-act *Newsboy* (1934), it gradually disappeared from the limelight.

By the mid-1930s, debates over the insufficiency of agitprop techniques had built up to a point where *New Theatre* (successor to *Workers Theatre*) felt compelled to announce that "the day of cliché and mechanical statement" was over: "An animated symbolic pantomime in a whirl of top hats and red-front fists punctuated with appropriate slogans may clearly illustrate to the intellectual the theory of surplus value, but the worker would prefer a vivid dialogue between a worker and a boss in terms of cash and cabbages."[35] The journal reminded its readers that the worker "also thinks in terms of love, life and death outside the shop—with his job always a conditioning factor."[36] Calling for new "characters that breathe, in situations that are real,"[37] *New Theatre* essentially outlined the aesthetic program for the second half of the decade, as we shall see in the following chapter. While the earlier agitprop influence still asserted itself in the emphasis on the immediacy of dramatic experience and the need for visceral vigor, most leftist theaters now began to look for greater realism in character and plot development, in the process also widening their thematic scope to the more quotidian aspects of workers' lives, to questions of "cash and cabbages."

New Theatre's call for new scripts was, of course, fueled by the need to attract a broader audience. With the adaptation of a united front platform (in accordance with Comintern policy), the radical left relinquished its former sectarian stance and adopted a more populist rhetoric that sought to mobilize all liberal forces in the defense of civil liberties, against fascism and war. "In organizing a stationary workers' theater," so critic Margaret Larkin pointed out, "it is supremely important to recognize the necessity of appealing to the *masses*, organized and unorganized."[38] The explicit goal was now to reach the non-revolutionary audiences, to draw the "unorganized workers into militant struggle."[39] For this, a move toward a broader subject matter and more profound character psychology was deemed indispensable. To an extent, this, however, also signified an alignment with the bourgeois culture industry. As Conrad Seiler insisted in *New Theatre*, "Non-revolutionary audiences—the kind we must attract—are used to the smoothness of the bourgeois theatre and the films, and consequently the lumbering, painfully trying performances given by some workers' groups will excite nothing but amused tolerance or derision."[40]

As the workers' theaters strove for greater mass appeal and professionalism, they began not only to espouse the aesthetics of the bourgeois stage ("the smoothness of the bourgeois theatre and the films") but also to appropriate its marketing strategies. Since they were now competing with Broadway for their audiences, they too sought the collaboration with professional theater people, developed full-length plays, and employed commercial publicity techniques (benefit parties and subscription services).[41] This vernacular impulse (to speak the language of the established sign system and to secure mass appeal) became most visible in the accompanying change in rhetoric. Abandoning their former sectarian stance, leftist theaters adopted a more inclusive Popular Front vocabulary. In changing its name to New Theatre League in 1935, the former League of Workers Theatres also switched its agenda from the class struggle of "the toiling masses" to "the struggle against war, fascism, and censorship."[42] *Workers Theatre* likewise became *New Theatre*. The same year WLT, one of the country's oldest and most militant amateur troupes, renamed itself Theatre of Action and went professional as well. This trend toward professionalization and vernacularization culminated in a heated debate over the new approach to form and public at the First American Workers' Congress in spring 1935. It would lead to the formulation of an indigenous theory of political theater, the doctrine of revolutionary realism.

For now, I shall discuss the New Deal production that most efficiently incorporated the agitprop aesthetics of the amateur workers' theaters while also already pointing toward its eventual abolition in the left's return to the "Western, Ibsen tradition":[43] the Group Theatre's landmark production of Clifford Odets's *Waiting for Lefty*. This play, hailed by Harold Clurman as "the birth cry of the thirties," most clearly marks the transition from agitprop to realism, from militancy to populism, from revolutionary Marxism to the reform politics of the New Deal.[44] In amalgamating militant agitprop aesthetics with the traditional "smoothness" of the bourgeois stage, *Waiting for Lefty*, moreover, sets up an important paradigm for vernacular political theater.

Stormbirds of the Revolution

Clifford Odets wrote his agitational masterpiece *Waiting for Lefty* allegedly within three nights in response to the New York taxi strike of 1934.[45] It won first prize at a one-act play contest sponsored by *New Masses* and *New Theatre* and was put on stage by Odets and Sanford Meisner (both members of the Group Theatre) for the *New Theatre* Sunday night benefits at the Civic Repertory on 14th Street. At its opening on 6 January 1935, it brought down the house:

> The first scene of *Lefty* had not played two minutes when a shock of delighted recognition struck the audience like a tidal wave. Deep laughter, hot assent, a kind of joyous fervor seemed to sweep the audience towards the stage. The actors no longer performed; they were being carried along as if by an exultancy of communication such as I had never witnessed in the theater before. Audience and actors had become one.[46]

For Clurman, this extraordinary communion between actors and audiences, culminating in the spectators' spontaneous assent to the stage's call to "Strike!" signaled nothing less than the inauguration of the "fervent years" of social commitment in American theater.[47] Inflected by the spirit of the time, Clurman's claim might be somewhat overstated, but he was certainly right in that the production marked a key moment for the American cultural front and for political theater in the United States. Enthusiastically received by radical, liberal, and conservative critics alike, *Waiting for Lefty* was one of the few radical plays to enjoy an extended Broadway run and to move labor from 14th Street into the heart of the American culture industry.[48] This public success was largely enabled by the skillful amalgamation of proletarian agitprop with bourgeois drama—an amalgamation that also anticipated a significant shift in the public of political theater, from the workers to the middle class.

Clurman's memoirs, cited above, indicate that *Waiting for Lefty* might have garnered its broad public success above all thanks to its enormous visceral appeal, which completely blurred the boundaries between stage and auditorium, fiction and reality. Odets, who witnessed the opening night from the audience, described it as follows:

> The audience stopped the show after each scene; they got up, they began to cheer and weep. [. . .] From stage to theater and back and forth the identity was so complete, there was such an at-oneness with audience and actors, that the actors didn't know whether they were acting and the audience didn't know whether they were sitting and watching it, or had changed position.[49]

Evidently, Odets had managed to build up visceral involvement in the dramatic action over the course of fifty minutes to such a degree that it could but erupt in the spontaneous and triumphant display of solidarity between stage and auditorium. The audience seemed transported, demanding some twenty-eight curtain calls. "[A]nd when they couldn't applaud anymore, they stomped their feet. And this was an old theater, a wooden theater, you know, and here are these hundreds of feet stomping on . . . all I could think was 'My God, they are going to bring the balcony down!'" cast member Ruth Nelson recalled.[50] Behind this extraordinary visceral affect were a few, well-placed techniques borrowed from the agitprop theater.[51]

First, like the amateur street performers, Odets radically dismantled the illusion of the fourth wall in the direct address of the audience. As the curtain opens, a large man is haranguing a group of men seated on the bare stage and leaning against the proscenium about the inopportune moment of going on strike. "That's why the times ain't ripe for strike," the man continues to exhort his listeners only to be interrupted again and again by plants in the audience, demanding an explanation for his caution.[52] Starting in *medias res*, Odets gives the impression that we have just stumbled on a strike meeting, that, in fact, the meeting does not end at the proscenium ramp but extends well into the auditorium. Union boss Harry Fatt is talking not just to the other characters but to us as well. Whether we want it or not, we suddenly find ourselves right in the middle of a union meeting. We are the taxi drivers assembled in a union hall to debate the question of strike. Just as in an agitprop street skit, the barrier between stage and auditorium, reality and fiction is completely taken down. The effect is one of great immediacy and urgency. In the presence of Fatt's gunmen menacing actors and spectators alike, we instantly feel an emotional bond with the beleaguered taxi drivers in front and around us. This sense of community is further enhanced, when at the very end Agate Keller turns to us directly, demanding, "What's the answer, boys?"[53]

When Agate's final call for "STRIKE!" is taken up by voices all around us, it is indeed hard to hold back one's wholehearted support for the striking cabbies—as was apparently the case at many *Lefty* performances at the time.

At the same time that Odets uses such agitprop techniques as apostrophe, bare stage, and plants in the audience, he also makes it clear that he understands them very much along the vernacular lines delineated by his American agitprop colleagues and not as modernist interventions. Similar to Shapiro, he insists that these very techniques effectively de-theatricalize the dramatic experience, presenting the play as life itself to the audience and, in this manner, enabling their spontaneous psychological and emotional identification.[54]

A second standard agitprop technique used by Odets is that of *typage*, the stereotypical portrayal of characters.[55] This technique, which has a long tradition in medieval morality plays, *commedia dell'arte*, and melodrama, serves the primary purposes of reducing characters to basic sociological or moral functions. Thus Fatt is characterized as "a fat man of porcine appearance" and is quite predictably equipped with the standard accoutrement of the cigar.[56] Constantly puffing smoke into the spotlighted play area, manhandling speakers and insolently pacing up and down the stage followed by a hit man, it should be clear upon first glimpse that Fatt "represents the capitalist system throughout the play."[57] As Odets details in his production notes, "The audience should constantly be kept aware of him, the ugly menace which hangs over the lives of all the people who act out their own dramas."[58] Similarly, the antagonists of the brief individual episodes, which unfold later in the play, are presented as clear-cut villains: the ruthless industrialist Fayette (an echo of Fatt), labor spy Clancy, the debauched theater producer Grady with "a big old rose canopy over his casting couch," and the callous hospital board.[59] Clearly, psychological depth is not what the playwright is after, at least not with regard to his villains, which come across as mere caricatures. Odets strives for utter simplicity of characterization, for a Manichean delineation of good and evil, which would facilitate audience identification.

However, such crude typification is not in play in Odets's portrayal of the "good guys." Although even his "very human heroes occasionally freeze into stained-glass attitudes,"[60] they are nevertheless each given the opportunity to distinguish themselves through personal stories. Thus, we do not simply encounter the stereotypical worker but meet cab driver Joe Mitchell, lab assistant Miller, the young hack Sid and his girl Florrie, the aspiring actor Philips, and hospital intern Benjamin. Sketching out a few intimate details in his protagonists' lives, Odets clearly answers *New Theatre's* call for greater realism in the portrayal of characters.

The third distinctive agitprop influence is Odets's use of montage. Interspersing the larger dramatic frame of a workers' meeting with a series of small, individual episodes, Odets persistently augments the militant rhythm of the play, building up dramatic suspense, moral argument, and emotional involvement toward a grand climactic finale. While the committee is waiting for chairman Lefty Costello, each member tells his story, explaining his reasons for going on strike. Significantly, these episodes reveal very personal motivations, mostly anchored in love and family life. Joe confesses that it was his wife Edna who "made up his mind" for him when she threatened to leave him unless he began to resist the constant wage cuts and to stand up to his bosses. Faced with the imminent dissolution of his family, Joe rushes off to organize his fellow cab drivers. For lab assistant Miller, strike is a symbol of personal and professional integrity. When bullied by his supervisor to spy on his colleagues, Miller responds by hitting his boss "and all his kind square in the mouth" and walking out.[61] In the next episode, young hack Sid shows us how, unable to provide for a family, he was forced to break up with his fiancée Florrie. Here, the action pauses for a moment in a melodramatic embrace, emblematic for a whole generation of young working-class lovers. After this, we are briefly returned to the "reality" of the strike meeting as one "audience" member unmasks another as a notorious labor spy—both of them, however, brothers. The fifth episode resumes the militant thrust of the opening scenes. After having been utterly humiliated by a theater producer, the young actor Philips is offered a dollar bill by the secretary. "One dollar buys nine loaves of bread and one copy of the Communist Manifesto," she explains, following up with the urgent appeal to "Come out in the light, Comrade."[62] A few minutes into the ensuing episode, Dr. Benjamin, a hospital intern who lost his job due to anti-Semitic prejudice, vows to his colleague to "[f]ight! Maybe get killed, but goddam! We'll go ahead." As the lights black out, he "stands with clenched fist raised high."[63]

These various snapshots effectively reveal the personal (and the sentimental) at the heart of the political. But it is not just the emotional force of each scene that matters but their deliberate and persistent build-up toward a powerful climactic finale. The cumulative energy of these eight vignettes prepares us for Agate Keller's final speech, in which he argues that surely enough (emotional) evidence has been accumulated to arrive at a decision independent of the still tardy Lefty. "What's the answer, boys?" he demands of the spectators. "What is it? An uppercut! The good old uppercut to the chin!" and with these words he raises his fist to the communist salute.[64] Up to this point,

Odets has steadily maneuvered the emotions of the audience through a skillful montage of quiet moments of personal tragedy and heated moments of spontaneous outbursts to a final climax: "Don't wait for Lefty!"[65] This resolution is now further enforced when the news arrive that Lefty has been murdered on the way to the meeting. It is the emotional impact of such ultimate martyrdom that allows Odets passionately and forcefully to drive home the message of the play: "HELLO AMERICA! HELLO. WE'RE THE STORMBIRDS OF THE WORKING-CLASS."[66]

Last but not least, *Waiting for Lefty* heavily relies like many agit-prop plays on repetition. Each episode reiterates, with different nuances, the same point over and over again: Don't take it anymore, do something! In this manner, Odets persistently drives home the message of the play, producing a sense of urgency that would ideally rally all spectators behind the political agenda of the play. Piscator, who successfully used this technique in his proletarian revues, once compared it to the wielding of iron hammers pounding out the same message as well as to a quick fire of examples modifying one and the same theme "so that it could escape no one."[67] Odets's use was not any subtler. Critic Richard Watts, in fact, called *Waiting for Lefty* a "dramatic machine gun," which "veritably bombards you with emotional arguments, grim humor and sheer theatrical forcefulness."[68] Increasing in militancy and urgency, all episodes essentially pound out the same call for action, which is finally taken up by actors and spectators alike.

Odets's calculated montage of episodes, persistent build-up of dramatic tension, and relentless repetition of the play's message are in fact very similar to Piscator's pedagogy of affect and Eisenstein's use of montage of attractions. Like them, he uses agitprop in order to bring about and trigger that moment of pathos "when the spectator is compelled to jump from his seat, [. . .] forced 'to go out of himself.'"[69] Piscator and Eisenstein, however, always made clear that affect, even at its most sweeping moment, always remained part of a theatrical experience, of a visceral spectacle. It was the product of a series of well-placed "aggressive units" (attractions) meant to break the *diegesis* of a play, to solicit the attention of the spectator, and to provoke that emotional shock that could bring about recognition. Like early cinema, theirs was an aesthetics of astonishment and confrontation that self-consciously exhibited its own artfulness.[70] For Odets, by contrast, affect derived from the growing absorption of the spectator in the fictional world of the play. It was the result of an utterly "human" experience, as Odets put it, and not of an Eisensteinian transcendence of the individual fate in the collective cause.[71] Instead of "going out of oneself," Odets's spectator was meant to lose herself in Diderotian fashion in the verisimilitude of the personal domestic tragedy of a married couple, of young lovers, of two brothers.

Reviewers and observers attested to the broad public success of Odets's vernacular agitprop dramaturgy. Even the conservative papers applauded: "Odets is holding—nay, commanding—your attention, and as an emotionalist he has a sweeping, vigorous power which is as welcome as it is thundersome."[72] The intense visceral energy of the play apparently swept away all ideological barriers. "No matter where you stand—to the left, to the right or indifferently in the middle— *Waiting for Lefty* is a keen and canny piece of theatrical legerdemain. [. . .] Is not 'Strike!' today's password to Utopia?" a baffled Robert Garland pondered.[73]

In light of such overwhelming applause for what is purportedly a militant play, it is indeed surprising that few months later Brecht's *Mother* (November 1935) and Piscator's *Clyde Griffiths* (March 1936) should fail. Surely *Waiting for Lefty* was no less militant in its rhetoric than *Mother*, also proclaiming in unambiguous terms, "It's war! Working class, unite and fight!"[74] However, in marked contrast to the detached epic argumentation of *Mother* and *Clyde Griffiths*, *Lefty* pleaded its case in decidedly emotional terms. Moreover, unlike the epic plays of Brecht and Piscator, *Waiting for Lefty* did not strike the American audience as entirely foreign and alienating in form and content because alongside the agitprop tradition it also shrewdly evoked familiar paradigms of classic bourgeois drama.

First, Odets infuses agitprop with Aristotelian mimesis and empathy. His characters do not simply exhort the spectators to action with the recitation of slogans, but they reenact (imitate) the various conflicts that prompted them to join the strike committee. As Joe begins to tell his story the house lights fade on stage and audience, and a single spotlight picks out the play area into which Edna steps. Moreover, in his portrayal of character, Odets relies heavily on the spectator's capacity for identification. His cab drivers are, in contrast to their antagonists, not mere stereotypes, but they have elementary biographies and rudimentary psychological depth. Above all, they are not simply militant workers getting ready for some serious class struggle but young couples trying to get married, young employees trying to do well in their professions, and families breaking apart under the pressures of the economic recession.

Second, the three prevalent themes of the play (love, family, and career) were familiar to everyone in the audience regardless of social standing or political allegiance. As Joe points out to the audience, "you guys know this stuff better than me."[75] It is the stuff of classic bourgeois drama, of Diderot's domestic tragedy and Lessing's *bürgerliches Trauerspiel*. Even the spectator who might be appalled by the militancy of theme and plot is, in this manner, drawn back into the action. At stake is, after all, not simply an abstract idea but also the well-being and prosperity of the American family. And this well-being is being threatened by an oppressive capitalist system, so illustratively embodied in the corrupt union boss Fatt, the ruthless industrialist Fayette, and the debauched theater producer Grady. By explaining the need for militant class struggle through the logic of sentimental domestic tragedy, Odets not only builds up melodramatic appeal but also lends great credibility to the plot development. "Life is like that!" one spectator allegedly exclaimed before fainting under the spell of such overwhelming verisimilitude.[76]

The sense of verisimilitude is further enhanced by two other distinctive characteristics: Odets's command of colloquial American English as well as the naturalist acting style of the Group Theatre. Atkinson, who reviewed the performance with his usual restraint, was greatly impressed by the utter believability of dialogue and acting: "The characters are right off the city pavement."[77] Such verisimilitude was certainly facilitated by the actors' training in Method acting, enabling them to recreate a character's emotional life with great verve and fine nuances. In addition, it was helped along by Odets's mastery of the East Side dialect: "The phrases are pungent, fresh, simple, mobile, the ringing speech of flesh and blood proletarians," Stanley Burnshaw wrote.[78] Joseph Wood Krutch likewise found the strikers "so real" and "so actual, that when the play is over one expects to find their cabs outside."[79] It must have been under the spell of the playwright's ability "to catch the accents and the feelings of life" that reviewer Richard Lockridge felt compelled to check up on the wages of a cab driver upon leaving the performance.[80] Not without relish he noted that Odets must have gotten the facts wrong after all. The cab driver he met could very well afford a family, a car, and weekly trips into the countryside and was, hence, surely not interested in a proletarian revolution. The occasional snide remark did, however, not diminish the general enthusiastic praise for the Group's realistic acting and the immediate mimetic appeal of Odets's writing, both of which made the play "stinging with reality."[81] As John Gassner confirms, it was precisely the emphatic realism of Odets's snapshots of American life in *Waiting for Lefty* that allowed the audience—in contrast to Brecht's *Mother* and Piscator's *Clyde Griffiths*—to cope with the more theatrical frame of the play and to accept its agitprop didacticism.[82]

Finally, Odets never lectures his audience the way that Brecht and Piscator do. Instead, he uses a more subtle and artistic didactic approach: the classic topos of conversion. Trying to bring about the overall conversion of the entire audience, Odets anticipates and rehearses it in miniature form in every individual episode. Each protagonist, cornered by a confluence of hostile circumstances, eventually comes to the realization that it is up to him to bring about change: Joe rushes off to organize his buddies; Miller knocks out his boss; Philips seems to be at the threshold of communist revelation; and Benjamin resolves to fight for social change. *Waiting for Lefty* thus becomes, as Lawson puts it, a "study in conversions"—individual conversions as well as group conversions.[83] While listening to each other's stories, the committee members become increasingly more resolute, eventually intervening together as Fatt's men attack Agate. Thus, their conversion from simple followers of Lefty into active strike leaders is complete as well. Simultaneously, the audience too is being converted. The precision and vividness with which Odets captures the malaise of the Depression have a deep personal effect on each spectator. Along with the protagonists, they are increasingly affected by the growing explicitness and persuasiveness of arguments on stage, and together with their heroes they resolve to resist and fight. The conversions on stage should thus lead to conversions in the onlookers, resulting in the final collective conversion of the audience in the union hall, the theater— and ideally the country as a whole. However, to what extent such *emotional* identification can lead to the spectator's *cognitive* endorsement of Odets's argument remains open.

I want to suggest that it was precisely the play's ambivalence as to how exactly emotional identification would translate into political commitment that enabled it unwittingly to appeal to a broad and diverse audience of organized and unorganized workers, middle-class sympathizers, and traditional theatergoers alike. Odets simultaneously operates on two levels. Using standard agitprop techniques, he clearly and swiftly delineates the main conflict of his play, establishes immediate communication with the audience, and facilitates their visceral absorption in the dramatic action. Drawing on familiar paradigms of classic bourgeois theater, he, moreover, enhances the verisimilitude of action and facilitates audience identification. Thanks to such shrewd amalgamation of the sharp, cartoon-like presentations of agitprop with the nuanced realism and sentimentalism of classic dramatic representation, *Waiting for Lefty* epitomizes, as Cosgrove puts it, "the archetypal American protest play and the logical conclusion of the fusion of social drama with agitprop"[84]—a fusion that was to be short-lived as we shall see in the next chapter.

Lefty quickly became a favorite of downtown and uptown audiences. Arthur Pollock was delighted that it found enthusiastic applause "right in the heart of the conventional theater district,"[85] and Atkinson strongly recommended the play to those wealthy patrons "who want to understand the times through which they are living."[86] In addition to playing some 168 Broadway performances, *Lefty* continued to be performed by amateur theater groups throughout the United States and even in Great Britain.[87] In New York, it became something of a fad among working-class audiences, with many spectators watching the play several times and joining the actors in their lines. The effortless adaptation of the play to the tastes of audiences on both sides of the "Macy-Gimbel line," however, begs the question as to the actual intention of the play and its targeted audience. Who was to be converted by the play's series of worm-turns situations, the uptown crowd along with the workers downtown? Was the play indeed a rallying cry to strike as the passionate audience responses on 14th Street would lead us to believe? Or was it written simply to facilitate understanding of one's times, as Atkinson suggests? In short, how viable is the ostensible militancy of the play?

Here, we stumble over the intrinsic contradiction between the play's form and message. Notably, Agate rallies his fellow strikers (on- and off-stage) to action by hailing them as "stormbirds of the working-class,"[88] deliberately evoking Maxim Gorky's revolutionary poem "Stormbird" (*Burevestnik*, 1901). But this appellation seems strangely at odds with the fact that only two characters of the play are strictly speaking working class (Joe and Sid) and that most of them decide to join the strike for personal reasons rather than out of the recognition of an objective economic necessity. Moreover, as Gerald Weales perceptively asks, if the function of agitprop was to elicit a particular audience response that could lead to concrete political action outside the theater, then what kind of action did Odets want to incite? "One not only shouted 'VOTE COMMUNIST!,' one presumably went out and did so. One not only shouted 'FREE TORGLER! FREE THÄLMANN!,' one did what one could about it. [. . .] One not only shouted 'STRIKE, STRIKE, STRIKE!!!' but . . . what?" Weales ponders.[89] Since the taxi strike was over and no new one was planned, there was no direct connection between the play's call for action and a concrete political agenda so typical of agitprop plays. Weales therefore concludes that the cry for strike must have been at best a symbolic call to arms.

If this, however, was the case, then the play's passionate finale most likely has to be read as a version of Aristotelian catharsis. The emotional and political climax of the play represented, as Weales puts it, a spontaneous "fulfilling of the audience, a moment of community that substitutes for direct action and makes it unnecessary."[90] In other words, the revolutionary energy aroused by various agitational techniques throughout the play most likely exhausted itself in the theater itself, in identification and empathy with the characters on stage (rather than the actual cab drivers outside). Seen from this angle, then, the play's revolutionary thrust was far from militant. On the contrary, the revolutionary energies that the play arouses are, in the end, domesticated in a generous humanist gesture: in a most general call for change. As Eberhard Brüning reminds us, although the strike was one of the most popular motifs of Broadway in the 1930s, it was rarely used and understood as an appeal for intervention but primarily as a metaphor for personal decision-making and conversion.[91]

At the time, only two reviewers picked up on the play's inherent contradiction between its dramatic form and revolutionary rhetoric, questioning the indiscriminate applause it received from left and right and wondering as to Odets's political intentions. Joseph Wood Krutch of the *Nation* suggested that while the play might be appropriate for turning the tide at a strike meeting, it was surely out of place on Broadway: "Its appeal to action is too direct not to seem almost absurd when addressed to an audience most of whose members are not, after all, actually faced with the problem which is put to them in so completely concrete a form."[92] Communist critic John Howard Lawson, on the other hand, insisted that the overwhelming emotional appeal effectively prevented the critical analysis of actual facts. The sheer force and excitement of rhetoric covered up the lack of logical substance, of "flesh-and-blood realities."[93] After all, could a militant strike committee really be made up of largely declassed members of the middle class (doctors, technicians, actors)? "One cannot reasonably call these people 'Stormbirds of the working class,'" Lawson protested.[94] He wondered whether the play even deserved the adjective "proletarian," which the press attributed to it. After all, it did not present a clear Marxist standpoint and did not argue its point on a sufficiently rational basis but represented a rather naïve and sloganized version of revolutionary commitment.

Who then was Odets writing for and with what intention? Surely, the play was not written for the Broadway carriage trade. But it is also doubtful whether it was written for a working-class audience. I want to suggest that Odets, who at the time was hailed by both left and right as "Revolution's Number One Boy,"[95] was in fact writing for just those declassed members of the middle class, whose presence in an ostensibly proletarian play Lawson so sharply criticized. *Waiting for Lefty* was above all a play about the economic and political demise of an impoverished American petit bourgeoisie. As Marxist critic Lewis Corey asserts in his study *The Crisis of the Middle Class* (1935), this was the class that was most derailed by the Depression.[96] Since the workers have hardly any property to lose and the very wealthy manage to hold on to their property even after considerable depreciation, the burden of an economic recession is usually carried by farmers and petit bourgeois. Corey, in fact, even maintains that "one of the objective functions of depression is the expropriation of the owners of small property."[97] During the American Depression, besides undergoing a growing pauperization and degradation of their living standards due to the loss of property, the middle classes also faced a phenomenon so far entirely unfamiliar to them: mass unemployment. Suddenly the identity of many lower-salaried employees, professionals, and farmers was no longer tied to the question of property but to the question of employment. From an economic point of view, these groups clearly formed the "new proletariat," Corey argues. Yet, from a sociological and psychological point of view, they often refused to acknowledge their changed social role and essential labor identity, clinging to the very middle-class ideology that had brought about their demise. According to Corey, the crisis of this derailed middle class consisted precisely in its inability to rethink its allegiance to a system to whose formation and rise it had been instrumental.

Waiting for Lefty reflects this fall of middle-class professionals (doctors, lab assistant, actors) into labor. Yet, in contrast to Corey, who argues that the only salvation for these new proletarians lay in breaking away from their middle-class allegiance and in throwing in their lot with organized labor, Odets does not quite advocate a similar solution. While the "Young Actors Episode" (in which the secretary hands Philips a copy of *The Communist Manifesto*) might suggest a Marxist stance similar to Corey's, it is important to note that this episode quickly disappeared from the text—probably as early as September 1935, some mere eight months after the play's triumphant opening at the Civic Repertory.[98] Aside from this concrete reference to a political platform, however, the play consists entirely of a series of individual (and sentimentally charged) regenerations, which in the romanticism of Odets's revolution seem to suffice for bringing about social change. What exactly this change would entail aside from a general sense of resistance remains unclear. In short, the thematic verve and rebellious form of his play, although certainly refreshingly and shockingly new on the professional stage in 1935, ought not to be mistaken for a solid ideological position. Odets's characters are, as Clurman asserts, "profoundly of the lower middle class with all its vac-illation, dual allegiance, fears, groping self-distrust, dejection, spurts of energy, hosannas, vows of conversion and prayers of release."[99] In this regard, "Revolution's Number One Boy" is also, as Gassner suggests, "the most authentic American author of *drame-bourgeois*."[100]

Odets's further career as playwright and screenwriter bears out his commitment to the American lower middle class. Born into a Jewish middle-class family in the Bronx, he was at his best in portraying the growing anxieties of a disintegrating bourgeoisie. His celebrated plays *Awake and Sing!* (1935), *Paradise Lost* (1935), and *Golden Boy* (1937) deal with its increasing social disorientation and growing emo-tional and intellectual turmoil. "The confusion created by the stock market crash and its sequel left the middle class with prayers and imprecations on their lips, but no clear answers in their mind or heart," Clurman commented. "They were waiting—and most of them didn't even know that."[101] What made *Waiting for Lefty* so appealing was its encouragement not to wait any longer but to take actions themselves—some kind of action, any kind of action, so it seems.

In the following plays, particularly after *Awake and Sing!*, Odets's dream of revolution became much more subdued than in *Lefty*. While his third play still ends on a note of general departure, it is nonetheless aptly titled *Paradise Lost* (December 1935). The Marxist fervor, even in its metaphorical evocation, is gone; instead Odets gives us a minute analysis of the psyche of an impoverished and disoriented American middle class.

In conclusion, the more Odets and the country's Marxist sympa-thies faded, the more *Lefty* switched its function from a "dramatic machine gun" to a bourgeois conversion drama. Random House editor William Kozlenko, who selected *Lefty* for his 1939 anthology of *Best Short Plays of the Social Theatre*, detected the play's social sig-nificance above all in its presentation of "living human values."[102] Forty years later, Clurman who had once hailed the play as "the birth cry of the thirties," located the play's political value in its empathetic depiction of the metaphysical longing of the middle class.[103]

Yet, despite its lack of a radical leftist position and despite its later transformation into the emblematic play of middle-class longing, at the time of its first production *Waiting for Lefty* vividly illustrated the spirit of the "fervent years." In its rhetoric, it embodied the vigor and energy of a young and vibrant workers' culture that was increasingly asserting itself in the cultural mainstream. In content and sentimental appeal, it spoke to the emotional and psychological need of many middle-class spectators—even if it failed to articulate a concrete solution. Its great power consisted in its proclamation (even though vague and general) of the need for change, for action. And it took this assertion right onto Broadway. Odets's play thus also illustrates the extent to which the "new" audiences and their "new" drama were capable of affecting the cultural mainstream. By 1935, within less than four years of the shock triggered by the Siftons' play, the professional American stage had become a public sphere in which contemporary problems could be addressed and discussed.

The dramaturgy of *Waiting for Lefty*, moreover, exemplifies the various aesthetic and political tensions that arose in the transition from amateur street theater to professional leftist theater as well as in the attempt of adapting the passionate leftism of the workers' movement to the economic situation and emotional concerns of the American petit bourgeoisie. The shift from agitprop to realism was part of this process and a surprisingly seamless one. In all these aspects, *Waiting for Lefty* stands as a pioneering and formative example of New Deal theater.

Chapter Four

Plays of Cash and Cabbages: From Proletarian Melodrama to Revolutionary Realism

The year 1935, the year Odets's *Waiting for Lefty* triumphed and Brecht's *Mother* failed, marked a turning point in the politics and aesthetics of American political theater. We notice a distinctive shift from the fervent sectarian stance of the agitprop sketch to the more populist appeal of the full-length realist play. The work of Theatre Union illustrates this shift very clearly. During its first two seasons, it developed a series of full-length plays, which, on the one hand, meticulously adhered to *New Theatre*'s call for new scripts portraying class struggle "in terms of cash and cabbages"[1] and, on the other hand, sought to infuse this demand for mimetic realism with the revolutionary energy and pathos so typical of the agitprop street theaters. The genre that seemed most useful for this endeavor was melodrama. But in the process of developing this form with plays like *Peace on Earth* (1933), *Stevedore* (1934), and *Black Pit* (1935), Theatre Union also increasingly shifted its aesthetic emphasis from emotive speech and action-driven plot to the photo-mimetic portrayal of character and situation. This gradual rapprochement with bourgeois realism was indicative of a general cultural reorientation of the left, which began around 1932 with the widespread resolution for professionalizing the workers' theater and culminated in the American Writers' Congress in April 1935, which succinctly epitomized the cultural and political transformations that took place in mid decade and set the tone for further developments in the American political theater. This chapter discusses the aesthetics and politics of proletarian melodrama, maps out the cultural factors that influenced its production and reception, and traces the short-lived evolution of the genre in the work of Theatre Union from 1933 to 1935, the time of the congress.

The Politics of Melodrama

In an essay of fall 1934, Michael Blankfort elaborated on *New Theatre*'s call for plays of "cash and cabbages" by asserting that the task of the newly emerging professional workers' theater consisted above all in dramatizing the common experience of the broad working masses in a language easily accessible to everyone. For him, this meant integrating the depiction of class struggle with domestic issues and particularly with the immediate and universal longing "for a home, for a woman, for children, for security, for love, happiness, etc."[2] Theatre Union responded to this demand of anchoring the political in concrete images of immediate sentimental and personal appeal by developing the popular genre of melodrama. Yet, while melodrama lent itself easily to the portrayal of such sentimental values, it also imposed structural limitations on the development of a genuinely revolutionary argument. In what follows, we shall see how Theatre Union expropriated the bourgeois genre of melodrama for a leftist agenda and how it thereby contributed to the formulation of a native theory of political theater. To begin with, I shall sketch out a few important observations on the aesthetic and political possibilities of melodrama for political theater.

Overall, proletarian melodrama closely follows the formulaic conventions of bourgeois melodrama, only that it transfers the primary conflict from the encounter between virtuous maiden (often working or lower middle class) and ruthless villain (often aristocratic or upper class) to that between workers and their bosses. Where formerly the melodramatic action was set in motion by a mysterious stranger attempting to subject virtue to his dubious schemes, it is now triggered by the excesses of an exploitative capitalist system weighing down on the workers. This bipolar pattern is triangulated by the figure of a noble young hero, who selflessly dedicates himself to the rescue of virtue and the punishment of villainy. In proletarian melodrama this gallant knight is usually played by a brave and self-sacrificing union organizer. Just like its bourgeois blueprint, proletarian melodrama also heavily relies on the family as its key trope. The family home stands in for a social order that has been temporarily disrupted by the threat and intrusion of external forces and is now in great need of reconsolidation. The melodramatic action seeks to identify, expel, and punish these forces and to restore the home of virtue or what Peter Brooks has termed "the old society of innocence."[3] In all these aspects, proletarian melodrama closely resembles its bourgeois predecessor. Above all, it strictly complies with the two most fundamental genre conventions: an overt emotional and moral teleology.

With this terminology, Brooks and Sergey Balukhatyi refer to the narrative's inherent desire to provoke in the spectator the utmost degree of emotional investment and moral clarity, both of which they see as intimately intertwined.[4] First, through a combination of a suspenseful plot, impassionate speeches, grand gestures, spectacular scenes, affective situations, and, above all, the constant evocation of basic sentimental values such as home, family, and romantic love, melodrama seeks to elicit vivid emotions in the spectator. This explains the high expressiveness of the genre, its penchant for excess and affect. In melodrama, so Eric Bentley reminds us, we find the root impulse of drama, its most quintessential expression and force.[5] Brooks likewise attests to the fundamental hyperbolic gesture inherent in the genre itself. In melodrama, nothing is held back but all is acted out, "nothing is *under*stood, all is *over*stated."[6] In speech and gesture, melodrama persistently seeks to break with the reality principle and to indulge desire itself in its "most transparent, unmodified, infantile form."[7]

Just as melodrama seeks to evoke the greatest possible intensity of emotions in the audience, it also attempts to channel this intensity toward a clear moral/political objective. The high emotional expressiveness of the genre is at all times accompanied by an infallible moral teleology, submitting everything (subject, plot, character, speech) to a binary worldview—its second defining characteristic. In melodrama, nothing less than the Manichean conflict of the forces of virtue with the forces of evil is at stake. In portraying the trials and tribulations of virtue, so Brooks explains, melodrama "strives to find, to articulate, to demonstrate, to 'prove' the existence of a moral universe which, though put into question, masked by villainy and the perversions of judgment, does exist and can be made to assert its presence and its categorical force among men."[8] Furthermore, in its endeavor to recover this "moral occult," melodrama knows no mediating point of view but operates entirely with the logic of the excluded middle. It is not interested in reconciling the opposition it sets up from the start but always seeks to eliminate one on behalf of the other; that is, it seeks to expel evil and to reward virtue.

It is the lack of subtlety that guarantees melodrama its broad success with audiences. Portraying virtue and her gallant knight in extremely sympathetic terms, and conversely villainy and its accomplices in extremely callous terms, melodrama commands the unequivocal identification of its audiences with the champion fighting for a noble cause and against the villain who is trying to block the fruition of this cause. As semioticians Henry Schoenmakers and Ed Tan point out, this crude "good guy/bad guy" dichotomy effectively sustains the involvement and interest of the audience by guaranteeing the pleasure of ultimately being on the winning side, for the dichotomy is always set up in compliance with the expectations of the targeted audience, and the result is hence predetermined at the outset of the play.[9] Even in the rare case where virtue remains unrehabilitated, the spectator retains the satisfaction of a vision that it could have come out differently after all. Melodramatic tears are thus not so much a sign of disappointment with the lack of final triumph but rather a sign of the spectator's profound investment in the very possibility of rehabilitation.[10] In this possibility, a moral universe, temporarily thrown into disorder, once more becomes legible. The formulaic application of the "good guy/bad guy" effect in melodrama allows audiences to surrender completely to the suspenseful plot development in the full knowledge that visceral gratification and moral satisfaction are guaranteed one way or the other.

It is evident to what extent these formulaic conventions are useful for political theater. Delineating fundamental oppositions swiftly and clearly and narrating intolerable social conditions in such a manner that spectators wish to see injustices alleviated, melodrama makes social conflict legible to everyone while simultaneously arousing the outrage and compassion that are necessary for political action. It is, moreover, an inherently egalitarian genre. As Balukhatyi observes, it "will inevitably work with any group of spectators whose hearts are open to such affecting emotional experiences, and such 'primitive' spectators constitute an extremely broad group, even if the range of their responses is limited."[11] Melodrama has thus traditionally brought together different classes and social groups, displacing class strife and social division in the shared visceral experience.

Not surprisingly, it has been the preferred genre of revolutionary periods ever since its emergence in the wake of the French Revolution. As Brooks points out, melodrama is particularly popular and useful in times, when "traditional imperatives of truth and ethics have been violently thrown into question, yet where their promulgation is also of immediate, daily and political concern."[12] Precisely for these reasons the genre was intentionally revived by the Soviet government during the Russian Revolution. Maxim Gorky (future father of socialist realism) and Anatoly Lunacharsky (Commissar of Education) saw in it an invaluable means of simplifying complex social relations and of recuperating a much needed clarity, even primitivism of feeling through which the desires and aspirations of the masses could be organized and directed. Of course, many of the qualities they appreciated in melodrama (e.g., "a fine, gripping subject; [. . .] richness in action; character traits defined with colossal relief; clarity and sharp expressiveness of all the situations and the capacity to call forth undivided and total emotional reactions of compassion and indignation; action connected to simple and clear ideological positions")[13] were also present in agitprop, which prospered on the Soviet stage at the time as well. In sharp contrast to agitprop, however, Gorky's and Lunacharsky's concept of melodrama did not stand for a sublime modernist aesthetics of shock and cognition but for a vernacular aesthetics of beauty and empathy.[14] As Gorky put it quite clearly, "The masses must be given *beautiful* theatrical performances in which their eyes can find *rest* and which will call forth in them the desire to put *beauty* into their own everyday lives."[15]

Gorky's and Lunacharsky's "revolutionary" concept of melodrama was, in the end, not all that different from the classic bourgeois concept of theater as a moral institution. It was to raise its spectators above "the chaos of the everyday and the ordinary" and to inspire them with basic humanist values.[16] The desired audience effect was therefore not the spontaneous singing of the "Internationale" as in agitprop but the weeping of "fine, purifying tears."[17] Not surprisingly, the role models for this new revolutionary melodrama were Dickens, Schiller, Rostand, and Dumas.

Revolutionary melodrama, or "melodrama permeated with an atmosphere of romanticism" as Gorky liked to call it,[18] was also very popular and influential on the New Deal stage. Here, it did not have to be promoted with the help of special playwriting contests, but thanks to the time-honored reign of Belascoism on the commercial stage melodrama seemed to be the likely choice for many socially committed playwrights on and off Broadway. The popular and critical success of the three Theatre Union melodramas, which were allegedly seen by some half million people, suggests that this genre best satisfied the demand for a vernacular aesthetics of political theater.

Yet, one wonders about the political value of such sentimental education. As many scholars of melodrama have pointed out, the genre's dramatic momentum is intrinsically conservative. In striving to expose and expel villainy from the melodramatic realm, it tends to restore a previous order and, in this manner, to reconfirm rather than challenge established social mores. The denouement is often but a return to the harmony of the beginning, and change appears to be cyclical rather than progressive. Moreover, melodrama tends to solve the social problems it touches upon in the spirit of what Balukhatyi calls the "ordinary morality" of the "common user" of melodrama.[19] But since this "ordinary morality" is firmly anchored in traditional values and established hierarchies and since the "common user" of melodrama is primarily of petit-bourgeois background, as both Brooks and Balukhatyi stress, then how viable is the genre for the implementation of *radical* social change? To what extent can it represent the interests of the working class? Is something like *proletarian revolutionary* melodrama even conceivable?

Jane Gaines sees the problem in using melodrama for revolutionary purposes in its lack of a dialectic argument. While the dualistic vision of melodrama lends itself to propagandistic didacticism precisely because it so quickly and clearly identifies basic contradictions, it also preempts their dialectic abolition in a Marxist sense. For melodrama can resolve conflict only by confirming one side of the binary that it has set up and by eliminating the other. But can "labor and capital be conceived of as a Victorian dualism and still function as a properly dialectical contradiction?" Gaines asks.[20] When used for political purposes, melodrama is thus caught up in a perpetual conflict between its own structural limitations as well as its revolutionary desire—a conflict apparent even in *Das Kapital*, when Marx stages the fundamental contradiction between labor and capital as a human drama between a ruthless capitalist and a cowering worker.

Thomas Elsaesser and John Cawelti detect a similar problem in the tension between melodrama's desire to present fundamental social evils and its generic inability (or avoidance) to question the very social structures that have led to their formation.[21] For Elsaesser, this constitutes the radical ambiguity of the genre. Depending on whether the stress is on the plot development ("the odyssey of suffering") or its *deus-ex-machina* resolution, melodrama can appear either as subversive or escapist.[22] Moreover, its continuing popularity suggests that while melodrama is very well capable of taking note of social crises, it also "refuses to understand social change in other than private contexts and emotional terms."[23] Distrusting intellectualism and abstract social theory, melodrama tends to emphasize the everyday primacy of visceral experience of social change (such as suffering and empathy). But more often than not its skepticism of *ratio* is simply indicative of a general ignorance of the proper political dimension and causality of such change. Lothar Fietz likewise asserts that precisely because melodrama tends to replace a hierarchically structured society (*Gesellschaft*) with an empathetic community (*Gemeinschaft*) anchored in compassion and structured by private connections, the main question about the actual source of evil often remains unasked, and questions of social relations and political structures are contained within the family, the individual, and the human condition.[24] In short, more often than not melodrama exhausts its critical potential by moving its audiences to tears rather than to action.

Political playwrights have struggled with these genre limitations in various ways and with varying degrees of success. As we shall see now, one popular solution on the New Deal stage was to supplement the melodramatic plot proper with a concluding image of revolutionary prophecy. Jack Conroy called it the trick of the fourth act. While the first three acts depicted the oppressive circumstances of the workers' everyday life as well as their preparations for some kind of struggle, the "fourth act" needed to suggest that victory was immanent and imminent even though it might not quite be within reach yet.[25] In theatrical practice, this meant that individual defeat had to be supplemented with a symbol of collective triumph, for example, a revolutionary tableau of collective struggle or some kind of fervent final speech, in which the vanquished hero dedicated his life to a larger cause. This larger cause was to supply the third term to the incomplete dialectic of melodrama.

I shall now examine how Theatre Union coped with these problems. Its first three proletarian melodramas mark a process of working out an effective form that offered both the visceral excitement of a melodramatic spectacle and a proper revolutionary outlook.

Melodrama on Fourteenth Street

Theatre Union was created "where nothing existed before."[26] Its founding manifesto established three professional goals: to produce plays that "deal boldly with the deep-going social conflicts, the economic, emotional and cultural problems that confront the majority of people"; to offer plays at low prices "so that the masses of people [. . .] can attend the theatre" (prices ranged from 30 ¢ to $1.50, with empty seats offered at no cost to the unemployed); and, finally, to organize and consolidate a broad working-class audience with the help of benefit parties and subscription services.[27] With this program, Theatre Union deliberately set itself up in opposition to and competition with Broadway, responding to a prevalent need to stage plays about the working class and for the working class, to put forth a working-class point of view, and to make the professional stage accessible to the broad masses.

Yet, even though considering itself a "revolutionary theatre," Theatre Union also carefully distanced itself from the sectarian stance of the Communist Party. "We stick to specific and limited tasks, functioning as a theater, not as a political party," founding member Listen Oak asserted.[28] Insisting that theirs was not an agitprop theater, the executive board (which included besides Oak, Michael Blankfort, Albert Maltz, Paul Peters, George Sklar, and Victor Wolfson) endorsed a non-sectarian, united front policy that "all honest militant workers and middle-class sympathizers" and particularly the unorganized and not-yet class-conscious workers could support.[29] This not only meant the avoidance of any blatantly "leftist" position but also the development of an aesthetics that would appeal to a broad and diverse group of spectators. In accordance with this policy, Theatre Union preferred to adhere to a classic, Aristotelian dramaturgy of verisimilitude, absorption, and identification, as seen with the example of the *Mother* adaptation. The melodramatic mode was a particularly effective vehicle for such vernacular pedagogy, allowing for the effective integration of political argumentation with visceral excitement.

Theatre Union raised its curtain at the Civic Repertory on 14th Street on 29 November 1933 with *Peace on Earth*, a play written by its members Albert Maltz and George Sklar. In its basic plot, *Peace on Earth* follows what Blankfort described as a typical "pendulum play"— a play about the conversion of a bourgeois intellectual from passive bystander into political activist.[30] Since the political effectiveness of a pendulum play depended entirely on the identification of the spectator with the plight and struggles of the protagonist ("The hero turns left; therefore the workers turns left. Q.E.D."[31]), Maltz and Sklar added a generous dose of melodrama in order to engender such empathy for protagonist Peter Owens.

Professor Owens is the somewhat artless and depoliticized American Everyman, who trusts in his government and the system it represents and keeps out of politics himself. "I am a scientist, I am a psychologist, I am not a champion of causes," he declares at the beginning of the play.[32] But the melodramatic logic of the play soon enmeshes him in a series of events that make it very clear to him (as well as the audience) that the democratic rights he so ardently upholds are no longer guaranteed. Through his friend Walter McCracken, a muckraking journalist, he gets drawn into a strike of local longshoremen against ammunition shipment. While he at first takes a purely academic interest in the strike, he is soon forced to choose sides when a student of his is arrested for publicly supporting the strike. Shocked by such blatant violation of free speech, Owens feels compelled to assert the country's democratic legacy: "I am an American citizen and I've got a legal right to say what I want."[33] But when he too gets arrested merely for reading out the Declaration of Independence, he suddenly realizes that the fundamental democratic rights of 1776 are no longer self-evident and need to be reclaimed from the very establishment he works for. By the end of Act One, the forces of virtue (Owens, MacCracken, students, longshoremen) are clearly demarcated from the forces of villainy (police, ammunition and shipping industry, university administration).

With Owens's arrest, the melodramatic action proper is set in motion. The rest of the play seeks to recuperate democratic values and to expose their deliberate obstruction by a corrupt industry and academy. In the process, the indictment of villainy becomes just as important as the public recognition of virtue. At a faculty ceremony, Owens passionately accuses his assembled colleagues of corruption and acquiescence:

> All right—don't protest. Don't protest, Howard, the University needs its endowment fund. Keep your art pure, Murdock, protest is propaganda. Don't protest, Bishop, Christ needs a new cathedral—Keep quiet all of you. There are too many people in this world. Let some of them die. What do you care? Hold tight to your honorary degrees. Keep quiet. Don't protest. Let another war come.—I won't keep quiet![34]

Such emotive speeches of moral indictment and self-vindication—delivered frequently throughout the play—are crucial to the melodramatic imagination. Virtue persecuted must speak its name, while villainy persistently seeks to mute its voice. In the heightened emotionality of such gestures fundamental ethical imperatives are made clear, urging the spectator to choose sides.

These emotive scenes are supplemented by classic affective situations, such as MacCracken's murder by militiamen. The death of the mentor marks Owens's rite of passage, allowing him to graduate from the role of disciple to that of a genuine activist. The scene is appropriately marked in melodramatic fashion by a *tableau vivant*:

> A small pool of light reveals a coffin. The rest of the stage is in darkness. Owens is sitting downstage of the coffin. Upstage of the coffin, a steady line of strikers moves past in silence. They move slowly. Each one stops for a moment, looks down at the body and moves on. Owens sits quietly.[35]

Needless to say, this interlude adds pathos to the story, which is important for motivating Owens's (and ideally also the spectators) conversion. But aside from that, the scene also serves as a crucial pause in the melodramatic plot development, allowing the ensuing denouement to shine forth the more forcefully. Already in the next scene, our hero bursts into a commencement ceremony in order to protest the giving of an honorary degree to the ammunition manufacturer responsible for McCracken's death—an act that propels the moral teleology of the play one step further.

Once the melodramatic struggle is clearly defined, it ought to be resolved in favor of virtue. This, however, brings us to the problem of the last act in revolutionary melodrama. What possibilities does the genre offer for advocating social change rather than the restoration of an existing social order? In classic melodrama, villainy should get punished and virtue rewarded. Not so in *Peace on Earth*. Here Owens gets framed, arrested, charged with murder, and sentenced to death. The play concludes with an expressionistic collage juxtaposing flashbacks of his show trial with the jingoism of a mounting war propaganda as well as with reports of rising stock market prices and frontline casualties. Contemporary capitalism, even though by now thoroughly exposed in its corruption and greed, seems to be triumphant.

Yet, just as Owens is led away to the gallows, we faintly hear the chants of an approaching anti-war demonstration: "Fight with us, Fight against War!"[36] Maltz and Sklar thus shrewdly end on a dual note: the hero dies, but his moral convictions live on in the collective struggle. Virtue triumphs after all; it triumphs in its martyrdom for a moral cause. In case anyone should miss the point, Owens is allowed one final emotive speech:

> You have no right to sentence me for murder because I haven't been found guilty of murder. But if my crime wasn't murder, if my crime was opposition to war, if my crime was association with workers fighting against war, then I am guilty. You can sentence me for those crimes, you can hang me—but you can't stop that fight.[37]

Here it is: the trick of the fourth act, the prophecy of future victory. Although villainy is obviously not vanquished quite yet, its ultimate demise seems to be looming large.

Without doubt, such final prophecy, particularly when delivered at the end of a compelling melodramatic plot, generates much revolutionary fervor: "You can't stop that fight." Over all, however, the play remains remarkably ambivalent as to the direction this revolutionary energy should take. What kind of social struggle is the play advocating? Is it rallying the audience to strike against an oppressive system? To protest against war? To the defense of freedom of speech?

As a play about class struggle, *Peace on Earth* is rather unconvincing. Although it calls for the political alliance of bourgeois intellectuals with the proletariat, the workers remain oddly effaced from *Peace on Earth*. Out of nine scenes, only two actually show the longshoremen in action. And while as motif the strike runs throughout the play, the actual strike is portrayed more or less *en passant*, reduced to a mere backdrop against which Owens's conversion unfolds. Moreover, in a genuinely Marxist argumentation, class struggle would be presented as the ultimate remedy to all forms of oppression and exploitation, including war. In *Peace on Earth*, however, class struggle (strike) stands merely as a symbol for anti-war protest. But if the play is primarily written in protest against the war as its subtitle also seems to suggest, then against what war is it rallying its audience? As an anti-war play *Peace on Earth* seems oddly displaced in 1933. The last war was fourteen years past, and a new war was not imminent yet. As Maltz and Sklar announce in their stage directions, the story is at this point purely hypothetical, a warning of things to come "in a year or so."[38] Besides, the anti-war demonstration never takes the stage but remains mere background noise. So if *Peace on Earth* is neither about class struggle nor about a concrete anti-war campaign, then what is it about?

I want to suggest that the play's militant anti-war and strike rhetoric are not meant as an incitement to concrete political action, not even as a call to leftist commitment. Rather, they serve as a reminder and reaffirmation of the ideals of Jeffersonian democracy, the very founding principles of American capitalism. Incidentally, the play is set in an unnamed "city in New England."[39] In one of the central sensational scenes, German sailors and American longshoremen join hands in throwing a shipment of ammunition overboard in imitation of the Boston Tea Party. Most importantly, Owens gets arrested for a public reading of the Declaration of Independence (and not the *Communist Manifesto*)—to be more precise, when reading out those lines from its preamble that emphasize the social contract between the people and its government. As he recites the words, "[w]hen, in the course of human events, it becomes necessary for one people [. . .] to dissolve those bonds which have—," a student of his joins in with a recitation of Lincoln's Gettysburg Address: "Four score and seven years ago our forefathers brought forth on this continent a nation created in liberty and dedicated to the proposition that all men are created equal."[40] Given the abundance of references to the American Revolution, the play's general call for action might really stand in metaphorically for the affirmation of the country's democratic legacy: the freedom of speech and the right to protest in times of national crisis—that is, when the constitutional rights to life, freedom, and pursuit of happiness are no longer guaranteed by the dominant social order.

It is in this context that we also have to read the deployment of the family as one of the play's key melodramatic tropes. *Peace on Earth* opens in the living room of the Owens home, with Owens returning home for lunch with his wife and teenage daughter. They are joined by journalist McCracken and a group of students who seek to enlist his help for their protest against the violation of free speech. The atmosphere is convivial and cheerful, and everyone soon joins forces in support of the strikers at the harbor front and the protesters on campus. By the middle of Act Two, however, this middle-class bliss is disturbed by four drunken alumni, who harass the daughter and get ready to lynch Owens as a "red." The anti-democratic actions of the establishment are here depicted as immediate threats to the American family, to the "universal longing for a home, a woman, children, safety, happiness."[41] If we are to understand the opening scene as a symbol of united front activism, then the scene in the second act suggests what could happen to the American family and, by extension, the American nation, should this united front fail to come about. The play's concluding call for collective struggle is then, above all, a rallying cry for the defense of American national identity. The melodramatic topos of the family not only imbues the political message of the play with moral relevance and sentimental value, but it also effectively translates collective action into the vernacular of American nationalism.

It is precisely in its melodramatic deployment of the family trope that *Peace on Earth* undermines its concluding revolutionary prophecy. In its appeal to safeguard one's home, to protect it from the violence of external forces, it suggests that oppression and exploitation are not indigenous to American capitalism but merely excesses that can be expelled. The politics of such allegorical rendering of the family home—a popular trope on the New Deal stage—are perhaps enunciated most clearly in Elmer Rice's *We, the People*, which opened on Broadway the same year as *Peace on Earth*. Rice concludes with the following exhortation: "We are the people, ladies and gentlemen, we—you and I and everyone of us. It is our house: this America. Let us cleanse it and put it in order and make it a decent place for decent people to live in!"[42] Clearly, what is at stake is not the tearing down and rebuilding but the cleansing and purging of the national home. In this regard, the allegorical use of the family also signifies the failure to imagine a fundamental transformation of society. In the end, the sentimental rhetoric of proletarian melodrama really cuts two ways: On the one hand, it effectively anchors the political in the personal and thereby facilitates identification with social conflict regardless of one's political allegiance. On the other hand, however, it also precludes a systemic critique of an existing social order.

Peace on Earth remains rather ambivalent in its political stance—and perhaps deliberately so. Thanks to a clear-cut moral teleology, it effectively exposes the failure of the current capitalist system to provide for "the people" and accuses it of the abolition of fundamental democratic rights for the profit interests of a few. Thanks to a strong emotional teleology, it also arouses in its spectators the outrage at social injustice and compassion for its victims that would be necessary for radical change. And thanks to the concluding prophecy, it even seems to tie this melodramatic energy to a revolutionary agenda ("You can't stop that fight."). For militant spectators, this might have sufficed as an endorsement of the revolution (labor press reviews suggest as much). For the more cautious spectator, the play however offers a rather different interpretation. Although *Peace on Earth* loudly gestures toward revolutionary change, it does not advocate revolution itself; at best, it proposes civil disobedience and the election of a new government as remedies for the current crisis. By explicitly linking social change to a confirmation of the ideals of the American Revolution, it moreover contains its critique of American capitalism in the very return to its founding principles in Jeffersonian democracy. Seen from this angle, the play is profoundly reformist rather than revolutionary in its political agenda, appealing to the better nature of American capitalism to save itself from itself.

In sum, *Peace on Earth* uses the melodramatic genre conventions in two different ways: while it employs the moral and emotional resources of melodrama for the indictment of the current political system and the arousal of the revolutionary sentiments of a broad public, it simultaneously deploys the sentimental rhetoric of family, home, and nation to redirect the energies it releases toward a revolution that has already taken place. Its dual goal is both the stimulation and the reassurance of the audience: villainy does exist and has to be purged from the current system, but such change does not require a fundamental transformation of society. Rather, "the old society of innocence," to use Brooks's term, can be restored as long as innocence and guilt can be clearly determined. The trick of the fourth act, the concluding revolutionary prophecy is really a red herring: deflecting from the fact that as so often in American melodrama, the melodramatic imagination even of a leftist play like *Peace on Earth* is intimately linked to an underlying project of national reconstruction.

Although leftist reviewers did not address the inherent cultural conservatism of the play, they nevertheless remained ambivalent with regard to its artistic and political merits. "*Peace on Earth* is not a great play. But it is a good play, and it has several scenes that contain the genuine stuff of life," Michael Gold diplomatically observed.[43] Indeed, a number of critics, left and right, objected that the play was too contrived to be politically effective: "One couldn't hear the theme for the noise they made in stating it."[44] Yet, while the bourgeois press simply dismissed the play as bad propaganda, the left made a concerted effort to rescue it for progressive labor politics. The *Nation* insisted that while the play might be "obvious and tiresome" for front row spectators, it was clearly received with "unanimous enthusiasm" by the rest of the audience, and this fact alone made it worth supporting.[45] William Gardener of *New Masses* suggested that insisting on the drama's weaknesses at this particular moment would only harm the emergent workers' theaters. He therefore decided to overlook its ideological shortcomings (such as its choice of a bourgeois hero) and to put his weight behind the first professional workers' theater production.[46] The labor press thus ardently rallied to the support of *Peace on Earth*, encouraging labor, liberal, and peace organizations to purchase entire blocks of seats. Thanks to such solidarity, the production ran for a total of 144 performances in New York. By January 1934, it had been seen by some 40,000 workers and sympathizers.[47] In short, *Peace on Earth* signaled the successful opening of the first professional leftist stage, and it was duly celebrated as such by the left. It succeeded in consolidating a broad working- and middle-class audience and established Theatre Union as a professional theater Broadway would have to reckon with.

Four months later, on 18 April 1934, Theatre Union followed up with yet another melodrama: *Stevedore* by George Sklar and Paul Peters. This time the play was enthusiastically acclaimed by left and right. "Here at last the American revolutionary movement has begun to find itself expressed adequately on the stage," *New Masses* rejoiced, while the Hearst press hailed *Stevedore* as the best propaganda play of the year.[48] But what for the labor press was the beginning of genuine revolutionary drama, "something to tell your Soviet grandchildren about,"[49] was simply good old melodrama for the bourgeois critics. Stimulated by "an evening of inevitable excitement, absorption, sympathy, stir," they conveniently overlooked the play's militant politics.[50] In terms of popularity, *Stevedore* was the most successful proletarian melodrama on the New Deal stage, but in terms of effecting critical thinking it also attested to what Elsaesser has called the genre's "radical ambiguity."

As a proletarian melodrama, *Stevedore* has two clear advantages over *Peace on Earth*: a gripping plot of "heroic simplicity"[51] and an unequivocal call to action. *Stevedore* opens with a violent squabble between a white woman and her lover. In order to cover up the beating from her husband, she accuses an unidentified African American man of rape. This incidence triggers a citywide manhunt and a number of riots against the black community. Among the men brought into the police station for investigation is protagonist Lonnie Thompson. From the beginning, it is clear that Lonnie is not only the embodiment of virtue persecuted but also of virtue ready to fight such blatant racism. The entire second act is taken up by the clash of the black employees of a New Orleans freight company with their white boss Walcott over covert wage cuts. Once again, it is Lonnie who vigorously speaks up on behalf of his co-workers. As is to be expected, he subsequently gets framed by his boss for the alleged rape of the opening scene. Lonnie manages to escape, and what follows is a series of narrow escapes and rescues and, in general, "enough pistol shots to keep you at the edge of your seat," as one reviewer put it.[52] All this is accompanied by increasing white mob fury, systematically stirred up by bosses, police, and media. It eventually escalates in the murder of Sam, Lonnie's closest friend. In the final act, the two themes of racial persecution and class conflict merge completely. As the white mob intrudes into the black neighborhood ready to lynch its inhabitants and burn down their houses, the black workers realize that flight is futile and resolve to fight back. But they also learn that they are unable to do so by themselves. In best melodramatic fashion, they are saved in the nick of time by the arrival of a group of white stevedores, rallied to the support of their black comrades by union organizer Lem Morris.

The political message of the play is once again sustained by an unforgiving bipolar viewpoint. As in classic melodrama, the authors swiftly delineate the fundamental moral opposition: the black stevedores (led by Lonnie and Lem) versus the white mob (led by gangster Mitch, superintendent Walcott, and the police). The character alignment not only suggests that the capitalist system (embodied by Walcott and police officers) cannot function without the support of gangsters, but it also points out that the virtuous black stevedores cannot triumph without the support of the labor union. Moreover, just as there is racial prejudice within the white union that keeps some of its members from supporting their black fellow workers, there is resistance among the black group to accept the help of any whites. To overcome these fundamental racial and class antagonisms, both black and white workers need to learn to put prejudice aside and join forces in the struggle against the true forces of evil: the capitalist system and its criminal agents. This is the point that Peters and Sklar relentlessly drive home by portraying the mounting violence and injustice against the black community and their futile search for solutions and escapes. But they also make very clear that without the support of the black stevedores, the white labor union too would stand no chance against the dominant system. The play concludes with a grand tableau on the barricades. "Black and white workers unite, for the first time on an American stage, to beat off their common enemy," an ecstatic Gold exclaimed.[53]

In contrast to *Peace on Earth*, which heavily relies on emotive speeches in order to clarify its political point and to maximize emotional effect, *Stevedore* generates melodramatic affect and political persuasion almost entirely out of the sudden twists and turns of a dynamic plot development, which persistently builds up dramatic suspense toward a climactic finale. The plot is underlined, as in classic melodrama, by a moving musical score. Throughout the play, we listen to "a negro voice singing wearily" and "low mournful blues from the radio."[54] Notably, these blues, jazz, and gospel melodies always remain diegetic (presented by workers on a dock, mourners at a wake, vocalists on the radio) so as to maintain the verisimilitude of the play and absorb the spectators in the action. Besides adding local color, such *melos* significantly underscores the emotional teleology of the play.

The melodramatic pathos, however, is saved till the very last scene. Here, the emotional energy of the plot is translated into revolutionary apotheosis. In the battle with the white mob, our hero falls. But his very death completes and corroborates the conversion of the black community into active participants in the class struggle. Led by Binnie, a resolute woman, and supported by the white union members, they resume the battle with "renewed frenzy." Before long, Mitch's gang is running, and black and white workers "stand in silence about [Lonnie's] body."[55] Tableau. Final curtain.

Similarly to *Peace on Earth*, the trick of the fourth act in *Stevedore* lies in ending on a dual note: the hero, who tellingly has been called "Black Jesus" all along, dies, but his individual sacrifice is transfigured into collective resurrection. In contrast to the former play, the political direction of this ending is forceful and clear: the curtain falls on a scene of active battle against racism and capitalist exploitation. Moreover, what remains embedded in the minds of the audience is the tableau of victory—even though it might only be temporary for now. "The play ends, but this powerful image of Negro and white working-class unity is stamped upon one's mind forever," an agitated Gold applauds.[56]

The final tableau stands, in many regards, as a grand symbol of revolutionary change. With its focus on Binnie, the armed woman leading her comrades into battle, it is evocative of Delacroix's *Liberté*. At the same time, the armed *black* woman guiding her black brothers and sisters to freedom is also reminiscent of the popular iconography of Underground Railroad conductor Harriet Tubman. Both allegorical figures embody the universal values of *liberté, egalité*, and *fraternité* and are thus powerful symbols of the liberation of black workers. And yet, in the end *Stevedore* too remains ambivalent with regard to the larger question, namely, to what extent such liberation has to be part of a radical transformation of society.

Once again, it is the sentimental trope of home and family that mitigates the militant thrust of the concluding scene. Lonnie's final speech, immediately preceding the revolutionary tableau, is remarkably un-revolutionary:

> We hyar to defend our homes. We hyar to fight fo' our lives. And we hyar to show'em dat we ain't gwine be kicked around, and starved and stepped on no mo'. We hyar to show 'em we men and we gwine be treated like men. And remember we ain't only fighting fo' ourselves. Dar black folks all over the country looking at us right now: dey counting on us, crying to us: "Stand yo' ground. You fighting fo' us. You fighting fo' all of us." Now how many of you gwine do dat? How many of you gwine stand hyar and fight? How many of you gwine stand hyar and never move if it's de last place on earth you ever stand? Raise your hands. Show me! Raise your hands.[57]

It is by invoking the familiar tropes of home and community (family)—underlined by the repeated cry of a baby and of children's voices throughout the scene—that Lonnie succeeds in mobilizing his listeners to action. Notably, he also presents the fight on the barricades, not in terms of class struggle but as the last stand of an embattled humanity ("Stand yo' ground. [. . .] You fighting fo' all of us."). In other words, by foregrounding Blankfort's insistence on expressing the universal longing for a home, family, security, and happiness, *Stevedore* deliberately sentimentalizes and universalizes its militant battle cry. In the end, it comes across not as the call for armed revolution but primarily as a powerful appeal to the defense of basic human rights and, above all, human dignity.

The effect of such vernacular pedagogy was extraordinary. According to the left, *Stevedore* advanced the need for the unionization of black and white workers "without equivocation,"[58] even with "glaring clarity."[59] The bourgeois press, by contrast, hardly took note of the play's clarion call to organized class struggle. Their reviews were, as Lawson put it, "fine examples of humanitarian vagueness."[60] While many of the reviewers seemed sympathetic to the cause of the embattled black stevedores, most of them denied that the play had any implications at all for New York audiences, since surely its problems were confined to the Deep South.[61] Only Gilbert Gabriel warned his patrician readers that *Stevedore* had "the smell of genuine, long-grown anger, [. . .] which should sharpen the nostrils of even that most inveterate sniffer, the casual theatergoer."[62] All others simply endorsed the play as "a very fine melodrama."[63] Even the conservative Arthur Pollock insisted in spite of his convictions that " 'Stevedore' ought to be patronized. It's pretty strong drama."[64]

It was particularly the climactic barricade scene that triggered the enthusiasm of critics and audiences alike. As Robert Garland pointed out, one would not be surprised "to see an embattled onlooker leap up on the stage and help those downtrodden Negroes defend their homes."[65] Several observers remarked that, "Upstairs there was cheering, and downstairs, where whites and blacks were scattered throughout the audience, there was a good deal of shouting and hand-clapping."[66] Such degree of audience agitation and participation was unparalleled on the American stage at the time—to be surpassed only with Odets's *Waiting for Lefty* a year later.

Amid general enthusiasm on the left for the high degree of emotional involvement achieved in *Stevedore* (which most leftist critics considered indispensable to the successful mobilization of the audience), some reviews, however, also revealed a new concern with the form of proletarian drama. According to Gold, it did not suffice for a workers' theater to differ from bourgeois theater simply in terms of content (a position advocated by Blankfort), but it also had to differ in style. It ought to infuse its subjects with the "new poetry of working class life."[67] Gold had in mind a sort of symbolic realism that transcended both the cartoon-like quality of agitprop and the photographic realism of the Belasco stage. In a couple of scenes, *Stevedore* already offered such sparse verisimilitude bordering on the poetic. This new concern with the degree of verisimilitude needed for the portrayal of characters and situations was to emerge even more vividly in the following Theatre Union production as well as during the Writers' Congress of the next year.

All in all, however, the left agreed that with *Stevedore* the proletarian theater could finally stand up to Broadway. "Isn't it a glorious thing to be able to say to bourgeois Broadway: here, from the depths of our poverty, [. . .] the struggling revolutionary theatre has matched you technically?" Gold triumphed.[68] The *New York Times* likewise conceded that Theatre Union had proven that "it will quickly make a place for itself in this town, not only as a labor group, but as a vigorous producing unit."[69] With 175 performances in New York alone, *Stevedore* was by far the most successful of all Theatre Union productions.[70]

With its next American production, *Black Pit* by Albert Maltz, Theatre Union completed its move toward greater verisimilitude in the representation of character and situation, albeit not exactly in Gold's sense. The play, which opened on 19 March 1935, was widely acclaimed for its moving and realistic portrayal of the plight of American miners. Just like *Stevedore*, it pitched workers against capitalists in a melodramatic struggle of good and evil, ending on a note of revolutionary promise: rebellion against oppressive working and living conditions in the form of a strike. Yet, unlike its two predecessors, *Black Pit* was not a pendulum play dealing with individual (*Peace on Earth*) or collective conversion (*Stevedore*); instead, it sought to portray the economic circumstances and character psychology of its protagonists in as detailed and accurate a manner as possible. For the sake of obtaining maximum verisimilitude, Maltz abandoned the agitprop schematism and revolutionary symbolism that still marked the previous two plays. Recreating "a slice of the coal country" on stage "with remarkable fidelity," he resumed the tradition of nineteenth-century European naturalism.[71] With *Black Pit*, the professional leftist theater in the United States entered a new aesthetic phase: in rigorously shifting the emphasis from action to character and situation, from presentation to representation, it abandoned the theatricality of popular entertainment for the mimetic illusionism of the bourgeois stage. And yet, despite Maltz's deliberate return to bourgeois realism, his play continued to draw abundantly on the melodramatic imagination that had marked the previous two plays.

Black Pit inaugurated a new dramaturgy in yet another aspect: it developed its political argument with the example of a "negative" hero. Its protagonist is Joe Kovarsky, a young union activist who returns home to his Appalachian mine after having spent three years in prison for a frame-up during a previous strike. Blacklisted, he can no longer find work but is in desperate need of work. He has to provide for his pregnant wife Iola as well as his sister's family since his brother-in-law, Tony, has been paralyzed in a mine accident. Superintendent Prescott, a cousin of Iola's, offers him a job in return for information on the miners' covert union drive. Forced to choose between steady employment and the expulsion of his entire family from the "patch," Joe agrees to work for Prescott, hoping to be able to deceive him. But Prescott proves a clever villain, keeping a tight grip on Joe by blackmailing him with a taped conversation and extra loans. Meanwhile, conditions in the mine worsen, gas is found in one of the slopes, a worker gets injured in an explosion, and the miners prepare to go on strike for stricter safety regulations and higher wages. This all happens the day before Iola's accouchement. When Prescott pressures him to reveal the name of the union organizer, Joe breaks down, scared of losing his job, the services of the company doctor, his family, and his home. But the miners discover Joe's betrayal and collectively turn against him. Upon Tony's advice, Joe leaves the mine. As he leaves, the miners gather at the picket line.

In its political agenda, *Black Pit* is as clear, uncompromising, and militant as *Stevedore*. Employing a rigorously bipolar frame of analysis, it demonstrates that the hardships of the workers' everyday life are the direct result of an oppressive capitalist system. Heroes and villains are clearly delineated from each other. On the one hand, there is a group of class-conscious workers such as Tony and union organizer McCulloh, and on the other hand, there is Prescott and company. At first glance, the workers' desires are very basic. As Joe puts it, "man got live lak man. Man got have eat, got have woman, got have house— man no can live in hole lak animal."[72] In themselves these are not revolutionary demands; they are the same things that Adam pleads for in *1931* and that the people demand in *We, the People*: the right to life, liberty, and the pursuit of happiness. Like the Siftons and Rice before him, Maltz shows how the forces of capitalism systematically obstruct the fruition of these demands. But unlike his Broadway predecessors, Maltz does not simply conclude by asserting the power of the people. Rather, he insists that since the capitalist system denies these rights to a majority of the American people, the workers need to unite and fight; what is more, they "got blow whistle" themselves, as Tony insists in his final speech.[73] Joe, however, fails to understand that his goal of "having a woman and a house" and of "living like a man" can be obtained only collectively. This is his fatal mistake that prompts him to throw in his lot with the villains—a somewhat surprising decision given Joe's militant union past. But the melodramatic worldview does not allow for correction or redemption. Once Joe has succumbed to the opposite site, he needs to be expelled.

This unyielding political argument is largely supported by the play's emotional teleology. In contrast to *Peace on Earth* and *Stevedore*, melodramatic affect is here generated and sustained not with the help of emotive speeches nor via a suspense-driven plot but entirely by way of a minute portrayal of the miners' lives. In classic naturalist fashion, Maltz uses extensive stage directions to evoke the deterministic milieu of a mine patch. Consider, for example, the following stage directions:

> Now that it is daylight, we see the company house in all of its squalor and ugliness. The shack is a rusty black from the coal smoke and sulphur fumes of the slate dump. The roof sags, the porch is broken in spots, the three little steps leading from the porch to the hard, bare ground look as though ready to collapse. Three of the chimneys are regulation, black cylinders—one is a makeshift hammered piece of tin. The shingles are decayed; a window is broken and stuffed with a rag; the rain gutters are twisted and full of holes—there is no end to the details of poverty.[74]

While such photographic naturalism is a far cry from Gold's demand for a minimalist, poetic realism, it is essential to Maltz's dramaturgy. By rendering as accurate a picture of everyday life as possible, the author hopes to drive home the brutal reality of the Appalachian coal mines to a mixed urban audience, to move them to identify with the miners, and to elicit their solidarity with their struggle.[75]

Maltz facilitates such audience identification by opening up with his minute portrayal of everyday family life a common ground between the reality of the West Virginia mines and the New York factories and offices. He, moreover, repeatedly zooms in on the strong bonds that exist between the various workers' families, most of them European immigrants of Slovak, Polish, Croatian, German, and Italian descent. We not only watch them work and scrape for a living, get injured and die but also laugh and dance—all in all, receiving a very intimate impression of the everyday life of an extended proletarian family.

Against this sentimental background, Joe's betrayal seems particularly dramatic, for he too desires nothing more than the security and happiness of everyday domesticity. Circumstances, however, trap him between a ruthless superintendent and his allegiance to his fellow union men and family of miners. As in classic naturalist drama, these circumstances are decidedly not of his own making (Iola's problematic pregnancy, Tony's injury, his own previous arrest). Furthermore, Iola is in desperate need of the company doctor, to whose help she is entitled as long as Joe is on the payroll—that is, as long as Joe sells out to Prescott. Joe's decision is thus turned into a question of life and death. Maltz adds urgency to the resolution of Joe's predicament by timing the gas explosion and impeding strike with Iola's accouchement. Time is ticking; Prescott wants names, and Iola wants the doctor. In the end, Joe is forced to betray his proletarian family in order to save his nuclear family. This is where *Black Pit* differs sharply from *Peace on Earth* and *Stevedore*, in both of which personal interest coincided with political interest. Joe, by contrast, emerges as the tragic hero who, trapped by fate, is no longer agent of his own (political) decisions. His tragic flaw, however, is nothing but a universal desire for a home, a woman, a family—the very things proletarian drama ought to advocate according to Blankfort.

This is ultimately also the weakness of Maltz's play. In the desire for a home and a family, the emotional teleology of the play collides with the moral/political one. As spectators, we feel empathy for Joe. After all, his wife's life is at stake, he is under enormous pressure from both sides, has no time to think, and ultimately does what, given the situation, we might have done as well. The more surprising it is when suddenly in the final scene Maltz lectures us that Joe never ought to have succumbed under any circumstances. As Tony explains to Joe, "Bett'r be Iola die from baby."[76] The emotional momentum that Maltz has so cleverly built up to this point now diverges from the accompanying moral argument. As one reviewer remarked, after having enlisted "every sympathy for poor Kovarsky for two acts, Mr. Maltz as propagandist is obliged at the last to kick him in the pants."[77] As good melodramatic spectators, we find ourselves caught in the middle. How can we suddenly switch our emotional allegiance from the individual to the collective?

The last act only partially compensates for this collision of emotional and moral argumentation. Joe's betrayal triggers a whole sequence of unfortunate events: union organizer Hansy McCulloh is beaten up and chased off the patch, which puts a halt to any strike preparation, which again allows for another gas explosion to occur, which again costs yet another miner's life. With this last victim, however, union organizer McCulloh reappears in deus-ex-machina manner and rallies the men to strike:

Hansy: The mine's hot. What're you gonna do about it? (Silence)
Barolla (in low, intense tones): Strike—I say strike. Strike! Strike![78]

There is much rejoicing and bustling as the miners rush off to get everybody out on strike. Their energy grips us as well, and along with the miners we abandon Joe to plead for absolution with Tony. Tony insists that it is too late to regain the confidence of the workers, and because we trust this veteran of class struggle, we halfheartedly agree with his verdict that Joe must leave. Tony's resolute decree spoken against the background of a revolutionary climax partially amends the previous dramaturgical blunder, shifting the emphasis back from personal to class allegiance, from individual ambition to collective action.

But the moral force of Maltz's argument has nevertheless been weakened. According to the play's melodramatic imagination, the hero should be able to triumph over his opponents or he should selflessly sacrifice himself to the greater cause. In *Black Pit*, Joe switches allegiances and consequently needs to be judged and expelled from the melodramatic realm in order for the proletarian moral occult to be reaffirmed. Yet, precisely because his character and situation have been sketched out in such intimate detail, we cannot wholeheartedly endorse such denouement. Was not Joe's frailty all too human? What choice did the playwright leave Joe? Might we not have crumbled under the pressure of circumstances as well? In the end, the relentless black and white dichotomy of the melodramatic plot clashes with the author's naturalist interest in gray zones of character psychology and situation.

While quite a number of reviewers noticed this problem, their reactions nonetheless ranged from favorable to enthusiastic. "The news today is that Theatre Union has done it again," Garland announced.[79] The bourgeois press was particularly impressed by the play's high degree of verisimilitude, its "careful realism," which it found emotionally very compelling.[80] "A play that cuts into the innards, pours salt into the wounds and leaves the observer with an agonizing hollow, a gnawing, grim feeling in the pit of his stomach," the *New York American* wrote.[81] Yet, while bourgeois critics almost unanimously hailed *Black Pit* as "the most theater-minded and least obviously propagandistic of all Theatre Union plays," hardly any of them discussed the play's politics.[82] As Garland put it most bluntly, any political value most likely got lost between West Virginia and West 14th Street: "I, for once, don't care about the tough-luckers of McCulloh's Run."[83] For most Broadway critics *Black Pit* remained "a typical Theatre Union play"—one that they valued primarily for its value as entertainment.[84]

Surprisingly, reactions in the labor press were mixed. While also applauding the new realism in dramaturgy and staging, leftist reviewers hotly debated the play's content. How useful was a "negative" protagonist for a workers' theater and for labor politics? What was the political value of a strictly realistic rendition of working-class life? Would it suffice for a revolutionary agenda or ought it to be supplemented by a heroic conclusion, an optimistic outlook to a classless future?

For Margaret Larkin of *Daily Worker*, the switch from "plot" to "character play" presented a great advance in the aesthetics and politics of a workers' theater, precisely because it allowed the theater to show "in personal, human terms [. . .] the corruptive influences of capitalism upon a certain type of worker."[85] Her colleague Carl Reeve, however, found that in focusing on individual failure rather than collective heroism, Maltz had severely compromised the political efficacy of the play. While his portrayal of the coal mines might have been "true-to-life," his focus on the exception rather than the rule did not represent reality adequately. As Reeve insisted, Joe's was not a typical case. The majority of miners heroically resisted the temptation of betrayal for individual gain. It was only Tony who ultimately saved the play for labor politics. He was the true "voice of the working class," and it was around characters like him and not around "a weakling like Joe" that Maltz ought to have constructed his play.[86] Reeve's position was shared by Joseph North, editor of *New Masses*. He too considered *Black Pit* severely flawed in its choice of protagonist. Joe's predicament would strike any worker as unconvincing since he had no more than the average share of daily hardships and since his betrayal was utterly inconsistent with the class-conscious worker introduced at the beginning of the play. According to North, such thematic considerations ought to be as important to proletarian literature as those of dramatic technique, if not more so. The flawed portrayal of American miners prevented "this fine play from attaining an excellence that would have rendered it outstanding."[87]

North's assessment triggered a heated response from Jack Stachel of *Daily Worker*, who insisted that the proletarian writer was free to choose any theme as long as it was in the interest of the working class. The scenario of betrayal "may not be the typical case, but it certainly is not an impossible one," and as such it should have a place in proletarian literature, Stachel maintained.[88] As a negative example, it was certainly of didactic value to workers, compellingly demonstrating that the bosses could trap even the most class-conscious union member. North riposted that proletarian literature was already full of the wounded and broken and therefore needed to take a more assertive stand. "I ask for our heroes—not for supermen or demi-gods. I ask only for what we have," he wrote, "They are not yet down on paper, not yet on the stage."[89] For North, the question of content was ultimately "a matter of degree of effectiveness,"[90] and at this particular moment proletarian literature needed positive role models and an optimistic rendition of class struggle.

The fervent discussion of Maltz's play anticipated the general debate over the function and goal of realism in proletarian literature that was to mark the American Writers' Congress of the same year. *Black*

Pit no longer offered the dramatic suspense, visceral spectacle, and pathos-laden speeches of Theatre Union's previous two proletarian melodramas but resumed the mimetic conventions of bourgeois drama, striving for mimetic breadth and depth as well as a high degree of verisimilitude and diegetic absorption. With this, it indicated a turning point in proletarian aesthetics in the United States—away from not only agitprop but also melodrama toward essentially bourgeois realism. This did, however, not mean that realism replaced melodrama entirely, as has so often been postulated in histories of American drama.[91] Rather, as we shall see, it absorbed it in the new concept of a romantic revolutionary realism.

Revolutionary Realism and the American Writers' Congress

In spring 1935, the New Deal stage was marked by two very dissimilar plays: *Waiting for Lefty* and *Black Pit*. The former was praised for its effective use of energizing agitprop techniques, the latter for its moving naturalism. However, the two were not all that different. Despite a different concept of mimesis (one presentational, the other representational), they both evinced a vernacular understanding of political theater. Both anchored the political in the domestic and sentimental; both sought to elicit identification with the protagonists and absorption in the dramatic action; and, above all, both relied on empathy as the crucial element in the political mobilization of the audience. Even with regard to their definition of verisimilitude the two were indeed similar. As shown earlier, to the makers and recipients of amateur theater, the crude and direct agitprop techniques presented the most "natural" way of interaction between worker-actors and worker-spectators. In this regard, the "realistic agitprop" of *Waiting for Lefty* already anticipated much of the mimetic realism of *Black Pit*.

In the mid-1930s, leftist theaters turned toward the latter. The year 1935 marked the watershed between the radical and sectarian proletarianism of the first half of the decade and the formulation of the doctrine of romantic revolutionary realism of the second. With the Writers' Congress, the transitional period during which the workers' theaters had tried to emulate the aesthetic standards and commercial methods of the bourgeois theaters, while still seeking to develop new forms for new contents, came to an end. The representational revolutionary drama that was to dominate the second half of the decade was firmly embedded in the tradition of bourgeois realism. It reflected the growing rapprochement of the workers' theaters with the Broadway stage as well as of American radicalism with bourgeois liberalism.

The American Writers' Congress of 1935, the first national convention of its kind, convened under the auspices of CPUSA in New York City at the end of April. That this was not merely a sectarian event but of central importance in American culture was attested by a front page article in the London *Times Literary Supplement* entitled "American Writers Look Left."[92] The call for the congress—endorsed by such eminent writers as Theodore Dreiser, Josephine Herbst, Michael Gold, Robert Cantwell, Erskine Caldwell, Malcolm Cowley, James T. Farrell, Langston Hughes, John Dos Passos, Nathanael West, Richard Wright—announced the general decay of capitalism and asserted in no uncertain terms that the task of the revolutionary writers consisted in accelerating "the destruction of capitalism and the establishment of the workers' government."[93]

On the agenda were two items: political action against war and fascism and the development of an aesthetics that aided the revolutionary cause. At this point, the fight against fascism was still considered to be synonymous with the fight against capitalism. As Earl Browder, chair of CPUSA, stated very clearly in his address to the congress, modern life was marked by only one basic antagonism, that between capitalists and workers. In the defense of civilization against the barbarism of fascism and war, which were ultimately products of a decaying capitalist system, the committed worker simply had to take the side of the workers.[94] Not surprisingly, the relationship of the writer to the workers' movement and the Communist Party was one of the main themes of the congress.

The various contributions bear evidence to the fact that by 1935 proletarian literature was largely considered synonymous with revolutionary literature. We thus perceive a strategic widening of the attribute from a narrow focus on strictly proletarian themes to a much broader and inclusive usage.[95] For Waldo Frank, chair of the congress, the attribute "proletarian" applied above all to "the key and vision" in which the work was conceived rather than its subject.[96] While his colleague Joseph Freeman still insisted that a proletarian writer needed to seek the "active identification" with the working-class movement,[97] Frank contended that a story of middle-class or intellectual life, as long as it presented a revolutionary vision, could be more effective for proletarians "than a shelf-full of dull novels about stereotyped workers."[98] Malcolm Cowley likewise asserted that for some writers like himself who were "strictly middle class" in background, family, and education, active identification with working-class characters might be problematic but that he could nonetheless contribute to the revolutionary cause by advancing the proletarian point of view. "I am not a proletarian writer and I doubt that I shall ever become a proletarian writer," he wrote. "But I believe that the interests of my own class lie in a close alliance with the proletariat."[99] All in all, the shift in terminology from proletarian to revolutionary was not merely cosmetic but indicative of a deliberate widening of its thematic scope as well as its potential readership. In this spirit, participants such as Freeman and Granville Hicks also stressed that proletarian writing and Marxist criticism were not recent imports from Moscow but the fruit of a long native tradition reaching back to the early socialist movement of the early twentieth century if not further.[100] Such calculated Americanization of proletarian writing and criticism was, of course, meant not only to corroborate the authority of its authors by anchoring it within the democratic tradition of American letters but also to widen its appeal for a more general public.[101]

The distinctive move toward broadening the concept of political literature from a narrow sectarian to a wider populist understanding is most apparent in the discussions over form, content, and audience. The general tendency was to insist on a more imaginative assimilation of content—that is, on abandoning the crude agitprop schematism that had marked the first half of the decade for a more representational approach that would recreate social forces in their entirety. In their contribution to the seminal anthology *Proletarian Literature in the United States* (1935), William Phillips and Philip Rahv called for the portrayal of "complete personalities" and of human relations "in their physical and sensual immediacy."[102] They insisted that a writer's achievement ought to be measured by the degree to which he succeeded in translating socio-political content into "images of physical life."[103] At the congress, this call for realism was further corroborated by Frank, who maintained that literature ought to portray not only the problems of working-class life but "all the richness and complexity of detail of life itself."[104] For him, such classic (bourgeois) conception of realism was the true measure of artistic and political achievement. Only by being effective as art could revolutionary literature effectively function as propaganda and prepare its readers for social change.

In the field of drama, Blankfort had long insisted that political theater ought to focus on the human conflict inherent in class struggle and that it ought to approach the subject through the "concrete, personalized and emotional appeal" rather than abstraction.[105] "There is no place for 'psychic distance' in a revolutionary esthetic," Blankfort argued already in 1934 in anticipation of the dismissal of epic theater. "If it were possible, the whole audience ought to be aroused enough to jump on the stage."[106] At the Writers' Congress, Lawson corroborated this position by suggesting that the goal of complete identification and absorption, of mimetic scope and human interest could best be achieved by returning to technique "in its most conservative and traditional sense."[107] For him, this meant adhering to the Aristotelian principles of conflict, action, and unity as well as emulating the analytic precision of an Ibsen play—that is, of bourgeois critical realism. *Waiting for Lefty, Stevedore*, and *Black Pit* were for Lawson vital steps in that direction.

Yet, at the same time that the conference participants endorsed the concept of realism, they also insisted that a merely realistic approach did not suffice. According to Jack Conroy, who had proposed the trick of the fourth act, "American proletarian literature must of necessity deal with prophecy."[108] The accurate portrayal of everyday oppression and suffering had to be supplemented with hope; temporary defeat had to be counterbalanced with triumph—a point that had already emerged most clearly in the debates over *Black Pit*. Blankfort had similarly insisted the previous year that unless "the promise of the future arises convincingly out of the struggles of the present," the playwright's good intentions were wasted.[109] As shown above, Theatre Union sought to solve this dual insistence on mimetic scope and prophetic endings by amalgamating realism and melodrama, by aiming for realistic effect while also retaining melodramatic affect. They had done so with varying degrees of success. At the congress, Blankfort and Michael Buchwald therefore pointed to the sharp difference between plays like *Stevedore* and *Black Pit*. In *Stevedore*, as in many other pendulum plays, the black and white schematism of ideological argumentation still hampered the realistic development of character and situation. But the play nonetheless "achieved greatness" with regard to the visceral excitement and revolutionary energy that it derived from a melodramatic plot development.[110] *Black Pit*, by contrast, lacked just that quality. On the other hand, however, it constituted an entirely new type of revolutionary drama. Rather than seeking the head-on fight, it revealed the forces of oppression in an indirect manner; rather than focusing on the hero's actions, it brought out his inner psychological conflicts. What remained to be done, so they argued, was to combine the melodramatic energy of *Stevedore* with the realistic scope and psychological depth of *Black Pit* and "to strike an effective balance between inner conflict and outer events, between the drama of the individual and the drama of his class."[111]

The American left's positive re-evaluation of realism and its amalgamation with romantic prophecy and melodramatic affect echoed the proclamation of Soviet socialist realism of the previous year, even though, as Ira Levine insists, the latter was not the decisive factor in the formulation of an indigenous doctrine of romantic realism.[112] Just as its Soviet counterpart, proletarian realism in the United States assumed that the mimetic portrayal of reality would inevitably mean presenting it in terms of revolutionary change. "You must not write because you want to be a 'mirror,' a 'camera,' but because you want to be an active moulder of life," J. M. Olgin exhorted his fellow writers.[113] For him, socialist realism was intrinsically romantic because it could see "the outlines of a future beautiful life in the present struggles of the workers."[114] Assertions like these prompted Mordecai Gorelik to suggest rather dryly that perhaps the new synthesis between realism and romanticism ought to be called socialist romanticism, since the so-called new realism was not so much mimetic as allegorical in character.[115] His colleagues, however, preferred to replace the term "socialist realism" with the terms "proletarian realism" and "revolutionary realism." The intrinsic irony, nonetheless, remained and was perhaps most clearly revealed in the suggestion of calling the new genre "objective romanticism."[116]

At the American Writers' Congress such discussions over form and content of revolutionary literature were framed by the need to develop a more complex and inclusive audience approach. Faced with the threat of fascism and war, it was clear that leftist literature could no longer limit itself to a position of militant oppositionalism but had to reach out to the non-proletarian public, particularly the middle classes, as well. As Philipp and Rahv argued with regard to the fundamental split in revolutionary writing between a more intellectual and a more popular approach, the committed writer had to work out "a sensibility and a set of symbols unifying the responses and experiences of his *total* audience."[117] The congress proposed various ways of achieving this end. Conroy, claiming that "the desperate striving for novelty of phrase and imagery" often only led to "a semi-private terminology almost unintelligible for the masses," maintained that proletarian literature ought to communicate its material as *simply* and *clearly* as possible to the *largest* body of readers it could command.[118] Kenneth Burke proposed to replace the symbol of "the worker" with that of "the people." According to him, the latter would be much more effective in pleading with the unconvinced precisely because it was inclusive, establishing a common basis of reference by evoking common values. Besides, while the symbol of the worker might have the great advantage of emphasizing the reality of existing class antagonism, it failed to evoke their future abolition in a classless society. By pointing to the direction of unity, the symbol of the people, by contrast, offered this incentive for change. For all these reasons, "the people" seemed to Burke a much richer and much more effective "symbol of allegiance."[119]

The Writers' Congress clearly marked a turning point in the debate over content, form, and public of political literature in the United States. The opening up of revolutionary literature to a broader audience, the widening of scope, and Americanization of themes, symbols, and traditions were indicative of the American left's attempt to adjust its agenda to larger political changes. Yet, as subsequent developments were to show, the new populism in proletarian literature was purchased at the price of a loss of radicalism. In endorsing the Popular Front platform, CPUSA sought the reconciliation with American liberalism. It now dedicated itself to the building of trade unions, the mobilization of broad support for New Deal legislation and for public vigilance against fascism and war. The shift in strategy became most apparent during the 1936 election campaign, when it changed its battle cry from "Towards a Communist America!" to "Communism is 20th century Americanism." Most importantly, Browder purposely presented the new populist platform of his party in the vernacular of American nationalism:

> To meet this danger [of fascism and war] to our liberties and welfare, we must unite our ranks. In common action we must go forward to overcome this crisis in an American way, in the spirit of 1776, in the interest of our people and of our country. [. . .] Democracy or fascism, progress or reaction—this is the central issue of 1936.[120]

Not only did Browder now seek to identify himself as heir to Jefferson, Lincoln, and John Brown, but he suddenly announced that "the life-needs" of workers, farmers, and petit bourgeois could be won "even under the present capitalist system."[121] While he still presented radicalism as an indigenous American tradition, as an inherent part of the nation's cultural and political identity, he redirected its energies into a program of social reform, into faith in the moral perfectibility of capitalism. With this rhetorical move, Browder deliberately tapped into the cultural nationalism of the period, adopting the broad liberal conception of social change, that had begun to manifest itself even among the more radical sectors of leftist culture as early as 1933 as for instance in plays like *Peace on Earth* and Granville Hicks's seminal study *The Great Tradition* (1933).[122]

With the official advent of the Popular Front in the party line, "the workerist turn"—to use Raphael Samuel's term—in American art was lost once and for all.[123] By the time of the Second Writers' Congress in June 1937, leftist art had been completely released from its "class moorings," as Rahv put it, and instead been transformed into "a pure endowment of democracy."[124] The frontline had been redrawn from the opposition between capitalists and workers to that between fascists and democrats. The second congress completely dissociated itself from the struggle against capitalism; the sole issue at stake was the defense of democracy against fascism. "Here in the United States all we had to do was to encourage trade unionism and defend what we already possess, namely our bountiful bourgeois democracy," Rahv remarked dryly. "On these foundations we shall build a 'great' American culture."[125]

The two congresses could not have been more different in rhetoric and politics. As Sam Smiley has shown, while the first was militantly pro-revolutionary and sectarian in its insistence on class struggle, the second was anti-fascist and concerned with building a united front.[126] While the first persistently conjured up the Soviet Union as the point of reference, the second congress corroborated its program in the repeated reference to the Spanish civil war. However, in the two years since the first congress, significant political changes, besides the alignment of CPUSA with the New Deal, had taken place: Franco's war against the Spanish Republic, the Italian invasion of Ethiopia, the first round of show trials in Moscow, and the formation of the Congress of Industrial Organizations (CIO). The growing menace of fascism and war, the visible onset of Stalinist repressions, and the new rank-and-file activism of the CIO contributed to mitigating the revolutionary fervor of the first half of the decade. Yet, it also needs to be pointed out that while all these factors prompted the American left to relinquish its earlier militancy and sectarianism in favor of a broad Popular Front and a strong CIO, this change in strategy also enabled it to gain a much wider radius of influence among American workers.[127]

Not surprisingly, what Rahv had termed "the blood and thunder style of blatant 'leftism'" was gone at the second congress.[128] The new congress was designed for all writers who generally agreed with the concepts of a united front against fascism and were supportive of the new power of labor in the United States. This, however, also meant that revolutionary thinking about art had virtually come to an end. Freeman, who was looking forward to a renaissance of political writing in the 1940s, even suggested that from a literary point the 1930s were drawing to a close.[129] Cowley, who only two years previous had thrown in his lot with the workers' movement, now found that the "great deal of wild talk about revolution tomorrow" had already started to ebb out in 1933. For him, as for many others, the "real fight" was now against fascism.[130]

However, not only the rhetoric and style had changed. With the adaptation of a moderate liberal program, the emphasis on Marxist content disappeared as well. Lawson lamented the dilution and concealment of social content for the sake of wider audience appeal as early as December 1936.[131] A few months later John Gassner likewise spoke of leftist theater as the "diluted theatre," which was more interested in character psychology than in making a point about current political issues.[132] Within a year Robert Forsythe was already yearning "for a time when plays were put on, in which ideas were expressed in the most violent fashion and without concern that somebody in ermine might be offended."[133] According to him, America once more "Wanted a Theatre" that shunned conformity with Broadway aesthetics in favor of pure emotions and vivid indignation. The slow defeat of the revolutionary spirit in form and content of American leftist art is most evident when considering the choice of keynote speakers at the three American writers' congresses of the decade: while in 1935, the congress was opened by soon-to-be party member Granville Hicks, in 1937 it was opened by Ernest Hemingway, and at the third congress in 1939 by Nobel Prize laureate Thomas Mann.[134]

In retrospect, the fervent spirit of the mid decade had shone forth most vividly in the proletarian melodramas on 14th Street. They had excited and offended their audiences and triggered lively debates among its critics. In this regard, these plays also show the extent to which leftist theaters like the Theatre Union both responded and contributed to larger cultural and political transformations during the New Deal. The American political theater of the 1930s was never merely a reflection of the social but always an active force in it.

All in all, melodrama was perhaps the form most conducive to a sentimental political education of a broad audience. Its strong emphasis on such universal and general values as home, family, love, security, and happiness effectively anchored the political in the vernacular language of the sentimental and the domestic. With its high degree of emotional expressiveness and suspenseful plot development, it moreover provided the emotional involvement and moral gratification that would make the political pleasurable. Above all, melodrama seemed to allow for a rather unproblematic alignment of labor interests with New Deal policy by enlisting the "revolutionary" energies of its audiences toward a project of national reconstruction.

Yet, in the end, the proletarian melodramas of the "revolutionary" Theatre Union forfeited their claim to radical intervention. Their reconciliatory political stance has as much to do with the concrete political moment of the American mid-1930s (Popular Front) as with a long tradition of cultural intervention in the United States in general. In the American Jeremiad critique and affirmation, change and conservatism have traditionally gone hand in hand. As part of this tradition, American melodrama has always tended to manage social crisis by anchoring national identity in a mythological locus of innocence and virtue, as Jeffrey Mason and Linda Williams have shown.[135] This is also true for the proletarian melodramas of the New Deal. Despite their leftist fervor, they reassured their audiences that change will be but a return to a previous just and moral social order.

Chapter Five

Why Sing of Skies Above?: Labor
Musicals and Living Newspapers

The triumph of realism on the professional stages of the American left in the second half of the 1930s did not preclude a certain amount of experimentation. Marc Blitzstein's proletarian opera *The Cradle Will Rock*, for example, was greatly inspired by the work of Brecht and Weill, while the Living Newspaper of the Federal Theatre purposely employed epic techniques reminiscent of Piscator's Volksbühnen productions. While some critics, such as Ira Levine, see in these experiments the belated arrival of epic theater in the United States,[1] I want to emphasize that these experiments were employed not so much in the spirit of modernist intervention but rather as part of a vernacular pedagogy of political theater. They effectively amalgamated the low and the high, art and commerce in a leftist middlebrow aesthetics. I will show that the use of epic techniques often enhanced the visceral appeal of leftist productions for Popular Front audiences by infusing them with revolutionary fervor. At the same time, however, New Deal theater knew how to anchor its occasional formal iconoclasm, its bold advancement of labor politics, and forthright exposure of social problems in a discourse of middle-class identity, consumerism, and cultural nationalism—all of which ultimately served to secure rather than undermine the status quo. This underlying dynamic becomes most obvious in the labor revue *Pins and Needles*—the most popular and commercially successful leftist production on the New Deal stage. The deliberate commodification of *Pins and Needles* thus also points to the limits of a vernacular praxis of political theater.

A Fairy Tale with Villains
and a Hero

Marc Blitzstein's "play in music" *The Cradle Will Rock* was widely acclaimed as one of the most radical cultural productions of the second half of the 1930s. It was radical, however, not so much by design as by virtue of the events surrounding its opening night. The story itself is a satirical allegory of middle-class rebellion, very much reminiscent of Odets's strike song *Waiting for Lefty*. It opens with the arraignment of an odd group of people in the night court of Steeltown, USA: prostitute Moll and town bum Harry Druggist along with the eminent members of the town's anti-unionist Liberty Committee, who were mistakenly arrested while attempting to break up a union drive. As the latter await bail by the ubiquitous Mr. Mister, who "owns steel and everything else," they each tell the story of how they sold out to the godfather of Steeltown.[2] Moll quickly realizes that the business of these bourgeois citizens is not all that different from her own. When union organizer Larry Foreman is brought in, Mr. Mister attempts to win him over too. But Foreman heroically resists, giving hope to Moll and Druggist. The play ends with the sound of "bugles, drums and fifes," announcing the successful end of the union rally as well as of Mr. Mister's autocratic reign.[3]

Cradle was originally conceived as a production of Project #891 of the Federal Theatre Project (FTP), a stage run by the young Orson Welles and John Houseman. It was to open on 16 June 1937 at the Maxine Elliott Theatre in New York. Four days before the premiere, with 14,000 tickets pre-sold, Washington suddenly decreed that no Federal Theatre play was to open before July, allegedly due to pending budgetary approval by congress. But Welles and Houseman quite clearly understood it as an act of censorship.[4] Blitzstein's musical was fairly explicit in its rhetoric, arguing in unmistakable terms for the unionization of steel workers at a time when labor strife was particularly intense. Since the fall of 1936, the CIO had been fighting it out with the auto and steel industry. According to cautious estimates, at least eighteen workers had been killed in strikes that year, ten of them alone on Memorial Day in Chicago.[5] Despite its official pre-approval of *Cradle* as a "magnificent" show, Washington must have felt ill at ease with a federal play that called for closed shops and revolutionary upheaval.[6] Besides, by early June 1937, signs of a congressional backlash against the Federal Theatre Project were already looming large on the horizon.[7] In view of these circumstances, Welles and Houseman decided to defy orders and to open the play as scheduled.

The ensuing events were not irrelevant to the public success and political glamour of *Cradle*. When Welles and Houseman found their theater shut down by federal guards on the morning of June 16, the day of the opening, they orchestrated the *déménagement* of the entire show. They rented the empty Venice Theatre on Seventh Avenue/58th Street, organized a used piano, and among much cheers from the assembled crowd, cast and audience walked the twenty blocks uptown. This theatrical procession has long since become legendary as a vivid testimonial to the freedom of the arts and the defiance of censorship.[8] The legend of the "runaway opera" is so colorful and perfectly dramatic that few attempts at revision have been made. Only recently, it has been rehearsed again by Tim Robbins, who in his film of the same title presents *Cradle* as emblematic of the rebellious spirit of the entire decade.[9] So far, only theater historian Barry Witham has tried to challenge the myth by suggesting that the "runaway opera" might not so much have been a case of political censorship than a well-orchestrated move by Houseman and Welles to turn an FTP project into a commercial production.[10]

Regardless of the motivation behind it, the spectacle of the opening night turned *Cradle* into a landmark event of American political theater and incidentally also a fine example of the possibilities of epic techniques—however, not so much by design as by circumstance. Welles and Houseman had originally planned a lavish production in the style of Broadway musicals, including a cast of sixty, an orchestra of twenty-eight as well as numerous fancy sets, including "a triple row of three-dimensional velour portals between which narrow, glass-bottomed, fluorescent platforms, loaded with scenery and props, slid smoothly past each other as the scene shifted back and forth [. . .]."[11] But without access to costumes and sets and faced with the strict regulations of Actors' Equity and the Musicians' Union, Welles and Houseman were forced to strip the show down to its bare essentials.[12] They resolved the dilemma with much ingenuity: the actors were asked to buy theater tickets and perform their pieces from their seats; the orchestra was disbanded; and a single piano was stripped of its front and hauled onto the stage. The composer himself then sat down at the piano in front of a faded backdrop of the Bay of Naples, and encircled by a single spotlight he began to play for an audience of 1,600. "I could hear an enormous buzz of talk in the house; when the curtains parted, I saw the place jammed to the rafters," Blitzstein recalls. "The side aisles were lined with standing cameramen and reporters. And there was I, alone on a bare stage, perched before the naked piano in my shirt sleeves."[13]

As Blitzstein played the overture, Welles introduced the setting and characters. Neither knew whether the actors would cooperate, but when Blitzstein began singing the first song, he suddenly heard a timid Olive Stanton take up the tune from the balcony. Immediately a spotlight swung over to her place. Encouraged by the spontaneous applause of the audience, Blitzstein announced "Enter Gent," once more prepared to sing the part himself. But again, actor George Fairchild stood up mid-center in the orchestra and began his dialogue with Stanton. "A scene, which three nights before, had been acted in a atmospheric blue light, around a pop lamppost, downstage right, was now played in the middle of a half-lit auditorium by two frightened relief workers thirty yards apart."[14] An enthusiastic audience "seethed with excitement," turning "as at a tennis match from one actor to another," as they sang their lines from different spots in the auditorium, so Blitzstein recalled.[15] Yet, since not all actors dared to defy Equity rules, the composer ended up covering some half dozen parts himself, while cast members improvised others. Such improvisations, however, only helped to enhance the iconoclastic character of the show and to capture the attention and sympathy of the audience. All in all, the labor opera "held up astonishingly under this brutal manhandling."[16] In its rudimentary mise-en-scène, it ended up resembling Brecht's epic theater: a bare stage, minimalist props, announcement of scenes, and direct address of the audience.

"Accident Starts New Style," *Daily Worker* raved along with other papers in its review.[17] The improvisations of the opening night proved highly successful with an audience already tickled by the sense of defiance and rebellion that lay in the air. According to *Daily Worker*, *Cradle* was "the most terrific wallop" since *Waiting for Lefty*.[18] "The best thing that militant labor has put into a theatre yet," Brooks Atkinson of the *New York Times* seconded.[19] Archibald MacLeish rejoiced in an off-the-cuff speech at the end of the performance that the American audience had finally been released from the deadly illusionism of the professional stage.[20] Houseman was quick to market the premiere's fortuitous mise-en-scène as a new concept of political theater, insisting that this "new" technique finally solved the long-standing problem of how to immerse an audience in a labor show.[21] The impromptu style of the opening night became the blueprint for all subsequent performances at the Venice Theatre as well as later on at Welles's and Houseman's own Mercury Theatre and during its following Broadway run. The actors remained in street clothes and were seated in oratorio fashion on a bare stage, where they awaited their cues, while Blitzstein played the entire score, announced stage directions, and sang several parts himself.[22] The very same style that had formerly been discredited in Theatre Union's production of *Mother* and the Group Theatre's production of *Case of Clyde Griffiths* as "too distant from [the] periphery of feeling" of American audiences, now met with the enthusiastic approval of audiences and critics alike.[23]

The incidental minimalism of the opening night seemed well suited to Blitzstein's score and libretto, both of which he had conceived in the spirit of Brecht. Blitzstein, who had studied modern music in Paris and Berlin, owed much to the *Gebrauchsmusik* of Kurt Weill, Hanns Eisler, and Paul Dessau as well as to the epic theater of Brecht. Like his German colleagues, he believed that modern music was to be functional. While it was composed for a mass audience, for the "man in the streets," it was not simply to give this audience what it wanted, "for what it wanted had been conditioned by generations of capitalist exploitation and treachery," Blitzstein explained.[24] Rather, it had to be used in a Brechtian sense, as a means of education and mass communication. Just like Brecht, he felt that for this purpose a new form was indispensable: "I have come to feel that the realistic theater of our day has about outlived its usefulness; and that a new sort of theatre, in which music must function as a special integrating force, is inevitable if there is to be any theater left."[25] The original impulse behind *Cradle* was therefore decidedly Brechtian, i.e., to educate the audience through form and content and to break with the diegetic illusionism of the bourgeois commercial stage.

Blitzstein had, moreover, met the German playwright during the latter's brief sojourn in New York in the fall of 1935. When Blitzstein showed him his song "Nickel under the Foot" about the plight of an American prostitute, Brecht allegedly suggested that to actual prostitution he ought to add the figurative one: "the sell-out of one's talent and dignity to the powers that be."[26] Inspired by this encounter, Blitzstein then wrote *Cradle* "at white heat during five weeks in 1936," dedicating it to his mentor.[27]

To break with the diegetic illusionism of the bourgeois stage was not all too hard for a musical play that by its very nature was presentational rather than representational. The education of the audience in form and content was a different matter. The form Blitzstein borrowed from the *Threepenny Opera*. He had seen its original production in Berlin in 1928. His proletarian opera was just like the former an amalgamation of various musical styles: "[R]ecitatives, arias, revue patters, tap dances, suites, chorales, silly symphony, continuous incidental commentary music, lullaby music—all pitchforked into it with a great deal of initiative from me," as Blitzstein remarked.[28] The final mix drew on Gilbert and Sullivan, American vaudeville, agitprop, oratory, and Weimar *Gebrauchsmusik* alike. While the syncopated modern tunes infused the opera with revolutionary pathos (particularly in the *Cradle* theme song), the classic and popular tunes functioned, just as in Weill's score, as critiques of the intrinsic commercialism of the genre itself. At times, the popular songs of each scene subverted the content of the play; at other times, they subverted their own form. Thus Editor Daily's inane "Honolulo" song, put on for the sake of indulging Junior

Mister, takes the clichés of the Hawaiian number *ad absurdum*. Reverend Salvation's off-the-cuff sermons on war and peace present a travesty of church chorales, gradually shifting from Bach-inspired solemnity to manic Turkey Trot.[29] The university scene in which Mr. Mister recruits the faculty for his war propaganda is set to the tune of a lullaby. Thanks to such humorous variety of musical styles, Blitzstein's rather crude and clichéd plot came to life. His clever parodies and travesties of popular and classical tunes not only provided an entertaining counterpoint to the by-now familiar agitprop rhetoric of the plot, but they also articulated a witty critique of the commercial musical theater and of middle-class values. "And even when you've stopped laughing, you haven't stopped thinking," one reviewer attested to the effectiveness of this approach.[30]

Upon Brecht's suggestion, prostitution became the guiding theme in content as well. *Cradle* deals with the "sell-out of one's profession, one's talents, one's dignity and integrity, at the hands of big business or the powers that be."[31] It opens with Moll's plaintive recitative "I'm checking home now, call it a night," in which she recounts how the economic recession has forced her into prostitution. She is quite surprised to find herself arraigned along with the venerable patricians of Steeltown, but as Harry Druggist explains to her, "We're in the same old trade as you."[32] The story of how Steeltown's middle class has prostituted itself to Mr. Mister is presented in a series of brief flashbacks in a manner similar to Odets's *Lefty*. We watch Reverend Salvation, "habitual prostitute since 1915,"[33] preach peace and war according to the demands of the steel market; Editor Daily, "procurer, also known as pimp,"[34] sell out the freedom of the press; violinist Yasha and painter Dauber crawl at the feet of their patroness Mrs. Mister; university president Prexy and his professors eagerly supply the propaganda for Mr. Mister's mounting war preparations; and, finally, Dr. Specialist fix the diagnosis of an injured machinist in order to prevent union trouble. We also learn that Druggist's acquiescence with Mr. Mister's schemes has led to the death of his son and the murder of a proletarian couple.

The theme of middle-class prostitution is played out against the background of an ongoing union drive. As we learn in the beginning, this is the night the workers will decide on whether or not there will be a closed shop in Steeltown. The necessity for such consolidation of labor forces is most emphatically explained in the song of Joe Worker, who "gets gypped" by Mr. Mister's thugs for his union activism. In agitprop fashion, his sister Ella Hammer turns directly to audience: "One big question inside me cries / How many fakers, peace undertakers / Paid strikebreakers / How many toiling, ailing, dying, piled-up bodies, / Brother, does it take to make you wise?"[35] The only solution to the ruthless exploitation and oppression experienced by the Joe Workers of the country, the play suggests, is organized labor, the closed shop. As union organizer Foreman explains,

> Open shop is when a boilermaker can be kicked around, demoted, fired, like that—he's all alone, he's free—free to be wiped out. Closed shop— he's got fifty thousand other boilermakers behind him, ready to back him up, every one of them, to the last lunch pail. The difference? It's like the five fingers on your hand. That's (Tapping one finger.) the boilermakers— just one finger—but this (Pointing to finger for each.) rollers, roughers, machinists, blasters, boilermakers—that's closed shop! (Makes a fist.) That's a union! (Thumbing nose with that hand.) O boy! O boy! O boy![36]

In the end, of course, labor wins the day. The sound of bugles, drums, and fifes announce that the closed shop has been won. Foreman falls in with the voices of the chorus converging upon the aisles, triumphantly singing, "That's a storm that's going to last until / The final wind blows . . . and when the wind blows . . . / The cradle will rock!"[37]

In the figure of Foreman, the two discrete themes of middle-class prostitution and labor struggle merge. Even though he does not enter the scene until the latter half of the play, he is the actual hero bringing the revolutionary theme song (until now played softly in the background) along with him. With the "Cradle Song," he insists that the proletarian revolution is imminent and, what is more, that it offers hope to a "rooked" middle class as well:

> You're in one of them racketeer unions, where you run all the errands and get maybe a dollar cigar for Christmas. You ain't made one real demand yet, you've only said, "Yes, Mr. Mister," up to now. You're caught there, boys; you're stuck like a sandwich between the top crowd pressin down and the bottom crowd comin up![38]

Similar to Odets, Blitzstein puts forth a compelling argument for the political reorientation of the American middle class, suggesting that it too would profit from an alliance with organized labor and that such alliance would eventually not only rock but also overturn the cozy cradle of unfettered capitalism.

To be sure, *Cradle* is fervently pro-labor in its rhetoric. Arguably, however, it is not this rhetoric alone that captured a wide audience and secured critical acclaim. Blitzstein's modernist endeavor to educate the masses about current political problems remains embedded in a vernacular concept of political theater. His is a middle-class allegory for middle-class people. Just as *Cradle* gives voice to their suspicions of being "rooked" by Mr. Mister, it also assuages their anxieties by providing them with the cathartic ending of a revolution accomplished single-handedly by a hero who is essentially just like them. However, as I will show now, in providing us with such a deus-ex-machina happy ending, the opera also exhausts its potential for stimulating a genuine social critique.

First, *The Cradle Will Rock* is, despite its prominent labor theme and nominal advocacy of revolution, just like *Waiting for Lefty*, only incidentally about unionism. "What I really wanted to talk about," Blitzstein admits, "was the middle class, [. . .] the intellectuals, professionals, small shopkeepers, little businessmen in the America of today."[39] Unions and unionism merely served as a symbolic solution to the plight of these petit bourgeois groups. "Where does their allegiance lie?" the author asks. "With big business, which is ready to engulf them, buy and sell them out exactly as it does labor, exploit and discard them at will as a sort of useful but inferior commodity?"[40] Blitzstein stages this question most dramatically in the person of Larry Foreman, the nominal labor hero of the play. Foreman is a middle-class character: a foreman who has a piece of property outside of town and chairs a committee of open-minded (and propertied) middle-class professionals, "farmers, city people, doctors, lawyers, newspapermen, even a couple of poets—and one preacher."[41] By presenting Foreman's committee as the very counter image of the proto-fascist Liberty Committee—as the uncorrupt, class-conscious, and progressive American middle class in alliance with the proletariat—Blitzstein recasts the question of political allegiance as a moral choice between corruption and integrity, fascism and democracy. In the climactic showdown between Foreman and Mr. Mister, the real issue is not whether the workers will win their union rally but whether Foreman too will sell out and become a corporate mercenary.

From a radical labor point of view, this is the main hitch in the play. When Foreman confronts Mr. Mister, he does so not as a spokesperson of labor but as a representative of the middle class.[42] The dramatic conflict has little to do with concrete labor politics. In fact, throughout the play, the actual workers are confined to supplementary roles, remaining off-stage, getting beaten (Joe Worker) or killed (the young Polish couple)—Ella Hammer presenting the one powerful exception in which labor directly challenges corporate capitalism (as well as the audience). In a strictly technical sense, *Cradle* is not a proletarian play, even though critics as well as Blitzstein himself repeatedly referred to it as such. Union drive and revolution fulfill, similar to the strike motif in *Lefty*, a metaphorical function, stressing the urgency for the middle class to choose sides.

Blitzstein's triumphant ending therefore has to be read *cum grano salis*. In terms of the libretto, Foreman's revolution comes as a surprise. Throughout the play, we are given a rather bleak picture of the moral integrity of the middle classes: journalists, doctors, artists, clerics, merchants—all selling out to the big money of Mr. Mister. Yet, somehow we are to believe that with the sounding of bugles, drums, and fifes, the middle class will march alongside the steel workers and begin to rock the cradle of capitalist autocracy. But how is this hopeful ending to come about? How and why would this corrupt (Liberty Committee) and confused (Harry Druggist) middle class suddenly mend its ways? The failure of dramatic logic, however, only reinforces Blitzstein's romantic rendition of what Michael Denning has termed the "folklore of unionism."[43] In the end, it does not matter that Ella Hammer's provocative question to the audience remains unanswered, that we still do not know how the change in middle-class consciousness is to come about. Nor are we as spectators forced to rethink our own class alignment or to seriously consider the predicament of the workers. Foreman supposedly takes care of the revolution for us, and we can simply let ourselves be swept along by the final revolutionary apotheosis. Seen from this angle, the main purpose of *Cradle* is then really the reassurance of the audience that change will occur all by itself. As Virgil Thomson suspects, it is the "hokum" of the ending, which secured the play's success: "That ending-on-a-hopeful-note is very close to a fairy-tale, to a sort of (dear Marc, forgive me the wisecrack) opium for the people, which makes the social bitterness parts hurt less."[44]

One of the reasons *Cradle*'s "fairy tale, with villains and a hero"[45] is so effective is that it recites with much passion the rhetoric and mythology of labor. Blitzstein's ardent deployment of what Denning has termed the "aesthetics of industrial unionism"[46] deflects from the actual reality of a middle class, which by prostituting itself again and again to Mr. Mister is in fact perpetually deferring Foreman's imagined revolution. It infuses the audience with a revolutionary fervor and romantic hope that is deeply gratifying for the duration of the performance. By the end, when the entire cast sings the theme song, "half the audience is ready to join in,"[47] even though, as one observer suggested, most of them "carried away no clear impression except that its theme was that steel workers should join a union."[48] Such romantic deployment of labor folklore, similar to Odets's *Waiting for Lefty*, was very much in accordance with the general aesthetic and political sensibility of the Popular Front public. It expressed the strong conviction that labor alone could save the day, that it would be able to solve the depression predicament of the middle classes and perhaps the entire nation—and that, in fact, it offered "the only chance for dignity, for survival in fact," as Blitzstein averred.[49]

Besides satisfying the revolutionary longing of middle-class audiences, there is a second factor that rooted the opera in the vernacular tradition and contributed to its popular success. The opera's grand allegory of middle-class salvation is emphatically enhanced by what Denning calls "the prostitute's lament."[50] While the "aesthetics of industrial unionism" served to infuse the work with the white heat of rebellion, the "prostitute's lament" secured the identificatory pleasure of a mass audience. Blitzstein frames the story of Foreman and the Liberty Committee with the sentimental story of Moll. She opens the play with her plaintive song "I'm Checking Home."[51] Shortly before Foreman enters the stage, Moll presents her famous "Nickel under the Foot" song (the original kernel for the opera):

> Maybe you wonder what it is,
> Makes people good or bad;
> Why some guy, an ace without a doubt,
> Turns out to be a bastard,
> And the other way about.
> I tell you what I feel:
> It's just the nickel under the heel.[52]

Moll, a cousin of Brecht's Pirate Jenny, demonstrates in *Lehrstück* fashion how morality, one's hopes and ideals have a firm economic basis: "For every dream and scheme's / Depending on whether, all through the storm, / You've kept it warm . . . / The nickel under your foot."[53] Although her song is far from being an *apologia* for the corrupted patricians of Steeltown, it nevertheless adamantly insists that personal integrity is not an inherent characteristic of human beings but a question of concrete economic circumstances and hence subject to change.[54] And yet, despite its inherent potential for a radical social critique, Moll's lament is rendered in such inconspicuous and sentimental manner that it comes across primarily as the lament of a working girl. "These bluesy working-woman's laments were neither folk songs nor topical protest songs. Rather, they borrowed the forms of Tin Pan Alley and turned them inside out," Denning comments.[55] It was the popularity of its tune and the mournfulness of its tone that captured the audiences. As the emotional backbone of the show, Moll's "Nickel Song" significantly contributed to its broad success.

A third factor anchored *Cradle* in the vernacular tradition of New Deal theater: the fusion of Weimar *Gebrauchsmusik* with vaudeville, revue, Tin Pan Alley, and jazz. According to music critic Philip Barr, it was this very fusion of the foreign and the native, the high and the low, that made *The Cradle Will Rock* "unmistakable American" music.[56] As "the first great music to bear the sign of jazz," it became the quintessential American opera in the vernacular.[57] Denning similarly points out that such "bastard unions" of the "modern and the middlebrow" were quite typical for the aesthetics and sensibilities of a broad cultural front.[58] In transcending the narrow confines of agitprop and translating radical issues into the familiar vernacular of the American musical theater, they helped to secure mass appeal as well as to Americanize the very concept of the revolution.

The concerted effort to vernacularize and Americanize a European and modernist concept of musical theater is also evident in Blitzstein's attempt to capture the rhythm of colloquial language in his songs. He substituted concert diction with the speech of the streets and, moreover, wrote his songs for actors rather than trained opera singers. The result, which strikes one as somewhat crude and uneven, is reminiscent of the popular style of hard-boiled fiction, and precisely this was its appeal. *New Masses* reviewer R. D. Darrell praised *Cradle* for its "simplicity, unaffectedness, and vivid realism."[59] Thomson called it "urbane music for urban people."[60] Flanagan likewise remarked, "It took no wizardry to see that this was not just a play set to music, nor music illustrated by actors, but music and play equaling something new and better than either. This was in its percussive as well as verbal beat Steeltown U.S.A.—America 1937."[61]

The labor and bourgeois press were extremely supportive of *The Cradle Will Rock*, hailing it as "the most exciting propagandistic tour de force" since *Waiting for Lefty*.[62] Such rave reviews had, however, little to do with the play's actual content, which was generally ignored or written off as a "common enough" propaganda drama.[63] The enthusiasm of the press was above all for the iconoclastic staging and acting. Richard Lockridge found that the "economic originality of the stagecraft" added freshness and energy to word and music that were after all not all that new.[64] Atkinson similarly asserted that *Cradle* would certainly "lose some of its direct fury in a normally accoutred performance."[65] Aside from its provocative mise-en-scène, it was above all its witty satire and good humor that drew a broad audience. "It is that laugh that gives the opera its inescapable force,"

Richard Watts wrote.[66] According to Sidney Whipple, it was thanks to its good-natured humor that the proletarian opera appealed to the most diverse sections in the audience: "downright left-wingers who care nothing for the acting provided the sentiment is 'correct,' theoretical radicals who regard their neighbors as 'Mr. Misters,' and conservatives who don't give a hoot about the philosophy but who enjoy good acting."[67]

In the end, however, it was the audience and not the critics that carried the show. "The audience alone is worth the trip," Thomson enthusiastically declared.[68] It represented "the newly amalgamated" urban left, which included such a broad spectrum as "the right-wing socialists, the communists, some Park Avenue, a good deal of Bronx, and all those intellectuals and worker groups that the Federal Theatre in general and the Living Newspaper in particular have welded into about the most formidable army of ticket buyers in the world."[69] By 1937, this Popular Front audience, which had gradually consolidated itself around the productions of New Theatre League, Group Theatre, Theatre Union, Labor Stage, and Federal Theatre, was clearly in place; what was more, it was conscious of itself as a public whose opinions mattered. When WPA authorities cancelled all subscriptions to *Cradle*, Welles and Houseman merely had to call up the various organizations that had already purchased tickets: "They needed no urging, for they were part of that new left-wing audience that had sprung up with the Depression [. . .] prejudiced and semi-educated but young and generous and eager to participate in the excitement which the stage alone seemed to offer them in those uncertain times."[70] This heterogeneous Popular Front audience now demonstrated its solidarity with the theater of the left by supporting its shows and joining WPA workers in numerous sit-down strikes through the spring of 1937.[71]

Cradle was a brilliant success of Popular Front culture. In assessing its politics, we, however, need to remember that this success owed much to the various political events that surrounded its productions as well as to Welles's and Houseman's bold defiance of censorship and cleverly staged relocation of the show. Thanks to these events, the spirit of iconoclasm and rebellion lay in the air well before Blitzstein played the opening chord at the Venice Theatre. If theater historians celebrate the form by which it finally became known as a radical experiment in non-illusory stagecraft, essentially epic in character, then they largely overlook the fact that in its original Federal Theatre design *Cradle* had been a very different concept. Blitzstein himself drew attention to the fact that the Spartan staging at the Venice "was really only a heightened reading, and as such, had no intended relation to the theories of Brecht or anyone else."[72] Although the successful (incidental) deployment of epic elements triggered some debate among theater makers about the usefulness of non-illusory staging techniques, in particular the "scenery-less" stage, it was the opera's distinctive vernacular qualities that informed its success with a broad public. Above all, it was the middlebrow aesthetics of Blitzstein's score and libretto, the successful amalgamation of "quickly singable and hauntingly difficult" musical tunes[73] as well as the idiosyncratic combination of middle-class satire, labor folklore, and sentimental lament that appealed and spoke to an educated urban working- and middle-class audience who took a lively interest in political culture and cultural politics. Although the play was shown in the steel towns of Pennsylvania and Ohio and even earned official praise from the CIO, it was and remained a middle-class allegory for middle-class people.

Can You Hear Us, Washington?

If *The Cradle Will Rock* elicited most sympathies among what Gassner called the "bourgeois-baiting 'bourgeois' *rive-gauche* tendencies that have barely touched the common man,"[74] then it was the Living Newspaper of the Federal Theatre Project that undoubtedly succeeded in reaching out to the average man and woman in the streets. Like no other cultural production of its time, it upheld and promoted the cult of the common person and in that regard was probably America's most vernacular form of political theater. In what follows, I will show that this vernacularity went hand in hand with a profound cultural nationalism and fundamental belief in the democratic possibilities of American capitalism.

"The Federal Theatre had its roots, not in an art theory, but in economic necessity," director Hallie Flanagan asserted with regard to the thousands of theater workers who had lost their jobs as a result of economic recession and a rapidly expanding movie industry.[75] In order to put them back to work, the government established under the Works Progress Administration (WPA) Federal One, the Federal Theatre Project (FTP), which began work on 1 October 1935. Besides providing relief, FTP was to stimulate the theatergoing of the lower-income public, to attract those who had never been to the theater or had not been able to afford it during the years of the Depression. Project One was to be "an American job, not just a New York job," WPA head

Harry Hopkins insisted.[76] Flanagan indeed accomplished an American job. With the help of five FTP centers (New York, Chicago, Los Angeles, Boston, New Orleans) and numerous touring companies playing the regions in between, she founded a theater "national in scope and regional in emphasis," providing theatrical entertainment for as little as ten to twenty-five cents and often entirely free of charge.[77] Already in spring of 1936, Flanagan reported that the project had put 12,500 theater workers back to work and was playing in thirty-one states, attracting an average audience of 500,000 spectators per week. The first government-sponsored theater thus also became the first national people's theater in American history.[78]

FTP covered the whole range of dramatic genres, but it was particularly one genre that stood out in its repertory for its innovative techniques and political subject matter: the Living Newspaper. The idea of the Living Newspaper was, just like the entire project, derived from the need to put a great number of people back to work. Flanagan suggested "the plan of dramatizing contemporary events in a series of living newspapers which would have a rapid, cinematic form and emphasis on many people doing small bits rather than roles demanding a few stars."[79] With its extensive research and editorial staff, an enormous cast, and dozens of people backstage, the Living Newspaper became one of FTP's most labor-intensive projects.[80] To Flanagan, it therefore seemed only logical "that a theatre which had its roots in economic need should be concerned in some of its plays with economic conditions."[81] It was thus the explicit goal of the Living Newspapers to illuminate the various social and economic forces that determine people's lives.

Out of twenty-two papers produced by FTP, the four New York editions became best known.[82] All of them dealt with highly sensitive political issues: agricultural crisis (*Triple-A Plowed Under*, 1936), unionization (*Injunction Granted*, 1936), public ownership of utilities (*Power*, 1937), and housing shortage (*One Third of a Nation*, 1938). The very first issue *Ethiopia* (1936) on Mussolini's invasion of Ethiopia was cancelled shortly before its premiere. Although Hopkins had assured Flanagan that Project One would be kept free from censorship, Washington worried that the issue might create "international complications."[83] While Elmer Rice, head of the New York Living Newspaper division, resigned in protest against such blatant censorship, Flanagan diplomatically asserted that she would not have the project used politically. FTP was to do "only such plays as the government could stand behind."[84] Such "non-political" mandate notwithstanding, the Living Newspaper became one of the most critical dramatic voices of the decade and a prime example of American political theater.

The Living Newspaper had its roots in the American workers' theater movement, from which it recruited many of its writers and directors. (Ironically, in drafting its most talented people, it also contributed to the demise of that very movement).[85] Its innovative modernist techniques, moreover, also recalled Piscator's multimedia spectacles at the Volksbühne and the agitprop pieces of the Russian Blue Blouses. It, however, embedded these theatrical elements in a vernacular aesthetics of identification. This was obvious in its choice of subject matter as well as of form. While it addressed a great variety of topics, the explicit goal of the Living Newspapers was a political one through and through, namely "to improve the social and economic lot of the average man."[86] With this goal in mind, it chose problems of immediate and pressing concern to the average person (e.g., housing shortage, the price of electricity and meat) and translated them into a language that was easily accessible and understandable to the common man and woman in the audience.

One Third of a Nation (1938) was by far the most successful of all Living Newspapers, with a run of 237 performances in New York alone. The issue was inspired by Franklin D. Roosevelt's second inaugural address of 1937, in which he drew attention to the fact that one third of the nation was "ill-housed, ill-clad and ill-nourished." In frontpage fashion, the play starts with a recent sensational event: a burning tenement. As the curtain opens, we watch people rush for water, cower in hallways, and fall to their death from broken fire escapes. A loudspeaker announces, "February 1924—This might be 397 Madison Street New York. It might be 245 Halsey Street, Brooklyn, or Jackson Avenue and 10th Street, Long Island City."[87] The scene then switches abruptly to the next episode: a committee investigating the fire but finding no violation of safety regulations. Instead, it concludes that the fire and its fourteen casualties were simply the tragic result of conditions long entrenched in the city's real estate history: "You'll have to go back into history and blame whatever it was that made New York City real estate the soundest and most profitable speculation on the face of the earth."[88]

After this prelude, designed to capture the curiosity of the audience by establishing the topic as one of immediate relevance, the plot proper sets in: a guided tour through the history of New York's real estate, from the first land grants in colonial times to the great migrations of the late nineteenth century, the tenement laws of the turn of the century and their persistent violation, right up to the 1930s. While the Loudspeaker provides the facts, actors illustrate them in scenic action. But as the play reveals the inefficiency of official laws and regulations, the corruption of administrators, and the greed of land speculators, the frustrated voice of the people makes itself heard. "Little Man" Angus K. Buttonkooper, who has strolled into the theater, hoping to find out how to improve his own living situation, steps onto the stage: "So I went down to see the Tenement Housing Commissioner. He told me the Living Newspaper was doing a show on housing and I ought to see it. . . . So here I am."[89] Buttonkooper now participates in the historical tour, discussing its highlights with the Loudspeaker. Realizing that the housing situation remains essentially unchanged, he begins to wonder about possible alternatives. These too are discussed with the Loudspeaker and acted out on stage (e.g., rent strikes, emergency rent laws, new tenement houses). Since these measures, however, only redress the symptoms of the crisis, they are all discarded as equally unsatisfactory. At the source of the ubiquitous lack of affordable and decent housing, so Buttonkooper discovers, is the profit system of a capitalist society.

But just as the plot is about to peter out in resignation, the Loudspeaker resolutely intervenes:

> Wait a minute! Hold it! Don't black out on that yet! Bring those lights up —full! (They come up) That's better. This scene isn't over yet. (Pause) Now, Mister Landlord, we know that the conditions you showed us exist. But we can't just let it go at that. We can't let people walk out of this theatre knowing the disease is there, but believing there's no cure. There is a cure! [. . .] If you can't build cheap houses—and you've just shown that you can't—then let somebody do it who can—and I mean the United States Government for instance.[90]

What follows is a brief survey of government initiatives, including various housing projects and the Wagner Bill for the elimination of slums and the development of safe and healthy housing. Although the Loudspeaker and Buttonkooper support government intervention as the only viable solution to the problem, they also quickly recognize that as practiced it is of limited effectiveness, at best improving two percent of the living conditions. Here, a determined Mrs. Buttonkooper steps in from the audience. She too has drawn her conclusions from the information provided and now suggests that the government ought to cut its military spending in favor of the housing budget: "You know what we're going to do—you and me? We're going to holler. And we're going to keep on hollering until they admit in Washington it's just as important to keep a man alive as it is to kill him!"[91] The play then ends with a powerful call for collective protest: "They'll hear us all right if we all do it together—you and me and LaGuardia and Senator Wagner and the Housing Authorities and the Tenant Leagues and everybody who lives in a place like that!"[92] Collective protest, so the play adamantly insists, is the only way of effecting change.

Like other Living Newspapers, *One Third of a Nation* freely borrows from the agitprop and epic theaters, as evident in its use of episodic plot structure, non-illusory staging, incorporation of original sources, and heavy didacticism. First, each scene dramatizes a different aspect of the larger problem; all of them, however, reiterating one and the same message: we cannot go on like this. At the same time, the plot gradually builds dramatic suspense within each scene, each act, and the play as a whole, eventually culminating in Mrs. Buttonkooper's holler for government intervention. Second, due to budget restrictions (only ten percent could be spent on production costs), the Living Newspaper normally worked without elaborate sets, props, and costumes, relying solely on light, sound, projections, and acting. *One Third* is exceptional in that set designer Howard Barker recreated a four-story tenement building on stage, vividly illustrating in naturalist fashion the crammed and unhealthy living conditions of urban slums. The play not only opens with the tableau of this burning tenement but also closes with it in order to drive home in a powerful image the point that, as Mrs. Buttonkooper puts it, "if we don't make them hear us you're going to have just what you've always had—slums—disease—crime—juvenile delinquency . . . and . . ."[93]

Third, the influence of agitprop and epic theater is also evident in the Living Newspaper's strong empirical bias as well as in its method of translating abstract facts and concepts into concrete visual imagery. Like other editions, *One Third* quotes extensively from newspaper reports, public speeches, statistics, laws, etc. At times, these facts are read aloud by characters or announced by the Loudspeaker; other times, they are projected in the form of photos or film footage on a screen. Supporting its argument with original documents and O-tones, the Living Newspaper underscores the authenticity and relevance of its presentations. In addition, it effectively visualizes abstract figures and terms. In *One Third*, Arthur Arent (author and co-author of several editions) vividly illustrates the callousness of real estate speculation with the help of a small grass carpet onto which more and more people crowd for ever-higher fees. In *Power*, he explains the concept of a holding company with the help of colored boxes, which are subsumed by yet other and ever-larger boxes. These educational scenes are often presented in slapstick fashion, skillfully masking their inherent didacticism. In *One Third*, the tenants of the above-mentioned grass carpet continue to go through the quotidian motions of shaving, dressing, and eating in ever-more restricted positions as the landlord meticulously clears a few more unoccupied blades of grass for yet another tenant. "A Very Fat Man hands over the money, kneels down, looks at it. He backs away to get a running start, then runs and jumps onto his spot. He bumps the Tenants who are annoyed. Then, music 'Home! Sweet Home!' "[94] The essence of the housing market is here translated into concrete visual imagery and burlesque physical action—an approach reminiscent of such basic agitprop devices as the election boxing match in Piscator's *Red Revue*.

Finally, one of the strongest echoes of epic theater is the Living Newspaper's basic didactic approach: its recreation of a student-teacher relationship on stage. Buttonkooper represents the American Everyman, "confused, belligerent, determined, but fundamentally innocent of malicious intent, never so complex that he obscured the point of the play."[95] Eager to learn, he demands explanations: "Every time something happens that I don't understand I'm going to stop the show and ask questions."[96] The Loudspeaker in turn functions as mentor, explaining events, commenting on decisions, and providing missing information; it is "helpful and sympathetic at one moment, bellicose, disdainful and sly at others."[97] Its main function is to teach Buttonkooper—and, by extension, the audience—to think and act for himself. As the Loudspeaker makes clear, while it can elucidate the problem, it cannot amend the situation. In the end, it is Buttonkooper and the audience that need to become active. This attitude is reminiscent of the speaker in Piscator's dramaturgy as well as of Brecht's favorite ruse of teaching the audience by teaching a protagonist on stage.

While the Living Newspaper is clearly influenced by modernist techniques of political theater, it nonetheless strives to expropriate them for an essentially vernacular pedagogy. This is most evident in the way it seeks to emulate in its dramaturgy the commonsensical process of problem-solving that it considers typical of the common spectator, the average citizen: it delineates a problem (real estate), acknowledges its importance (fire), determines its causes (land speculation), examines alternatives (rent strikes), and arrives at a conclusion (government intervention).[98] The pragmatism of this approach is further underlined by the introduction of an average plebeian protagonist, someone who is just like the people in the audience, someone with whom most of them can easily identify. Naturally, this character usually enters from the auditorium and carries an allegorical name like Timothy Taxpayer, Homer Bystander, John Q. Public, or Angus Buttonkooper. White, male, married, and with children, this Little Man exemplifies the audience's pattern of what John Dewey has called "reflective thinking"[99] and also serves as the human correlative to the statistical data provided by loudspeaker and screen. He is the main point of audience identification.

In addition, abstract thought is brought to life not only in slapstick skits but also in a series of fictional scenes, which movingly complement and enhance the documentary character of the play. "For the love of Mike, let's see some people!" Buttonkooper impatiently demands at the beginning of his lesson.[100] So whenever the Loudspeaker reads out statistics on cholera epidemics and juvenile delinquencies in urban slums, actors enact the story from the perspective of the people suffering from them. In brief melodramatic scenes, they show the devastating impact of cramped housing conditions on the dreams, morale, and health of the tenants. These naturalistic vignettes provide dramatic suspense and highlight the human dimension of the story. Similar to *Waiting for Lefty*, this humanist dramaturgy allows for the breakdown of a complex problem into tangible personal stories, enabling the audience to access the play not only on a rational but also on an emotional level.

In short, in choosing a common-man protagonist who is just like the average spectator, in developing a dramatic structure that emulates his commonsensical understanding of problems of immediate daily relevance, and in enhancing the basic documentary style of their issues with fictional, yet highly realistic vignettes, the Living Newspaper turns the analysis of a current problem into an individual dramatic adventure, providing its audience with a comprehensive factual and yet entirely personal and sentimental (and therefore vernacular) education on current political issues.

Arguably, we have in the Living Newspaper an effective synthesis of modernist and vernacular strategies of political theater. It is therefore particularly intriguing that the makers of the Living Newspaper purposely downplayed the modernist influence on their work, highlighting instead its inherent vernacularity. Arent bluntly denies that agitprop and epic theater had any impact at all, asserting that the staff of the Living Newspaper was completely unaware of the sources of its techniques.[101] Flanagan, who had studied modernist theater overseas, acknowledged the "occasional reference to the Volksbühne and the Blue Blouses, to Bragaglia and Meierhold and Eisenstein," but adamantly insisted that the Living Newspaper was "as American as Walt Disney."[102] With regard to its skillful amalgamation of epic elements with a classic humanist dramaturgy, of the modernist and the middlebrow the Living Newspapers was indeed an idiosyncratic product of the American theater. However, in the purposeful elusion of its modernist roots, we also sense the presence of a profound cultural nationalism, to which I shall return shortly.

According to Ira Levine the prominent presence of epic elements in such cultural productions as *The Cradle Will Rock* and the Living Newspaper was, in fact, indicative of a growing interest among leftist circles in epic theater, enabled by the Popular Front's shift to a middle-class audience (this audience was thought to be more receptive to non-realist writing than a working class audience).[103] Indeed, the non-illusory staging techniques of *Cradle*, the Living Newspaper, and Thornton Wilder's *Our Town* (1938) were widely discussed among leftist theater makers at the time. However, as Flanagan also insists, the Living Newspaper used these techniques for primarily economic reasons and not as part and parcel of a new concept of political theater.[104] Therefore, I want to suggest that the use of epic elements had little to do with a sudden appreciation of modernist political theater nor with the rediscovery of a middle-class audience, as Levine maintains (after all the Living Newspapers were produced for the impoverished "one third of a nation"). Rather, they were understood as stylistic innovations that remained firmly embedded in a native concept of realism, one that privileged fact and experience over theory and abstraction. Barbara Foley has called this concept of realism the American "cult of authenticity."[105]

As Foley has shown in *Radical Representations* (1993), leftist writers of the 1930s did not consider realism a homogenous concept but remained open to formal innovation, particularly when this innovation served to enhance the immediacy of experience and primacy of fact, both of which they considered crucial to a "truthful" rendition of reality. "Truth to the object, rather than arousal of the reader, constituted the principal determinant of value in a proletarian text— although it was assumed that arousal might well result from the reader's encounter with truth," Foley writes.[106] In other words, as long as the text avoided the direct, unmediated exhortation of the audience (which was often dismissed as "propaganda"), as long as it rendered its facts in a believable and compelling fashion, factual truth could very well be presented in the non-illusory form—as proven by the mainstream success of *Waiting for Lefty* and *The Cradle Will Rock*. It is therefore not surprising that the highly theatrical issues of the Living Newspaper were often praised precisely for their "realism." "Realism in this context" did not function as a mimetic concept (a photographic reproduction of reality) but as a palpable visceral effect, as an affect that "makes you, sometimes, hold your breath," as one spectator described it.[107]

In this regard, the direct address of the audience by the Loudspeaker in *One Third of a Nation* was most likely perceived less as an unmediated didactic voice than as the voice of fact and reality. As such, spectators seemed to accept it as part of the diegesis of a play. Worker John Mullen, for instance, compares his experience of watching a Living Newspaper to that of watching a Piscator play: "What's got me stumped [. . .] is this: there's a 'speaker' in the *Triple-A Plowed Under* and the acting is episodic as in *Case of Clyde Griffiths*. But there the similarity stops. The WPA show is so good that it makes your hair tingle and sits you on the edge of your seat."[108] Whereas Mullen was clearly annoyed by the constant lecturing of Piscator's Speaker, he was strongly moved by the stark reality of the facts presented by the Loudspeaker in *Triple-A*. Emulating the commonsensical logic of the common person, evincing the "truthfulness" of everyday American lives, the latter simply did not carry the connotations of heavy-handed didacticism and abstract theorizing that epic theater was commonly associated with in the United States. In this manner, the Living Newspaper managed to garner the attention of a mass audience that Brecht and Piscator had sought in vain in the mid 1930s. But aside from such difference in aesthetic perception, there were other political and cultural factors that also embedded the modernist techniques of the Living Newspaper in an essentially vernacular concept of political theater.

One Third of Nation was very popular with audiences and critics. In New York alone, over 200,000 people flocked to see it between its opening on 17 January 1938 at the Adelphi Theatre and its closing in October that year.[109] Most reviewers, who now enthusiastically applauded the production as "exhilarating showmanship," had only two years previously vehemently attacked and condemned the epic plays of Brecht and Piscator as dramatically unexciting, overtly didactic, schematic, and blatantly propagandistic.[110] But these very same qualities now earned almost unanimous approval. Sidney Whipple, conceding that *One Third* was "frankly propaganda," insisted that "propaganda to be forceful must necessarily present its case strongly and without compromise."[111] Richard Watts likewise admitted that "the Living Newspaper method is, of course, earnest, partisan, bitter and given to a Left Wing point of view" but that it was nonetheless "almost invariably forceful, striking and remarkably skillful in dramatizing what might seem to be undramatic ideas."[112]

Why such sudden acceptance of didacticism and propaganda? What made the very principles of epic theater (such as episodic structure, non-illusory staging, instruction, topical content), which had previously greatly angered the American public, now socially and theatrically acceptable? How to explain the enthusiasm of a conservative press for a decidedly political genre, which at first had been considered "controversial dynamite" and whose launching had been accompanied by heavy police presence?[113] I want to suggest that by 1938 the leftism of the Living Newspaper had become acceptable, even fashionable, for the following reasons: it was "safe" propaganda on behalf of the government; it presented political issues as consumer interests; and it asserted its critique in the familiar form of the American Jeremiad, which was ultimately affirmative rather than subversive of the existing system.

First, as a government-sponsored project, the Living Newspaper presented propaganda on behalf of the government, which in the minds of many Americans could hardly be a source of alarm. "Propaganda? Precisely . . . and excellent propaganda. Propaganda with a strong pulse to it, doubled fists, a tough jaw and a fighting jag," Gilbert Gabriel raved about *Power*.[114] John Mason Brown likewise endorsed attendance of *One Third of a Nation* as "every good citizen's duty."[115] Such semantic recharging of the term propaganda had to do not alone with its integration into a vernacular aesthetics but also with a general political reorientation in the public sphere, as evident in reviewers' distinctions between good and bad propaganda—that is, propaganda on behalf of the government versus propaganda of the radical left. Good propaganda was without "breast-beating indignation and tearing down of a system of government as we always get it from the leftist playwrights, but a straightforward and sensible narrative of abuses existing under a government that is seeking to prevent them," Douglas Gilbert explained.[116] Many reviewers therefore preferred the propaganda of the Living Newspaper to that of Brecht and Piscator.[117] What was the difference? All of them depicted the oppression of the working population under capitalism. Yet, where Brecht and Piscator suggested that man can be truly free only under a non-capitalist system, the Living Newspaper shied away from what would be the logical conclusion to its empirical analysis. As Ulrich Halfmann has shown, in *One Third of a Nation* the systemic critique of capitalism is translated into a system-immanent solution, namely the shifting of the budget from military spending to Wagner's housing bill—a rather naïve solution given the mounting war preparations in 1938.[118] Naturally, such propaganda did not pose a threat to the dominant economic and social order; on the contrary, by calling on the government to amend the situation, the Living Newspaper asserted its faith in American democracy. Seen from this angle, it becomes clear why what had once seemed "dull," "ugly," and "schematic" in Brecht and Piscator could suddenly be acclaimed as "theater-mindedness" and a "fascinating dramatic lecture"; what was once dismissed as "preaching to the converted" could now be lauded as "instructiveness" and "partisanship."

This brings us to a second factor for the overall acceptance and celebration of the Living Newspaper by press and audience. Although its main goal was to improve living conditions for workers, farmers, and petit bourgeois, it rarely argued along class lines. Rather, it consolidated these various groups under the umbrella term "consumer." America's "Little Man" is the average consumer struggling with utility bills and the housing situation, marveling about the price of milk and meat. In *One Third*, he is most tellingly called Buttonkooper, the buyer of buttons. As suggested most clearly in *Triple-A*, the consumer was the crucial link in the economy; by strengthening his purchasing power, the agricultural crisis could be amended and business revitalized. In general, the political argumentation of the Living Newspaper was thus very much in line with Roosevelt's Keynesian reform program. More than any other form of political theater in the United States, it sublimated class consciousness into consumer consciousness. What is more, it presented this consumer consciousness as part and parcel of a democratic national identity. When Hopkins congratulated Flanagan on a successful *Power* premiere, he praised it above all for its consumerist propaganda: "It's propaganda to educate the consumer who is paying for power. It's about time someone had some propaganda for him. The big power companies have spent millions on propaganda for the utilities. It's about time that the consumer had a mouthpiece."[119] Appealing to the democratic consumer consciousness of its spectators, the Living Newspaper managed to elicit wide popular support for Roosevelt's New Deal.

Third, the widespread acclaim of the Living Newspaper was also enhanced by its rehearsal of a long-standing, native tradition of cultural intervention: the American Jeremiad. With this term, Sacvan Bercovitch describes a body of literature that exhorts its readers to live up to the Puritan founding ideals of their society.[120] For Bercovitch, these texts fulfill a dual function: lamenting the decline of the national dream, they celebrate and affirm its very essence. Underneath all exhortation, they reveal an unshakeable optimism and belief in American progress and democracy and, in this manner, function as moral correctives rather than the visions of doom and destruction they purport to be. The Living Newspaper is heir to this tradition. Despite its forceful critique of private profiteering and rugged individualism, it asserts an essential faith in American democracy and government reform, putting its weight behind the Soil Conservation Act (*Triple-A Plowed Under*), the Tennessee Valley Authority (*Power*), and the Wagner Act (*One Third of a Nation*). Its political intervention thus never violates the basic republican consensus of American democracy.

The final scene of *One Third* evinces this Jeremiah character most clearly. After a *tour de force* lesson in Marxism that exposes the economic conditioning of the housing crisis, the play surprisingly concludes that "the thing that's made these slum conditions possible for the last hundred and fifty years" is not capitalism itself but something as vague as the "inertia" of the American citizens.[121] And it suggests that all that is needed to amend the situation is to "holler" out loud: "Can you hear me—you in Washington or Albany or wherever you are! Give me a decent place to live in! Give me a home! A home!"[122] In short, while the Living Newspaper might remind its audience that the American people have revolted "for slighter causes" than the lack of home, work, and food,[123] it also assures them that what is needed is not another revolution but sufficient clamor on part of the average citizen and consumer to move the elected government to reforms that can make the system work on their behalf.

In conclusion, by adapting modernist techniques for a vernacular praxis of political theater, the Living Newspaper asserts a fundamental critique of American capitalism and calls for change, while at the same time affirming the very system it criticizes. It attacks the corporate system but not capitalism itself. On the contrary, it maintains that under the supervision of the government a moral capitalist system could prosper to the benefit of every consumer. It is not surprising that the Living Newspaper was widely accepted as a critical but essentially democratic mouthpiece for the average American citizen and consumer. Its primary purpose was not incitement to revolution but the reassurance of it audience of the intrinsic regenerative power of American democracy. It is precisely in this regard that it was most dissimilar to modernist political theater proper. Monitoring social shortcomings while at the same time affirming the system's economic foundations, as was typical of the American Jeremiad, the Living Newspaper was indeed, as Gassner put it, "the most native form of theater this country has produced."[124]

Yet, its fundamental Americanism and widespread public support notwithstanding, the Living Newspaper was discontinued along with Federal One by act of U.S. Congress on 30 June 1939. "A project which from first to last had stood on American principles of freedom, justice and truth was accused of being through its plays, its audience and its personnel, subversive, communistic, and indecent," Flanagan wrote.[125] The backlash began already in summer 1938 with various allegations about a "communist subversion" of the Federal Theatre. Two congressional committees investigated the matter, concluding that "a rather large number of the employees on the Federal Theatre Project are either members of the Communist Party or are sympathetic with the Communist Party."[126] Although this rash verdict was clearly based on the dubious statements of a handful of biased witnesses, the committees refused to hear any evidence on behalf of the project, just as they also declined invitations to the shows under debate. Among the FTP productions questioned were the four New York Living Newspapers. By government standards, however, they were by far not the most subversive ones. Most dangerous of all turned out to be the children's play *The Revolt of the Beavers* (1937) by Oscar Saul and Louis Lantz, in which "woodless" beavers revolted against the cruel "wooded beavers."

Since the Federal Theatre was not allowed to engage in publicity on its own behalf, Flanagan had no chance of defending the project against such absurd allegations. When she was finally allowed to speak at the hearing, she stressed, as always, her and the project's allegiance to the American government. It was to no avail. Flanagan's time was cut short and the hearing turned into an anti-communist crucible—its outcome determined well in advance.[127] The federal advocacy of New Deal reforms had long become a thorn in the side of many conservative legislators.

The spectacular ending of the Living Newspaper once more confirmed that it presented a powerful and vital form of political theater. It brought important current issues up for debate, teaching its audience how their lives were historically determined by a confluence of various social, economic, and political factors. Its didactic role consisted above all in enabling and encouraging the public to voice an informed and authoritative collective protest and to exert pressure upon its government. While it represented the interests of an exploited "one third of a nation," it deferred the interventional power to the government. As a mouthpiece of public concerns it nevertheless played an important role in political debates of the time, functioning as a moral corrective and political commentary on Roosevelt's New Deal politics.[128] In all these regards, it was an expression of a Popular Front liberalism, reformatory rather than revolutionary—with occasional radical overtones.

Or We Won't Love You

By far the most popular proletarian show on the New Deal stage was the musical revue *Pins and Needles*, which over the course of four years played a total of 1,108 performances, including two national tours. Originating in the drama workshops of the International Ladies' Garment Workers' Union (ILGWU), it was staged by amateur actors for their work peers at the union Labor Stage.[129] But within weeks of its opening in November 1937, it became the talk of the town attracting the carriage trade as well. *Pins and Needles* eventually became the longest running musical of the 1930s (upstaged only by *Oklahoma!* in 1943), making some $1.5 million in clear profits. Like no other leftist production of the time, this labor revue demonstrates the capacity of a vernacular theater praxis to mobilize a broad and diverse audience in support of a national reform program. It also vividly illustrates the extent to which vernacular political theater is capable of adapting itself to the socio-cultural parameters of its time. Similar to the Living Newspaper, *Pins and Needles* spoke compellingly on behalf of the workers while also asserting its faith that the very system that had subjugated them could be made to work for them. However, it also points to the limits of vernacular political theater. For what began as an amateur performance in the garment shops on Seventh Avenue ended up as one of the most profitable Broadway commodities of the time—a career that raises a number of questions about the relationship of commodification to political viability as well as the various ways for assessing political value.

The primary impulse behind *Pins and Needles* was to provide entertainment for workers and by workers. "The worker is just like everyone else. When he goes to the theater he wants to be entertained," Louis Schaffer, director of Labor Stage insisted.[130] In addition to providing entertainment, the show sought to "blaze a wide trail to an understanding of labor's ideals among the most divergent sections of our country's population."[131] To accomplish these two goals, Labor Stage called on prominent leftist theater workers of the time to help put together a colorful revue; among them were Harold Rome as composer; Marc Blitzstein, Arthur Arent, and Emanuel Eisenberg as writers; Sointu Syrjala as set designer; Benjamin Zach as choreographer; and Charles Friedman as director. Out of this collaboration came a lively labor show, which with satirical skits, torch songs, and dance routines attempted to provide a labor point of view on socially significant issues.

The program of the revue consisted of three main categories: political satire, portraits of urban work life, and parodies of leftist culture. While the sequence of numbers remained essentially the same throughout the run of the show, some of the political sketches were modified in response to the changing political climate. Thus, the number of angels in the popular burlesque "Four Little Angels of Peace" varied according to foreign affairs, at some point including Stalin as angel number five besides the other four angels: Hitler, Hirohito, Mussolini, and Eden (later Chamberlain). Their "angelic" routine, however, remained the same. After stating their peaceful intentions ("Four little angels of peace are we / There is one thing, on which we agree / With foe and with friend we will fight to the end / Just for peace, peace, peace"), the angels would habitually resolve their peace convention in slapstick fashion with a general scuffle and beating.[132] In similar fashion, the original sketch "Stay out Sammy," which opposed U.S. intervention in Europe, was replaced in 1940 by "History Eight to the Bar," rallying the audience to its support. Such changes allowed *Pins and Needles* to provide its audiences with a running commentary on current events. All in all, the show offered a total of forty to fifty different sketches, culminating in two updated editions: *Pins and Needles 1939* in spring 1939 and *New Pins and Needles* in fall 1939. Returning to watch the new numbers and enjoy old favorites, audiences attested to the revue's successful combination of political cabaret, vaudeville, slapstick, and urban romance, to its "bastard union" of various styles and genres that was so typical for the cultural front.

Although decidedly labor in content, in form and style *Pins and Needles* aspired to be Broadway—a labor version of the great *Ziegfeld* and *Grand Street Follies* of the 1910s and 1920s. In addition to witty political satires, it offered catchy rhythms, energetic dance routines, and elaborate sets and costumes. It was particularly the musical score that stood out. While the two act finales had been inspired by the radical German music theater (with its syncopated rhythm the semi-finale "Men Awake!" being strongly reminiscent of the "Internationale"), the key songs of the show were drawn from the popular sound of Tin Pan Alley. It was especially these catchy tunes that captured the audience and prompted the critics to praise the show as "smart, satirical and melodious, offering shrewd popular music in clever and captivating fashion."[133] Indeed, songs like "Sing Me a Song of Social Significance," "One Big Union for Two," and "Sunday in the Park" soon made the radio charts.

It was particularly the following three characteristics that made the show attractive to a mass audience as well as to Broadway: its emphasis on love and romance, its unshakable humor, and ironically also its amateur cast. In the tradition of Tin Pan Alley, most of these songs sing about love and romance. "Sunday in the Park" reclaims

New York's Central Park as a working couple's retreat for leisure and romance, while the torch song "What Good Is Love?" poignantly asks what good are fashionable love songs when "you haven't got all that makes life worth living?"[134] In the second edition, the more upbeat "I've Got the Nerve to Be in Love," nonetheless, insists that love is not the prerogative of the affluent few: "Our economic standing / Won't need investigation / We know that we're included / In one-third of a nation / It's very plain to see / But still I've got the nerve to be / In love with you."[135] That love and romance can very well function as effective vehicles for social critique is most apparent in the theme song "Sing Me a Song of Social Significance" (also known as "Why Sing of Skies Above"). Here, the chorus girls complain that they are tired of their suitors' crooning and would rather be wooed with verses of "social significance," with verses that are in tune with their time. "It must be packed / With social fact," so the girls insist, or "We won't love you."[136] As the song gently critiques and parodies the culture industry's penchant for meaningless "moon and June songs," it nevertheless insists that love and romance are as essential to labor culture as songs of social significance, that, in fact, love songs are of social significance.

Aside from the Tin Pan Alley songs, the show's strongest asset was its sense of humor. Regardless of whether it ridiculed fascists abroad or reactionaries at home, whether it made fun of consumer culture, leftist aesthetics, union squabbles, or government politics, its tone was light and playful, "indicting with a song and a smile."[137] It was particularly its capacity to laugh not only at capitalists and reactionaries but also at left-wingers (as in the union sketch "Papa Lewis, Mama Green" or the Brecht spoof "Little Red School House") that endeared it to its liberal critics. "'Pins and Needles' shows that garment workers can act and that propaganda can be palatable," the bourgeois press rejoiced.[138] Richard Watts found it "an immensely likable show," which once and for all refuted the charge that "Left Wing boys and girls lack a sense of humor."[139] John Mason Brown considered its humorous method "twice as effective" as the "the sober routine methods of agitprop drama."[140] That *Pins and Needles* was widely considered "propaganda in its most winning fashion"[141] was most vividly attested by the ready attendance of the Broadway crowd. Sidney Whipple slyly remarked, *Pins and Needles* "ribs the moneyed classes so beautifully that it has begun to attract the limousine trade."[142] The First Lady herself flew to New York to see this "delightful" performance. "No one could be disappointed by this entertainment," she wrote, "the actors are having such a good time, the audience must of necessity reflect their good spirits."[143]

The amateur cast, which charmed Eleanor Roosevelt and many other critics, was indeed crucial to the popular success of the revue. As stated in the opening song, these worker-actors were "plain, simple, common, ordinary, everyday men and women who work hard for a living."[144] But overnight these "dressmakers, cloakmakers, cutters, underwear workers, knit-goods workers, neckwear makers, embroiderers, stampers, checkers, examiners, graders, pressers, trimmers, binders, pinkers" managed to sing and dance their way into the heart of America.[145] Their lack of professional training and theatrical experience was very much to their advantage. "The fact that they were amateurs and rather awkward gave the show an impact which helped," Rome conceded.[146] The bourgeois press praised the actors' "fresh, straightforward and unaffected" manner[147] as well as "the pleasure they take in what they are doing."[148] The labor press, too, was impressed by their valiant attempt of appropriating a classic Broadway form for labor purposes. As Ben Irwin saw it, the occasional "awkward spots" in singing, acting, and especially dancing only enhanced the overall appeal of the show, reminding the audience that this was a labor revue for and by workers that could easily compete with Broadway.[149]

The producers of *Pins and Needles*—Louis Schaffer (director of Labor Stage), David Dubinsky (president of ILGWU), and Julius Hochman (vice president)—quickly recognized the attraction of its amateur cast and began to advertise their spectacular rise from Seventh Avenue to Broadway accordingly. "A year ago they led the prosaic lives of needle trade workers," they wrote in the Souvenir Program,

> They got up early, they traveled to work in the crowded subways, they sewed, they cut, they operated their bonnaz embroidery machines, all without thought of a career on stage. And then they heard about the drama groups set up by the unions. [. . .] Who can tell but that their children will be born within the smell of grease paint. Anything is possible now, especially with the kind of favorable reception they've had.[150]

If a dressmaker could turn Broadway star, so the program suggested to its readers, then indeed anything was possible. As a labor union version of the American Dream, *Pins and Needles* naturally greatly appealed to a mass audience. "If these worker-actors don't look out they'll find themselves capitalists before they know it," one reviewer quipped.[151]

Indeed the worker-actors soon turned professionals. While at first they continued to work a thirty-five-hour week, rehearsing at night and performing on weekends, they soon performed three nights a week to satisfy the growing demand. Taking a leave of absence from their jobs and joining Actors' Equity, the former amateur performers were now semi-professionals working full-time on stage. At some point, the show included a nostalgic skit, in which Millie Weitz mourned the "Good Old Days" in the shop, a world without "two songs a night and diction worries."[152] Of course, she whispered at the end, she would rather be an actress than a seamstress. The greatest distinction in the acting career of the needle workers came with the White House command performance in March 1938. For the cast, "it was like being given an Academy Award!"[153] The Roosevelts were just as thrilled: "President in Stitches or Sew It Seams," a witty *New York Times* header declared.[154] When the show ended in 1940, most performers returned to their workplace, while some joined another show. As expected, the careers of the worker-actors were abundantly documented and commented upon by the press. After all, here was the classic solution to the crisis of capitalism: any ordinary worker could—with a little help from the union drama classes—become a star or starlet and, in this manner, overcome the general economic crisis. Once more, it was individual success that won out over collective effort.

As *Pins and Needles* grew more popular, its producers were more and more intent on polishing the show for Broadway standards. Not only did Schaffer move the show to the larger Windsor Theatre in 1939 and send two companies on the road, he also began to hire professional actors, singers, and dancers. "The cast was changed. Schaffer wanted to make the show more palatable. He put in new, sweeter material, good-looking girls, and talented non-union people," cast member Nettie Harary remarked.[155] In the process, Schaffer also "weeded out those people with thick, ethnic accents. People who looked Jewish were also weeded out."[156] But the more the show was groomed and polished for the Broadway market, the more it lost its distinctive working-class and ethnic markers. Harary was asked to get a nose job and other Jewish performers to change their names, prompting Hyman Goldstein to become Hy Gardner. A number performed by the black actress Olive Pearman was deleted from the White House performance.[157] The show thus drifted further and further away from its origins in New York's ethnic working-class communities. When "the new, pretty girls" were asked to stand by a sewing machine for some publicity shots, they "didn't even know which side of the machine to stand on!" Pearman recalled.[158] In the end, the show was as professional as it could be, but the price of such professionalization had been the persistent whitewashing of its cast, the glossing over of all those distinctive ethnic and class markers, which had once endeared it to labor audiences and critics. The audience changed accordingly as well. "It was like a Cinderella story. We were playing to packed houses, mostly New York carriage trade. We were the hit show of the town."[159]

But what social significance did the show have when performed by a white professional cast for a white upper middle-class audience? How to assess the political value of an amateur show that became one of the greatest Broadway successes of the decade? What kind of political agenda could a labor revue affect when it played at venues where workers could no longer afford the price of a ticket?

Whipple slyly mused, "If, by the quality of their art, these worker-players can lure chinchilla and other fur-bearing females into their theater on 39th St., this may be the beginning of a rapprochement leading to an era of social peace and good will."[160] What he overlooked, however, was that it was hardly the revue's social agenda that attracted the carriage trade but its entertainment value. As the *Brooklyn Daily Eagle* aptly pointed out, *Pins and Needles* was "propaganda without an irritant."[161] Its satirical indictment of dictatorship and fascism ("Four Little Angels of Peace," "Mussolini Handicap"), its spoofing of American reactionaries ("We'd Rather Be Right," "Call it Un-American"), and its parodies of squabbles on the American left ("Papa Lewis, Mama Green," "Little Red Schoolhouse") were all presented without sting, "more concerned with providing entertainment first."[162] If the show did indeed contribute to social peace among the various strata of society, as imagined by Whipple, then this harmony did hardly extend beyond the walls of the theater. And yet, it was precisely this illusion that the show sought to nourish.

Leftist critics, in fact, became increasingly more annoyed with the show's rapprochement with Broadway. Heywood Broun, who like many of his colleagues was very fond of the labor revue, suggested that it might simply be too funny for its own good: "I wish it had less entertainment value and more bite as propaganda. *Pins and Needles* has attracted the carriage trade, but the carriage trade eats it up. There ought to be one number, at any rate, which would send some dowager screaming into the night at every performance."[163] Mary McCarthy writing for *Partisan Review* put it more acerbically: "The dictators have turned comedians, and the indictment of capitalism is subdued to a genial spoofing of Macy's, militarism, Americanism [. . .], popular love songs, high-pressure advertising, social snobbery, and etiquette books. Ingratiation is the keynote of the performance."[164]

It was precisely this sense that *Pins and Needles* was trying to entertain the Broadway crowd at any price that eventually also triggered the ire of the labor press. *Daily Worker* withdrew its support for the show in 1939 when it realized that as a professional Broadway production it was about to sell itself out politically. Surprisingly, the target of its objection was less the CIO satire "Papa Lewis, Mama Green" nor the inclusion of Stalin among the "Little Angels of Peace" (both of which it naturally considered in utterly bad taste) but above all Weitz's song "Give Me the Good Old Days," which "painted a picture of factory joy which few astonished members of the ILGWU are going to recognize."[165] This *New Pins and Needles*, so the reviewer declared, was going out of its way to deride the sources from which it had evolved. "The strange malice at the Windsor Theatre" was, for him, "as startling and out of place [. . .] as it would be to see a friend kick his mother downstairs."[166] Such objections, however, were of little concern to the makers of the show. As leftist critics protested that *Pins and Needles* had abandoned its labor origins for the Great White Way, Dubinsky and Hochman considered their goals achieved and congratulated the cast on having made the grade: "In your own sweet, intimate manner you have laughed your way into the hearts of multitudes by mingling gaiety with 'social' significance."[167]

How to assess these two contradictory perspectives? This question is not easily answered, for here we also arrive at the problem of methodology in our evaluation of the political in political theater. In what follows, I shall show how depending on our theoretical angle, we can arrive at very different conclusions with regard to the political value of *Pins and Needles*.

According to Denning, it was its enormous popular success that made *Pins and Needles* politically relevant. By moving labor from Seventh Avenue onto Broadway, it established working-class identity in the cultural mainstream and asserted proletarian agency within modern consumer culture. In this regard, the show's "social significance" consisted not so much in its political satires about Hitler and Stalin or about the squabbles between CIO and American Federation of Labor (AFL) but precisely in those seemingly apolitical songs like "Sunday in the Park" and "I've Got the Nerve to Be in Love," with which the workers boldly and joyously reclaimed leisure and romance from the affluent few. They did so in a manner that was witty, entertaining, and self-confident. For example, when Weitz complains in her ironic lament "Nobody Makes a Pass at Me" that the ads do not seem to hold what they promise, she ultimately asserts herself as a female working-class consumer who can see right through the tricks of consumer culture:

> I wash my clothes with Lux
> My etiquette's the best,

I spend my hard earned bucks,
On just what the ads suggest.
O dear what can the matter be?
Nobody makes a pass at me.[168]

In "Chain Store Daisy," Ruth Rubinstein laments that her college education only got her a job at Macy's ("I used to be on the daisy chain / Now I am just a chain store daisy,") but she nonetheless retains the capacity of poking fun at her clients and herself: "Once I wrote poems that put folks in tears / Now I write cheques for ladies' brassiers."[169] The Cole Porter–style duet "I've Got the Nerve to Be in Love" similarly reclaims romance from Hollywood for urban labor culture: "I buy my things at Woolworth's, no charge account at Saks's / I never have to juggle reports of income taxes / That maybe so but why should I deny myself a try at love."[170] These songs constituted, as Denning writes, the show's emotional backbone. While the political satires were perpetually modified and changed in accordance with shifting domestic and foreign politics, the sketches dealing with love, romance, and urban work life remained unchanged. They, moreover, quickly made the charts and became the folk songs of the garment industry.[171] Their popularity owed much to the fact that they reflected the everyday experience of the young performers—most of them second-generation Italian and Jewish immigrants, who had grown up steeped in American popular and consumer culture. In these regards, the quotidian aspects of labor culture were certainly among the show's strongest political assets.[172]

As Denning furthermore reminds us, at the center of the show was the working girl. Although women represented the majority of workers in the garment industry and union, they remained almost completely effaced from its public image.[173] On stage, they, however, asserted their presence. The indisputable stars of *Pins and Needles* were female performers such as Ruth Rubinstein, Millie Weitz, Lynn Jaffe, and Nettie Harary, who performed the major skits and interpreted the best-liked songs. Weitz and Rubinstein greatly contributed to the show's success by inflecting their songs with the distinctive sound of an urban ethnic music tradition, of popular Jewish singers like Fanny Brice and Sophie Tucker. These women and their songs made *Pins and Needles* essentially a woman's show. A number of songs represented young, urbane working women who were acutely aware not only of their personal problems but also how these related to the larger social, economic, and political situation. Denning therefore rightly concludes that "[t]he success of *Pins and Needles* lay in its union of class, ethnic, and feminist energies, in the way it sang for young Jewish and Italian working-class women of the garment trades."[174]

By choosing a popular form (the grand musical revues of the 1920s and the catchy Tin Pan Alley sound of the 1930s), *Pins and Needles* elicited what Grant Farred described as the "intense identificatory pleasure" with the political without which political struggle would "not only be tedious but perhaps also entirely unsuccessful."[175] By infusing the political with the pleasurable, by conjoining labor politics with urban consumer culture and proletarian romance, the show contributed to what Denning calls the overall "laboring" of American culture—that is, the greater visibility of the influence and participation of working-class Americans in modern consumer culture and in the public sphere. Such laboring of American culture sustained the social movement of the Popular Front and generated broad public support for Roosevelt's New Deal. Seen from this angle, *Pins and Needles* was not entirely inimical to a leftist agenda, as suggested by the leftist reviews discussed earlier. On the contrary, from this perspective a seemingly apolitical song like "Sunday in the Park" asserted a political position. It stood, as Denning writes, as an "allegory of the entire show, the reclaiming of leisure and entertainment from the leisured classes and the celebration of the common pleasures and ordinary songs of working class life."[176] *Pins and Needles* succeeded in transmitting this assertion of labor identity to thousands of Americans, including the president.

Yet, I am hesitant to join Denning in his unreserved applause for the political efficacy of the show's vernacularity. For his argument can only be maintained if we bracket off its deliberate commodification for Broadway audiences, a process during which actual labor identity was replaced by a commercially produced image of labor that was thought to be most appealing to Broadway and the president.[177] But even if we ignore the whitewashing of the cast, the substitution of Jewish and Italian amateurs with professional Anglo-Saxon actors who had never before operated a sewing machine, we still have to wonder to what extent this professionalized labor revue continued to sing and dance for the workers in venues where they could no longer afford the price of a ticket.[178] Can we still speak of a propagation of working-class culture if this very culture is turned into a luxury item to be consumed by the upper middle class only? Does the show still reclaim leisure and entertainment *from* the leisured classes *for* the working classes, as Denning insists, when it increasingly caters to the tastes of the former? For me, these questions also point to the limits of a vernacular praxis of political theater.

At this juncture, I am tempted to modify Denning's interpretation by returning to a Frankfurt School–inspired analysis of cultural production that focuses on the ideological work accomplished by the commodity form. I want to suggest that *Pins and Needles* most likely owed its broad public success not so much to its labor politics but to what Fredric Jameson and Richard Dyer have referred to as the "utopian sensibility" of entertainment.[179] According to them, entertainment (the reification of the commodity for the purpose of consumption) is never simply a diversion and distraction from reality but a response to real needs created by society. As Jameson puts it, "Works of mass culture cannot be ideological without at the same time being implicitly or explicitly Utopian as well: they cannot manipulate unless they offer some genuine shred of content as a fantasy bribe to the public about to be manipulated."[180] In other words, in order to manage existing social or economic anxieties, mass cultural entertainment first needs to give them some kind of rudimentary expression. However, at the same time that it addresses concrete needs, it also delimits and defines these very needs. Thus it typically tends to ignore questions of race, gender, and class, focusing instead on economic or romantic wants—wants that it can easily fulfill in the construction of narrative and visual solutions. Most importantly, entertainment suggests what utopia should *feel* like rather than how it should be concretely organized.[181]

One of the most prominent solutions for providing the audience with the feeling of utopia is the creation of a spectacle of consumption. Drawing on the work of Hans Magnus Enzensberger, Dyer shows how entertainment in Western society manages with the help of representational (narrative) and non-representational means (costumes, movement, light, sets, etc.) to turn scarcity into abundance, exhaustion into energy, dreariness into intensity, manipulation into transparency, and fragmentation into community. At the same time, the excess and extravagance of the spectacle make clear that there can be no question that this promise could be fulfilled in reality. In the end, consumption as spectacle is a mere parody of utopia, as Enzensberger writes.[182] It chooses to present those categories of a "utopian sensibility" that capitalism itself promises to meet: abundance in consumerism, energy and intensity in individualism, and transparency in the freedom of speech. At worst, Dyer concludes, "entertainment provides alternatives *to* capitalism which will be provided *by* capitalism."[183]

Pins and Needles too addresses the crisis of capitalism in a dazzling spectacle of consumption. The glamorous costumes, jazzy tunes, elaborate dance routines, and even the wit and energy of the biting political satires and the thrilling romance of its moon songs momentarily suspend the stark reality outside the theater, suggesting that scarcity, want, and social inequality could disappear. At the same time that the show evokes and fulfills the wish for an alternative to the real, it also contains and controls it in the visceral affect of a general utopian sensibility. This stands out most clearly in the theme song "Sing Me a Song of Social Significance." While the chorus girls chide their suitors for being out of tune with their times, they nonetheless eagerly change from their work clothes into evening gowns ready to be whisked away into an elaborate Hollywood dance routine. The crisis of "wars, breadlines, strikes and last minute headlines,"[184] ever so carefully alluded to in the lyrics, is thus easily dissolved in the sparkle of the performance, evoking the energy and optimism, cheerfulness and faith that were conspicuously missing on the other side of Broadway. However, the actions of the performers not only belie their interest in the actual social crisis they are singing about; in the end, even the demand for social significance is undone, when it is contained in and supplanted by the ultimate demand for love: "It must be pact / With social fact / Or we won't love you."[185] Just as in the popular backstage comedy *Gold Diggers of 1933* (1933) social significance is suddenly reduced to a witty backdrop against which a conventional boy-meets-girl story is played out.

And yet, while glamour, romance, and wit supersede scarcity, want, and inequality, they do not entirely erase them. After all, as Jameson reminds us, mass culture never just functions as empty distraction from reality or mere false consciousness but actively manages and represses social and political anxieties and fantasies in the narrative construction of imaginary solutions and, most of all, the projection of an optical illusion of social harmony.[186] That this projection had less to do with reality than with wish fulfillment remained obvious to its most astute critics.

It is in this sense that we have to read Eleanor Roosevelt's sigh of relief that "*Pins and Needles* talks a good deal about 'social significance' but none of it is very deep."[187] It was, as director Charles Friedman put it, "the voice of the American people laughing themselves out of their misery."[188] From this perspective too, *Pins and Needles* was indeed a deeply political show, however, not in any interventionist sense. On the contrary, by offering the spectacle of consumption as a remedy to the crisis of capitalism, it effectively deflected from the necessities of class struggle and the responsibilities of organized labor, affirming instead a fundamental belief in capitalism itself. As McCarthy dryly suggested, *Pins and Needles* is in the end but "the group expression of a large, well-run, relatively contented labor union, whose union contracts are signed without much trouble and whose demands do not exceed decent minimum wages, decent maximum hours, the closed shop, and the right to picket."[189]

Pins and Needles shows the extent to which our assessment of political efficacy is also contingent on our choice of methodology. By examining the moments of popular agency contained in this vernacular leftist revue as well as the politics of its form, we arrive at not only a very complex but also ambivalent picture of its political value. To be sure, it did suggest proletarian agency within consumer culture. But it also did sell out to the culture industry, affirming the dominant ideology. Does this constitute a contradiction in terms? Will we have to come down on one side or the other of this theoretical divide?

Not necessarily. For the dilemma of form and public is ultimately tied to the question of what kind of social change cultural praxis considers viable and seeks to accomplish. A Frankfurt School–inspired analysis (like that of Jameson and Dyer) would ultimately debunk a show like *Pins and Needles* for its complicity with a capitalist culture industry, precisely because of this methodology's urgent interest in forms of radical cultural critique that can resist and undermine the ideology of the culture industry. We here detect the influence of Theodor W. Adorno and Max Horkheimer, whose goal it was to reveal the intrinsic commodity character of modern mass culture and to show to what extent precisely this commodity character perpetually cheats its consumers out of that which it perpetually promises.[190] To lay bare this dialectic of utopia and ideology is also at the heart of a critique like Jameson's and Dyer's. Their theoretical approach allows us to expose the ultimate failure of radicalism in the reification of a show like *Pins and Needles*, which is not just "*also* a commodity but commodity through and through."[191] As Adorno and Horkheimer assert, the main problem with the commodity is that it produces conformity rather than resistance, impeding the development of independent and autonomous individuals who consciously judge and decide for themselves. In its sweeping critique of hegemonic commodity structures that produce such conformity, this approach, however, also tends to overlook the various ways in which individuals and collectives nonetheless decode and appropriate the commodity for their own purposes.[192]

The strength of Denning's approach lies in creating an understanding of these processes of decoding. In the spirit of Stuart Hall, he enables us to locate popular agency even in a polished commodity like *Pins and Needles*. As seen, Denning measures political value not by the deliberate refusal of the commodity structure but by the articulation and deployment of popular agency in the processes of cultural production and reception, which can enable negotiation with and transformation of the dominant system. This approach is informed by the goal to examine to what extent cultural practices not only constrain and subjugate people but also offer them resources and possibilities for resisting and undermining those constraints—a goal that joined the diverse interests in working-class and popular culture of scholars such as Richard Hoggart, Raymond Williams, Paul Willis, Dick Hebdige, and Stuart Hall at the Centre for Contemporary Cultural Studies in Birmingham and later fueled the work of numerous American scholars as well (John Fiske, Lawrence Grossberg, Janice Radway, etc.). Shifting the emphasis from the critique of the commodity to the analysis of the various intricate ways in which cultural practices interact with and within relations of power, Denning allows us to read and appreciate (rather than simply dismiss) a non-modernist/vernacular praxis of political theater in the first place. Yet, arguably, his keen interest in forms of agency that can emerge from the constant negotiations with the culture industry also effaces the larger question: to what extent can such agency indeed engender a radical, systemic transformation of society?

This, however, is really the most important question at stake in a discussion of political theater. What kind of political agenda motivates the choice of form and public in leftist productions? In what kind of social change are they interested, and what are their visions of a new and better society?

I, here, want to return briefly to my analysis of the American translation of Brecht's epic theater for the New Deal stage, with which I opened this study. This translation was indispensable to address the particular cultural and social contingencies of the American theater and its public at the time. In this context, it was not incidental that in the final scene of *Mother*, Theatre Union insisted that the workers remain unarmed, unlike in the original Berlin production of 1932. Brecht's non-Aristotelian aesthetics of alienation, developed in the Weimar Republic, were meant as a militant critique of capitalism itself and aimed at nothing less than the proletarian revolution. For reasons that I have shown to be embedded in American cultural and political history as well as in the confluence of various cultural and political vectors that led to the emergence of the Popular Front, this agenda could no longer be sustained in the New Deal of 1935.

Pins and Needles addressed this particular cultural moment much more carefully than Brecht. In the grand finale "We've Only Just Begun," the needle workers modestly but firmly assert, "In the future to be built we intend to have a voice!"[193]—not exactly a call for revolution but nonetheless a passionate affirmation that labor is a force to be reckoned with. However, it is also quite telling that by 1939, when the U.S. economy had reconstituted itself, the more militant first act finale "Men Awake" was replaced by the joyous celebration "Back to Work": "Ain't had such good news since Lord knows when / For the strike is over boys / Back to work again!"[194] In the end, *Pins and Needles* cheerfully affirmed the possibilities of capitalism even while insisting that it required the collective power of labor culture to secure its democratic foundations. Its grand finale, "There are millions of us / Yes we'll have something to say," was very much in line with the agendas conveyed by other New Deal finales. Along with Odets's call for "Strike," Blitzstein's assertion that "The cradle will rock!" and the Living Newspaper's appeal for government intervention, "Can you hear us, Washington?" it was an ardent reminder that by affirming the nation's democratic legacy, capitalism could be made "moral."

Chapter Six

Toward Postmodernism: The Political Theater of the 1960s

The Return of Modernism

As established structures of hegemony began to crumble in the 1960s under the pressure of student protests, anti-war and Civil Rights movements at home, and liberation movements abroad, profound changes took place in the cultural realm as well. On the American stage, it was the year 1959 that signaled what critics have called the disruption of "the bourgeois dream of unproblematic production" (both with regard to industrial and cultural production).[1] That year saw the premiere of Edward Albee's *Zoo Story*, the Living Theater's staging of Jack Gelber's *The Connection*, Allan Kaprow's yet unclassifiable *18 Happenings in 6 Parts*, and the belated break-through of black theater with Lorraine Hansberry's *A Raisin in the Sun*—all of which shook Broadway out of the complacency of a "well-made" bourgeois realism that had marked its repertoire throughout the 1940s and 1950s. While critics were still unsure what to make of these various attacks on white middle-class drama, they agreed that this new theater was certainly an "uncomfortable" and "confrontational" one. According to observers such as Howard Stein, "The middle classes were attacked in ways that were deliberately disturbing and provocative, whether through bizarre forms (Kopit), unseemly characters (Gelber), or vicious relationships (Albee)."[2] Aside from offending bourgeois morality and confronting WASP politics, this new theater also sought to upset the aesthetic sensibilities of its audiences, "stretching our minds until it strains our imagination, stimulating our senses to the threshold of pain," as another reviewer put it.[3] Whether it was the intense hyper-realism of Gelber, Kenneth Brown, and LeRoi Jones, the unsettling surrealism in the work of Kaprow and John Cage, or the turn to the ritualistic in the Living Theater, the common goal was the decisive break with the hegemony of Broadway's unproblematic realism, the radical disruption of established traditions, and the stimulation of the audience's senses and perception—an endeavor reminiscent of the project of the historical avant-garde half a century earlier.

Part of this new avant-garde departure was the revival of a vibrant political theater movement after two decades of effective repression under the onset of the cold war and McCarthyism. The new political theater, which just like the iconoclasts on Off and Off-Off Broadway also took a vivid interest in formal experimentation, was, however, less interested in *épater les bourgeois* than in developing theater into a concrete means for social action and political intervention on behalf of the marginalized and oppressed. Its commitment to social change took various forms: on the one hand, it continued the tradition of social realism (which had run from Ibsen via Gorky to Odets and Arthur Miller)—and here it was particularly an emergent black theater that appropriated this dominant paradigm as a form of protest and intervention (Hansberry, James Baldwin, Alice Childress). On the other hand, the political theater of the 1960s also rediscovered the modernist experiments of the 1920s and 1930s, which they sought to fuse with contemporary popular and mass culture. In this concluding chapter, I want to look at this particular strand of political theater and investigate to what extent it connects the fervent years of New Deal theater with contemporary, postmodern political theater.

The renaissance of a distinctly modernist praxis of political theater is particularly evident in the work of street theater troupes such as the San Francisco Mime Troupe, the Bread and Puppet Theater, and El Teatro Campesino—all of which defined themselves in classic modernist fashion as fundamentally anti-bourgeois, anti-capitalist, and anti-commercial leftist theaters. Their primary goal was to educate their audiences about existent economic, political, and social issues and to incite them to political activism. With low-budget productions and performances in public spaces (streets, parks, churches, meeting halls, farms), these theater groups, moreover, attempted to remain outside commercial venues and to retain a high degree of autonomy from the culture industry. "We are not 'professional' in that we do not wish to end up on Broadway or commercial TV or on film," Ron Davis of the Mime Troupe insisted.[4] All three groups furthermore asserted the Brechtian credo that political commitment could ensue only from the audience's constant awareness of the very theatricality of the spectacle on stage. With non-illusionist productions (which heavily drew on techniques of alienation), they attempted to make the spectators aware of the presence of the actors (not just their characters) as well as of the world around them so that a community of interest could be formed between actors and spectators—a community that could serve as a model for future political action.[5]

What made this sudden return of modernism in political theater possible? How could a praxis that proved to be incommensurable with the cultural politics of American leftist theaters in the 1930s suddenly become a source of inspiration to many committed theater artists? I suggest that, among other things, the return of modernism in political theater was enabled by the belated advent of something akin to Bürger's historical avant-garde on the American stage. As Arnold Aronson suggests, the art that began to emerge in the 1950s was something very different from the Little Theater movement of the 1910/1920s and the leftist theaters of 1930s. "There was a bold spirit of experimentation— a rebellion against the mainstream commercial system and the utter rejection of the *status quo*."[6] Defining itself in vehement opposition to Western dramatic conventions and the bourgeois cultural apparatus behind them, this new American theater avant-garde "radically altered both the aesthetic and organizational basis upon which performance was created," Aronson maintains.[7] I, furthermore, suggest that thanks to this fundamental adversarial position to established cultural traditions and venues, the categories of rupture and renewal, which had been so crucial to the historical avant-garde forty years earlier, now became available for artistic production and broad counter-cultural social formations in the United States as well.[8]

In their endeavor to break with the hegemony of realism and to disturb Broadway's "bourgeois dream of unproblematic production," the American avant-garde of the 1960s turned to their modernist predecessors: they discovered the ritual force of Artaud's theater of cruelty (soon leading them to Grotowski's poor theater), and they began to study Brecht's theories of epic theater. By 1959, the attitude of the left to Brecht had changed significantly—thanks to the dissemination of his theories and plays by leading artists and intellectuals in the United States and thanks to the international success of his work.[9] Moreover, a number of artists had gained first-hand experience of epic acting and staging in Erwin Piscator's Dramatic Workshop at the New School for Social Research in New York; among them was Judith Malina, co-founder of the Living Theater. In short, epic theater was no longer considered an alien irritant but a source of inspiration and potential renewal. Along with Artaud, Brecht now became the leading theorist for American avant-garde theater.

However, at the same time that the artists of the 1960s rediscovered the modernist spirit of iconoclasm and experimentation as a mode of resistance and renewal, this very modernism was being institutionalized in museums and university curricula across the nation. By the 1960s, abstract expressionism—even while still paving the way for Fluxus, pop art, and many other subsequent movements—had essentially been assimilated by the cultural mainstream. The shock of the modernist New had been absorbed and mediated. The once so notorious Armory Show of 1913 could now be restaged with great success in New York City as well as in Utica, New York, and Amherst, Massachusetts.[10] Numerous exhibits of expressionism, surrealism, and Dadaist art in leading museums and galleries of the country followed. At the same time, campus theaters nationwide (alongside Off-Off Broadway theaters) began to revive Brecht and other modernist playwrights.

The institutionalization of high modernism had two consequences. On the one hand, the public became more educated in and ideally also more receptive to its aesthetics than in the 1930s. On the other hand, it also meant that modernist aesthetics were now available not only as a form of radical critique and potential renewal but also as a new form of middlebrow culture. Furthermore, during the Kennedy years high modernism also became part of the official state culture designed for continuing the cold war on cultural terms alongside military ones. As Andreas Huyssen explains, it was only now that modernism itself had entered the mainstream via the culture industry that a "European-style avantgardist revolt against tradition made eminent sense."[11] Yet, as Sally Banes points out, the institutionalization and commodification of modernism also made the position of the avant-garde of the 1960s an inherently contradictory one: while vehemently protesting against the establishment, it was already part of it, "simultaneously rejecting *and* reproducing middle class culture."[12]

These tensions and contradictions were also evident in the political theater of the period. While certainly inspired by European modernist theater, it did not simply revive the praxis of its predecessors but transformed it by bringing it into a productive alliance with vernacular modes of cultural critique. Bread and Puppet, for example, combined puppetry with medieval morality plays seeking to create "a language, a mythology that is to everybody's understanding."[13] El Teatro Campesino and the San Francisco Mime Troupe took up the broad gestures, crude stereotypes, farcical humor, and populist sentiments of what Peter Brook calls the "rough theater" (as found in vaudeville, *commedia dell'arte*, circus, and melodrama).[14] The San Francisco Mime Troupe, again, sought to popularize the very notion of an avant-garde by presenting itself as a powerful combination of "theater, revolution, and grooving in the parks."[15] While perhaps reminiscent of the praxis of the Living Newspaper and other more experimental New Deal productions, the combination of modernist and vernacular approaches in the work of these three groups was nevertheless very different from that of

its 1930s predecessors. The Living Newspaper used epic techniques of
alienation and documentation to *enhance* its fundamental vernacular
pedagogy of providing the common person, the American consumer,
with a sentimental education on contemporary political issues. Bread
and Puppet, Teatro Campesino, and the Mime Troupe, however,
attempted nothing less than the *fusion* of what were once considered
antithetical approaches to the dilemma of form and public in political
theater, namely, of mass culture and modernism. Moreover, in contrast
to their New Deal ancestors, these 1960s theater groups were not
interested in integrating leftist and mainstream culture for the sake of
governmental reform politics, but, on the contrary, they were interested in producing counter-cultures that could serve as alternatives
and correctives to the status quo.

Of course, the 1960s did not present the first challenge to what
Huyssen has called the "great divide" between high art and mass culture. As seen vernacular theater has always freely borrowed from mass
culture and high culture alike. Modernist political theater, on the other
hand, has, to a degree, attempted to challenge this divide by incorporating elements from popular entertainment into its iconoclastic aesthetics. Piscator, for example, used a boxing match in his *Red Revue*
(1924) to defamiliarize and satirize the election campaign of that year.
Brecht refunctioned the popular genre of the operetta into an effective
critique of the bourgeois cultural apparatus with his *Threepenny
Opera* (1928). In his staging of Nikolay Ostrovsky's *Wise Man* (1923),
Eisenstein used film clips as popular attractions that would simultaneously excite a broad audience as well as defamiliarize the very
experience of stage drama. Ruses like these not only broke with the
conventions of the bourgeois stage but also served to undermine the
strategy of exclusion by which high modernism constituted itself vis-à-vis
an ever-expanding mass culture. In the 1960s, however, this engagement with mass culture took on a whole different dimension. The goal
was to merge the vanguard in the arts with the vernacular syntax and
lexicon of American mass culture—that is, to collapse the divide
completely. In the political theater, this endeavor meant not only the
revival but also the critical engagement with the two older traditions.
We shall see how in the process our previous notions of both the
vernacular and the modernist were redefined.

In what follows, I shall examine the transformations that took
place on the political stage with the examples of the Bread and Puppet
Theater and El Teatro Campesino. (I will forego a discussion of the
Mime Troupe since Teatro Campesino, at least in its early work, is a
direct heir to its aesthetics). Both Bread and Puppet and Teatro Campesino

purposely revive a modernist concept of political theater, particularly in their insistence on alienation and abstraction as the main principle of breaking with the hegemony of realism on the bourgeois stage while at the same time attempting to fuse their political and aesthetic agendas with the cultural experience of their audiences (a heterogeneous urban public, on the one hand, and an ethnic farm workers audience, on the other). Their reworkings of modernist and vernacular traditions of political theater are, however, very different from each other.

"Une sensibilité du cœur": The Sentimental Modernism of Bread and Puppet

Among the above-mentioned street theaters of the 1960s, Peter Schumann's Bread and Puppet Theater is perhaps most indebted to his modernist predecessors. When Schumann moved from Germany to New York in the early 1960s, he brought with him a distinctly avant-gardist and European notion of space, movement, and form. His concept of political theater had been decisively shaped by his training as a sculptor, his experience in abstract dance, his interest in Oskar Schlemmer's theory of the body as art figure, and Kurt Schwitter's Dadaist Merz collages—all of which inform his typical preference of the image over narrative. Schumann explains his predominant work method, "We are starting from forms—pure musical movement and ideas—and then we proceed slowly to something that, we feel, becomes understandable, becomes communicable."[16] Because of its non-literary, abstract, image-based approach, its prevalent lack of dialogue and action, critics have even called his work "anti-theater."[17] Deliberately negating conventional forms of theater, particularly the commercialism of Broadway, Bread and Puppet has, however, created a new form of theater that is at once decidedly modernist and vernacular.

"Alienation is automatic with puppets," Schumann remarks when asked about Brecht's influence on his work.[18] Indeed, in the streets the eight- to fourteen-foot tall puppets and solemn masks of Bread and Puppet appear to be "louder than traffic," while the carefully choreographed, slow movements of the performers interrupt and halt the quotidian flow of urban life.[19] "It stops people in their tracks—to see those large puppets, to see something theatrical outside of a theatre. They can't take the attitude that they've paid money to go into a theatre to see something. Suddenly there is this thing in front of them,

confronting them," Schumann asserts.[20] In the confrontation with the
unexpected and the extraordinary, bystanders are turned—at times
involuntarily so—into spectators, into an audience of the most diverse
constituency.

Consider, for instance, Bread and Puppet's Second Fifth Avenue
Parade, which was part of an anti-war march in March 1966. On that
day, a casual onlooker on Fifth Avenue in New York would behold in
the midst of thousands of marchers a few black-clad men with skull
masks dragging along a group of performers draped in white and
wearing the large pale masks of a Vietnamese woman's face. Bound,
blindfolded, and chained together by a single rope, the women would
trudge along until suddenly attacked by a large black papier-mâché
airplane with shark teeth carried by a third group of performers in
black. The women would sway back and forth in unison, bend over
and fall, only to be yanked up again by the men in skull masks and
dragged on. This sequence would be repeated in slow motion over and
over again, all the while accompanied by a cacophony of noise produced by makeshift instruments, such as gasoline cans filled with nuts
and bolts. Throughout the sequence another group of tall "Vietnamese"
women with masks, persistently chanting a high tone, would follow the
group like a Greek chorus.[21] This choreography of mask, mime, and
sound must have struck any chance observer as strange and unusual.
With the help of compelling abstract imagery and silent gestures,
Schumann effectively defamiliarizes and distances not only the familiar narrative of war espoused by the media but also the very experience of an anti-war protest movement (usually that of marchers
holding placards and shouting slogans). What the spectator encoun-
ters in the Fifth Avenue parade is surprising, shocking, new, and as
such worthy of her attention.

"The mask has always had a denaturalizing effect, but it made whatever it represented unrecognizable in order that it might be known,"
Ernst Bloch writes.[22] Indeed, looking more closely, the spectator would
detect in the traveling tableau of masks and mime a rudimentary but
nonetheless emotionally and morally compelling interpretation of the
Vietnam War. Similar to the Brechtian *Gestus*, Schumann distills the
substance of political conflict into a few distinct and compelling gestures
and images, creating what Roland Barthes refers to as a series of "pregnant moments" or, more specifically, "a gesture or a set of gestures
[. . .] in which a whole social situation can be read."[23] In the Fifth
Avenue Parade these gestures consist of a set of stark dichotomies: white
versus black, woman versus man, East versus West, suffering versus
aggression, humanity versus technology—all of which taken together

effectively denounce the American war effort not only as imperialistic but also as inherently immoral. In marked contrast to Brecht, however, who uses the *Gestus* as a way of distilling the essence of social and economic relations between people, Schumann uses it for the illumination of an archetypal moral situation in which any spectator can immediately recognize the Manichean forces of good and evil and identify accordingly. The underlying moralizing gest is most apparent in the contrast between male/Western aggression and female/ Eastern passivity. In other performances, it is vividly expressed in the frequent contrasting of the puppet of Uncle Fatso (a tall, Georg Grosz–inspired rendition of Uncle Sam, complete with top hat and cigar) with the puppet of Jesus Christ or that of the Gray Mother/Gray Lady.

Schumann's visual language operates on two levels: alienation and empathy. Without doubt, the gigantic puppets and intricately sculpted masks present a compelling *Verfremdungseffekt*, commanding onlookers' attention by defamiliarizing political conflict and creating a critical distance to the representation itself. Watching the puppet and the puppeteer entails a double vision that forestalls immediate identification with the story and absorption in the spectacle and requires critical reflection. At the same time, however, the imagery and symbolism of a Bread and Puppet performance is intensely familiar to anyone watching, including a five-year-old child, which is precisely the effect Schumann is striving for. Its representations of mothers with babies, Jesus figure, and Mother Earth alongside those of airplanes with shark teeth, men with skull masks, and the grotesque figure of Uncle Fatso draw on deeply ingrained archetypes of good and evil, victimhood and aggression. They represent archetypal moral oppositions such as that of male perpetrator versus female victim and of technocratic society versus rural community—oppositions that elicit spontaneous (and therefore unreflected) archaic emotional responses in the audience: empathy for the victims, antagonism toward the aggressor, the desire to protect the defenseless females and to stop the intruding males, to destroy the machine and restore the garden.

Significantly, these archetypal images are not so much referents to a concrete socio-political reality (as they would be in classic agitprop) as of general ethical concepts, which steer the reception process of the audience by referring it back to "universal" moral values. The primary opposition is always between innocence and evil; it is an opposition inscribed into our collective imagination by endless replications from fairy tales to biblical stories to Hollywood. Our initial alienation (triggered by the mask), notwithstanding, Schumann's allegories of modern warfare and oppression tend to facilitate our empathy, regardless of our political position, for they activate a common language of myth and archetype and the basic emotions attached to them. Precisely, this is Schumann's goal: to elicit the "direct emotional response to what is happening."[24] He believes that political commitment can ensue only from "une 'sensibilité à' qui vient du cœur tout entier et complètement engagé";[25] or, in other words, from a sensibility of the heart, which fueled by moral conviction and intense emotional concern, can trigger if not immediate political action then at least ethical responsibility. This sensibility of the heart constitutes the fundamental vernacular element in Schumann's political theater.

It is not only in its emphasis on the moral affect of political conflict that the approach of Bread and Puppet differs from a Brechtian understanding of political theater. In contrast to Brecht's clearly defined social *Gestus*, the rich imagery of Bread and Puppet defies a clear political interpretation. Its masks, costumes, sounds, and choreography suggest a surplus of meaning beyond the concrete political comment at hand that exceeds both the production and interpretation process. This excess of meaning stems, above all, from Schumann's idiosyncratic collage style. In the manner of Schwitters, he assembles the most diverse material and miscellaneous objects. "Any garbage can, any music, anything we can find, any smallness and bigness" are juxtaposed in order to "get a communion out of it, not by creating atmospheres and moods and dialogues and tales, but by leaving these things as pure as they can be."[26] Collage is a classic modernist technique that is used by Dada and surrealism to estrange the familiar, to subvert established mimetic modes, and to provoke new modes of perception. It has also been widely used in political theater. But rather than synchronizing his materials into a Piscatorian *Gesamtkunstwerk* or structuring it in the manner of an Eisensteinian montage of attractions, Schumann deliberately forgoes any kind of unity or pathos. Instead, he prefers the incongruous collage of signifiers (of figure, gesture, sound, object) that stresses the very dissonance of materials, their "tense confluence."[27]

The result is, on the one hand, very Brechtian. Brecht too insisted on the strict separation of theatrical elements so that each element could be evaluated by the spectator independent of its teleological function within the overall narrative. Like him, Schumann wants to sharpen the critical awareness of his spectators by impacting them "through eyes & ears, on emotion" in order to "agitate rather than lull the creative drive in the audience."[28] But in addition, it is, as John Bell rightly points out, "the frisson of ambiguity, the bit of unclarity about what exactly an object represents that allows the political theater of Bread and Puppet its possibilities of subtlety, of inexactness, of open-ended interpretation."[29] It is precisely with regard to such ambiguity and open-endedness of meaning that Bread and Puppet differs most significantly from classic political theater—both its modernist and vernacular predecessors. It rejects the positivism inherent in Brecht's theater for it does not provide the spectator with "a workable picture of the world."[30] At the same time, it also eschews the short-lived cathartic empathy of a sentimental approach to theater, which rarely extends beyond the perimeters of the performance. The images of Bread and Puppet, by contrast, "haunt one for weeks afterward," as one reviewer asserts.[31]

Audiences have responded to Schumann's stylized moral accusations with a mixture of empathy and unease. After watching *Fire* (1966), a short indoor mime with puppets that portrays everyday life in a Vietnamese village, its destruction by an air raid, and the slow death of a Buddhist nun immolating herself in protest against the war, a reviewer wrote, "Suddenly we 'feel' the 'reality' of the war, more than any ideological speeches, well-meaning films or pictures of napalmed children could convey."[32] Another critic similarly remarked, "All the theatre is now in darkness. The play is over and everyone knows it, yet not one applauds or moves. The silence is ours as well as theirs. We are unwilling to part with it. Finally the houselights are turned on. Some few clap their hands. Others move shufflingly. We make our way to the door, walking like convalescents."[33] Without doubt, the accusatory silent images and slow mimes of Bread and Puppet are emotionally stirring and morally provocative. Images such as that of a white-robed figure with the mask of an aged Vietnamese woman's face slowly enveloping herself in red paper tape until it covers her mouth and eyes, until she can no longer move and topples over (*Fire*) are at once easily understandable and deeply perturbing to anyone, regardless of cultural background and education. For Schumann, they display "life in its clearest terms."[34] The baker and puppeteer then seems to have found an effective model of political theater for American audiences: at once stirring up empathy and provoking critical reflection.

However, in its emphasis on maximum moral decipherability, Bread and Puppet at times also runs the risk of reductiveness and naïve simplification. In distilling the elemental, its tableaux often bypass the historical. Anti-war performances like *King Story* (1964), *A Man Says Goodbye to His Mother* (1965), *Fire* (1966), *Wounds of Vietnam* (1967), and *Johnny Comes Marching Home* (1968) largely efface the concrete political and economic determinants of the Vietnam War, instead focusing on human suffering. In this manner, they also run the risk of transforming war from a function of actual geopolitical interests into a basic allegory of Western man's growing estrangement from nature and of the alienation of the self in a modern technocratic society. At its best, this ahistorical methodology can raise relevant ethical questions, but it can also end up naturalizing that which ought to be shown as historical and changeable.

Yet, it is particularly the impression of being "haunted" by its images that points us to a new understanding of the political in the work of Bread and Puppet. In the density of his collages, Schumann actively negates the world as we know it. The purposeful contradictions of his fables (e.g., the depiction of fire as both death and transfiguration in *Fire*, the image of motherhood as the source of both life and death in *A Man Says Goodbye to His Mother*) and the predominant silence of his mimes (narration is used occasionally in indoor performances) evince a profound skepticism toward language, the logic of causality, rationality, even toward mimesis itself, that we do not encounter in classic modernist or vernacular political theater. Barthes once wrote with regard to Bunraku puppetry that it "does not represent but signify."[35] The same can be said for Schumann's use of puppetry, particularly since he acknowledges the influence of Bunraku on his work; that is, Bread and Puppet does not aim to reproduce mimetically the world for the spectator but to create a series of undetermined significations. In combining analytical precision with deliberate semantic ambiguity and auratic allusion, so critic Gerd Burger suggests, Schumann aims to strike at our unconscious, to lay bare an archaic mythical counter-world, remnants of which still reside in our collective unconscious. In returning us to the ritual and shamanic origins of theater, Bread and Puppet seeks to recover these very traces of the auratic and the mythical that have been erased by technical progress and the cold logic of rationality.[36]

While the undecidability of Schumann's significations thus heightens our awareness of absence, it also has the potential to open up a space for the very forms of thought and actions that the dominant society represses. In this space, "an image of the heretofore unthought, unseen, begins to appear," Beth Cleary writes.[37] Cleary, in fact, understands the political project of Bread and Puppet as one akin to the theories of the Frankfurt School. Both insist on negation and contradiction as basic means of resisting the culture industry's resolution of all representation into identity and conformity; both represent the world "as defiantly un-reconciled, and demonstrate through their respective media the urgency of dwelling in and acting from places of unreconcilability."[38]

According to Cleary, the undetermined significations of Bread and Puppet thus beckon us towards what Bloch has described as "the contents of a future which had not yet appeared in its time."[39] It is here that Cleary (from a decidedly Blochian point of view) locates the political value in the work of Bread and Puppet. Schumann's dramaturgy thus urges us to reconsider our previous concept of the political in political theater. Seen from the angle introduced by Cleary and Burger, the collagistic dramaturgy of Bread and Puppet is then (despite or maybe precisely because of its ahistoricity) not only a source of ritual renewal but, more importantly, a training ground for our utopian imagination.

Schumann transforms our previous concept of political theater in yet another regard. His visions of suffering and compassion are never simply expressions of political commitment. On the contrary, he remains skeptical of the instrumentalization of his theater for concrete political purposes. "We are not very interested in ideology," Schumann asserts.[40] For him, theater needs to fulfill a dual function. On the one hand, it is a practical tool that allows him to communicate his views about relevant political issues, "to scream and kick and participate in our century's struggle for liberation in whatever haphazard way we can."[41] On the other hand, he insists that "theater must do more than protest."[42] It has to be a form of religion. This is one of the primary reasons for his use of puppets. While they are capable of stopping the traffic in the street, they cannot be instrumentalized. In the tradition of Heinrich von Kleist and Edward Gordon Craig, Schumann understands them as "God's music, eternal hands, faces from inside."[43] Critics, such as Gerd Burger, perceive this simultaneous insistence on a utilitarian *and* transcendent function as a fundamental contradiction in Schumann's concept of political theater. I want to suggest, however, that the duality of political and religious commitment might be Bread and Puppet's most productive incongruity and indeterminacy. Political theater is no longer solely defined in terms of commitment to the concrete political comment and intervention at hand but also in terms of what possibilities it offers for the retrieval of a more ancient function of theater: the ritual that is both cleansing and community building.

As in many other alternative theaters of the 1960s, the community is at the heart of Schumann's political vision—and, more specifically, the counter-community—that is, one that opposes dominant modes of production and consumption.[44] Bread and Puppet embodies it in its lifestyle as a self-supporting commune as well as in its work ethics. Deliberately "poor" in its aesthetics, materials, and finances, the theater relies extensively on working closely with local communities. On

a more symbolic level, Schumann emphasizes the communal spirit
when he distributes homemade bread during Bread and Puppet performances. "Something is shared, and the audience is jarred out of
passivity by the act of eating together," one participant writes.[45] The
Eucharistic overtone of the ritual is intended, pointing us to the cen-
trality of regeneration and redemption in the theater praxis of Bread
and Puppet.[46] Above all, the bread is supposed to nourish the communal spirit so that it can grow into collective action. At the same time,
however, Schumann takes great care to stress that his "theater of the
stomach" has little to do with the quick culinary satisfaction offered
by mainstream entertainment, which he calls the "theater of the
skin"[47]—on the contrary, like bread it is to be a deeply felt necessity.
In short, Schumann approaches his audience from two ends. Where
puppets are meant to elicit the critical engagement of the spectator,
challenging their utopian imagination, bread signifies the ritual basis
of his project. In this manner, he also emphasizes that the quest for
utopia is an inherently communal endeavor.

Last but not least, Schumann originally developed his collagistic
iconography and moral allegories particularly for a broad and heterogeneous urban audience (to be supplemented later on by the rural
communities of New England) and in this regard seems to be fairly
mainstream in his choice of public. His puppet performances, however, are far from endorsing a mainstream politics. On the contrary,
regardless of whether they are performed in the streets of New York or
on the farms of Vermont, they seek to inspire a counter-cultural spirit
that can nourish alternative social and political visions. In this spirit,
the puppets and masks of Bread and Puppet, which formed an integral
part of the iconography of 1960s anti-war protest, have continued
to haunt their spectators well beyond the epoch, as, for example, in the
anti-imperialist critiques *The Triumph of Capitalism* (1991) and *Mr.
Budhoo's Letter of Resignation from the IMF* (1995).[48]

In conclusion, Bread and Puppet has significantly changed American
political theater. With regard to its commitment to iconoclastic experimentation as well as social change, it has participated in and merged
both the aesthetic and the political avant-garde of the 1960s. Its aesthetics evince traces of its modernist heritage and particularly of the
tradition of modernist political theater. We detect the influence of
Schlemmer and Schwitters alongside that of Brecht and Piscator. Most
importantly, however, Schumann significantly vernacularizes the
latter's concept of political theater for contemporary audiences by
infusing it with the archetypal and the religious. Although Bread and
Puppet has perhaps not completely collapsed the great divide between

modernism and mass culture yet, it has certainly attempted to bridge it—with varying degrees of success. This is evident in the ways that it seeks to forge a productive alliance between its modernist emphasis on alienation, abstraction, and stylization and the vernacular demands for identification, empathy, and visceral gratification. Yet, while it aims for broad accessibility and sentimental affect in its representations of the political, it also resists complete readability and easy consumption (the perpetual risk of a completely vernacular praxis) by emphasizing the semantic excess and heterogeneity of its images. When Schumann "pits papermache [*sic*] against government, [. . .] wooden swords against status-quo-thinking machines,"[49] the moral dimension of dramatic conflict can be grasped immediately by anyone. But beyond that, Bread and Puppet neither provides simple answers nor poses succinct questions. Schumann understands the political function of his theater as "opening something up"—this critical and creative aperture, however, has to precede consciousness and stem directly from the heart; it has to be "une sensibilité du cœur."[50] His concept of political theater is then at once more modernist (in a Blochian and Adornian sense) and more vernacular (in a sentimental sense) than that of his modernist predecessors of the 1930s.

Cantinflas and Brecht: The Modernist Vernacular of El Teatro Campesino

"We don't think in terms of art, but of our political purpose in putting across certain points," Luis Valdez, founder of El Teatro Campesino, asserts.[51] Indeed, El Teatro Campesino was born out of the necessity of mobilizing Chicano and Filipino farm workers for the Delano Grape Strike of 1965. The theater was to serve as an entertaining and didactic means of strengthening the morale of the strikers, of urging field workers to join the strike, and of soliciting solidarity with the strikers among urban audiences. These political objectives along with practical considerations determined the aesthetics of its early performances. Working with amateur actors and seeking to maintain a high degree of mobility (of being able to pack the entire theater in the trunk of a car), Valdez developed short, improvisational agitprop skits. He referred to them by the Spanish term *actos*—primarily to emphasize the particular politico-cultural context from which they derived but also because "skit" seemed to him "too light a word for the work we are trying to do."[52] The *actos* were designed to fulfill the complex task of illuminating social problems, showing solutions, inspiring the audience to social action, and in general expressing what people were feeling. Its political program as well as its "rough" aesthetics (performing without script, scenery, and curtain, with only minimal costumes and props) firmly situate Teatro Campesino in the tradition of American and European amateur agitprop theaters as well as the popular performance tradition of Mexican working-class culture.

Aside from the concrete demands of providing workers with an entertaining political education and of maintaining a highly mobile troupe, Valdez—who studied drama in college and worked with the San Francisco Mime Troupe before joining the strikers in Delano—brings a distinctly modernist and, more specifically, Brechtian understanding of political theater to his work. "Chicano theater must be revolutionary in technique as well as content," he insists.[53] For him, this means the radical break with the "*gabacho* culture" of the commercial American stage, with what he calls the worship of an "antiseptic, antibiotic (anti-life)" realism.[54] Not surprisingly, he stresses the affinity of his "unbourgeois" theater with that of Brecht: "In a Mexican way we have discovered what Brecht is all about."[55] With its high degree of theatricality, its systematic use of *Gestus* and *Verfremdung* (in the form of apostrophe, placards, masks, and songs), his theater strikes one indeed as inherently Brechtian. Jorge Huerta even calls Valdez's *actos* the Chicano equivalent to Brecht's *Lehrstücke* (learning plays).[56]

But Valdez does not simply revive a Brechtian praxis of political theater. Remarkable in his aesthetics is the abundance of elements of lowbrow, popular culture. As mentioned earlier, such elements were, of course, already present in the rough street theater of agitprop, in the political revues of Piscator and Eisenstein, and to an extent even in the epic theater of Brecht. But in the early work of Teatro Campesino slapstick, clowning, and the burlesque carry almost the entire show, at first glance suggesting a greater affinity with a Bakhtinian carnival than a Brechtian *Lehrstück*.

This is most evident in two early examples: *Los Dos Caras del Patroncito* (1965) and *La Quinta Temporada* (1966). *Los Dos Caras*, one of the very first *actos*, was designed to dismantle the grower's self-assured display of power, to reveal such standard accoutrements as a big truck, shot gun, sun shades, and armed guard—which would often intimidate the farm workers to the point of preempting their capacity for critique or resistance—as performative symbols of power rather than as power itself. In this burlesque *acto*, the grower El Patroncito in a spur of romanticizing the campesino's life as one free from the growing financial demands exerted upon him by a spoiled wife and steep property taxes suggests trading places with the worker. He picks up the campesino's pruning shears and dons his hat and cardboard sign (which ironically reads "Esquirol," scab, in reference to the farm hands trucked in from Mexico to replace the striking workers). In return, he hands him his "Patroncito" sign, his whip, cigar, and coat. When he even takes off the pig mask he has been wearing, the farm worker exclaims in surprise, "Patron, you look like me!"[57] At this moment, the dismantling of the insignia of power and with it their defamiliarization is complete: underneath it all, the farm worker is now able to see a person just like himself (this effect of sameness was vividly reinforced when Luis Valdez and his brother Danny played the parts). But the campesino also quickly realizes that power consists above all in the performance of power. Along with the cigar, whip, and pig mask, he now also adopts the voice and demeanor of someone in power, undeterred by the protest of a dismantled boss. With "I said get to work!" he kicks the Patroncito.[58] The grower at first plays along, even attempting to imitate the Chicano idiom of his worker, but when the new Patroncito claims his car, house, and "blonde in a bikini," and suggests that he instead take up the long work hours, low wages, and unsanitary living conditions of the migrant worker, he calls for his bodyguard. Alas, all the ape-like guard sees is the wearer of a pig mask molested by someone wearing the hat of a campesino. As the latter is dragged off stage by the guard, he cries out for help: "Help! Where's those damn union organizers? Where's Cesar Chavez? Help! Huelga! HUELGAAAAAA!"[59] The campesino, however, pulls off the pig mask, content to have taught his boss a lesson: "Bueno, so much for the patron. I got his house, his land, his car—only I'm not going to keep 'em. He can have them. But I'm taking his cigar. Ay, los watcho."[60] With this Brechtian gesture of smoking a cigar, he concludes the *acto*.

Los Dos Caras is brief but effective. In a few strokes, it sketches out a basic power constellation familiar to everyone in the audience: an (illegal) immigrant farm worker at the mercy of the whims of an American grower. The ironic reversal of this quotidian relationship, however, defamiliarizes these basic power structures, revealing that power is not a "natural" constant but a historically grown formation, sustained in daily reenactment, and as such clearly subject to change. The answer to how change can be brought about is ironically given by the grower himself: Huelga! Strike! For now, the campesino might retain only the cigar, that one most symbolic accoutrement of capitalist power, but he certainly has the last laugh in the confrontation with El Patroncito.

If *Verfremdung* of power (its defamiliarization and historicization) is the central concern of *Los dos Caras*, then the distillation of the fundamental social *Gestus* is at the heart of the next major *acto*, *La Quinta Temporada*. Here, Teatro Campesino uses (just like Bread and Puppet) basic allegories, reminiscent of medieval morality plays, to illuminate the Chicano's position in the agricultural economy, particularly his relation to the much disliked farm labor contractor, called "coyote"—a mediator between grower and worker, who in bypassing the regular process of union hiring halls shamelessly exploits the need and ignorance of the workers. The *acto* begins with Don Coyote hiring a campesino for the Patron's summer crew. Summer enters as an actor covered from head to toe with paper money. As he crosses the stage, the farm worker frantically attempts to pick as many bills off him as possible. Just as he stuffs them into his own back pocket, Don Coyote sneakily extracts them from there and hands them over to the grower. When Summer finally exits, the farm worker is shocked to find his pockets completely empty. This brief slapstick sequence humorously illuminates the fundamental *Gestus* of the farm worker's position in the agricultural economy: his double exploitation by contractor and grower.

Valdez continues to develop this gest further in the allegory of the seasons. Autumn enters, a somewhat thinner man and less bedecked with dollar bills, and the same process is repeated. Even though this time the worker catches Don Coyote red-handed, he is powerless to act against such obvious exploitation. When a lean and mean Winter steps onto the scene, demanding money, the farm worker, abandoned by Patron and Coyote, is completely at his whim and mercy. "Winter drags the farm worker [downstage], kicking and beating him, then dumps snow on him from a small pouch. The farm worker shivers helplessly."[61] Next, a lovely Spring (the only female actor in the troupe so far) comes skipping along, chasing Winter off stage and admonishing the worker to resist such treatment and fight for his rights. So when Coyote and Patron return from their winter vacation and get ready to recruit the summer crew, the campesino sits down in strike. Summer and Autumn return dressed in dollar bills as in the previous scene, but he boldly insists, "Estoy en huelga!"[62] Much to the grower's despair, the seasons exit untouched. Naturally, Winter too comes back with a vengeance, but this time a visibly weakened campesino is aided by the figures of Spring returning as "The Churches," of Summer as "The Unions," and of Autumn as "La Raza." Unable to harm the worker, Winter goes after Patron, who despite handing over "wads and wads" of money gets a good kick and beating and is covered by snow. Shivering and frightened he turns to Churches, Unions, and La Raza for help, and after being threatened with more snow, he finally signs a union contract. As the triumphant seasons carry the campesino away, a crushed El Patron crawls off stage. In the meantime, Winter has caught up with Coyote. Ever the trickster, Coyote tries to bluff him by pointing out that his season is long over. "Winter slaps his forehead stupidly. Don Coyote laughs and starts to walk out. Then suddenly Winter snaps his fingers as if realizing something."[63] "I'm the fifth season," he declares, flipping over his cardboard sign and revealing a new inscription: "La justicia social!"[64]

I described this second *acto* in detail to show that Teatro Campesino is also a very physical theater, a "rough" theater of "noise and smell,"[65] abundantly employing the simplistic and bawdy gestures of the burlesque and the circus. It uses a language full of slapstick violence (frequent beating of characters), sexual innuendo (Winter addressing Spring with "Mamasota"), and gratuitous, self-referential clownery and humor (Winter announcing his return with " 'Llego el lechero!' And my name ain't Granny Goose, baby!"). This copious use of the burlesque reflects the extent to which Teatro Campesino sees itself in the tradition of Mexican popular culture—particularly of the *carpa*, a traveling circus show that combines circus acrobatics with slapstick comedy and that found its most colorful expression in the *rascuache* humor and antics of the popular film clown Fortino Mario Alonso Moreno, alias Cantinflas.[66]

Valdez's enrichment of Brechtian didacticism with the crude physical gestures and uproarious laughter of the *carpa* is far from being gratuitous or a mere stylistic flourish. While perhaps less obvious in their function, these bawdy, comic gestures fulfill the same purpose as the Brechtian *Gestus*: they illuminate the everyday reality of the farm worker in clear and manageable images. Consider, for instance, the image of a desperate and hysterical grower "on the floor, kicking and snorting like a wild horse," being ridden by Don Coyote "like a bronco until [he] calms down and settles on all fours, snorting and slobbering incoherently."[67] To the farm workers such slapstick interludes vividly demonstrate the extent to which the grower's power is dependent on their work. Moreover, in the spirit of the Bakhtinian carnivalesque, these burlesque episodes momentarily invert social relations and suspend, if not overturn, power itself—El Patroncito being reduced to a slobbering animal. The recognition inherent in the laughter about such silliness might be just as powerful as that triggered by the recognition of the social *Gestus*.

More importantly, by deploying the *rascuache* humor and carnivalesque antics of the *carpa*, Valdez significantly vernacularizes his political agenda. In drawing on the linguistic and cultural lexicon and syntax of Chicano working-class culture, he appeals to the cultural expertise of his audience, and by emphasizing the amateur character of the performances, he enhances their accessibility and relevance to the farm workers. To the Chicano farm workers, the Cantinflas-inspired burlesques of Teatro Campesino are as "homegrown as chile and frijoles," as playwright and critic Carlos Morton remarked.[68] The use of the local vernacular of working-class culture is further underlined by the troupe's use of the Chicano idiom, its playful mixing of English, Spanish, and *caló* (slang). "If there was anything unique about the *acto*, it was the fact that it addressed the concerns of the Mechicano in the language of the fields and the barrios," Huerta similarly writes.[69] Using the local vernacular of his audience, Valdez consciously appeals to their cultural expertise.

Moreover, Teatro Campesino's spectators are not only familiar with the slapstick of the *carpa*, but they also take an acute interest in who is slapping whom. The image of Don Coyote at the mercy of Winter (who underneath his allegorical function is always clearly visible as a worker) or of El Patroncito reduced to a slobbering animal triggers laughter that is both full of comic relief and of recognition of the very possibility of role reversal. On the other hand, when they witness how Don Coyote and El Patron steal the money out of the campesino's back pocket, they also laugh, however, "not because it's funny, but because they recognize the reality. They have been caught," Valdez explains.[70] It is for this reason that Valdez considers humor and satire Teatro Campesino's "major asset and weapon."[71] They not only expose the underlying power relations of the campesino's everyday work life, but they also momentarily reverse them, thus intimating the possibility for change. By infusing "slapstick with a purpose," Teatro's *actos* are at once liberating and empowering.[72]

In addition, it is the amateur character of the performances, their deliberate makeshift mise-en-scène and acting, that enhances the relevance of the performance for the campesino spectators and establishes a community of interest between stage and audience. "Huelguistas portrayed huelguistas, drawing their improvised dialogue from real words they exchanged with esquiroles (scabs) in the field every day," Valdez emphasizes.[73] Ironically, the very lack of all aspirations to stage illusionism is here perceived as highly realistic by the spectators—an effect that we have also seen in place in the American amateur street theaters of the 1930s. When the worker turns into an actor, the distinction between audience and stage, actual life and its representation seems to disappear. At the same time, the fact that this very transformation takes place in front of the spectators also heightens the critical awareness of the latter. This sense of critical participation was particularly evident in the early *actos*, when spectators were invited to contribute to the development of a scene through commentaries and improvisation. All these devices—the use of the vernacular language of Chicano working-class culture, the appeal to the cultural and political expertise of the farm worker, and the heightened verisimilitude of the *acto* in the amateur character of the presentation—combine to tease out and enhance the spectator's identification with the political, an identification that is at once pleasurable and critical.

Valdez has famously described his theater as "somewhere between Brecht and Cantinflas."[74] This remark underlines his effort to vernacularize his essentially modernist understanding of political theater, to combine the political with the pleasurable and the highbrow with the mass cultural, to make propaganda entertaining and palpable for an ethnic community as well as to politicize Chicano popular culture. For critics of Chicano theater, however, the remark has become a bone of contention. Some scholars, such as Jorge Huerta see "the influences of both the great German playwright/theorist and the superlative Mexican comedian" at play in Valdez's work, particularly in the *actos*.[75] Huerta, in fact, considers this amalgamation of European modernism with Mexican popular culture for the purposes of political performance one of the greatest assets of Chicano theater. Lately, however, this emphasis on aesthetic hybridity has come under attack. Yolanda Broyles-González, for example, insists that "although some affinity may be sought and found between El Teatro Campesino and European models [. . .], it seems spatially and temporally more compelling to investigate the question of origins in our own backyard first, especially when the Mexican lineage is more than evident."[76] Given the prominent influence of the *carpa*, of an expressive Mexican culture of orality, of the underdog humor and motley *rascuache* aesthetics of Chicano working-class culture, she not only finds any Brechtian influence "less than negligible,"[77] but the continuing preoccupation of scholars with the European modernist heritage short of neocolonial appropriation. In other words, to her, Teatro Campesino is pure Cantinflas and devoid of any traces of a modernist European heritage.

Both positions have their critical appeal, particularly with regard to larger debates on Chicano identity and cultural nationalism. Broyles-González derives much force for her Chicanismo argument from the strategic equation of modernism with European colonialism. This strategy enables her to read the *carpa* as an indigenous means of contesting dominant Anglo and European culture, of opposing its cultural colonialism with the counter-hegemonic aesthetic of the *pelado* (the Mexican underdog). (Yet, she nonetheless supports this approach with yet another Eurocentric theory: that of the Bakhtinian carnivalesque). Huerta's emphasis on hybridity, on the other hand, marks Chicano identity as inherently bicultural, in this manner, also anticipating later theories of borderland identity that seek to reassess the heterogeneity of Chicano culture as one of empowerment.[78]

This theoretical scuffle over the aesthetic heritage of Teatro Campesino (pitching Brecht against Cantinflas or seeking a strategic alliance between the two) points to a continuing investment of scholars in the great divide (European modernism versus local vernaculars), an investment that prevents us from seeing the most astonishing thing about Teatro's work: the way that it teases out and utilizes the great affinity that has always existed between Brecht and Cantinflas. Brecht, a great admirer of the antics of Munich clown Karl Valentin, defines "the popular" ("das Volkstümliche") as what is "intelligible to the broad masses," as what is useful to them.[79] In this regard, the popular (including the mass cultural) has always been an essential component of his theater praxis.[80] Yet, in order to be useful popular/mass cultural forms have to be invested with a purpose, they have to be able to illuminate social relations in such a way that they become subject to change. Without that purpose, that impetus for social change, the wittiest slapstick remains at best carnivalesque in a Bakhtinian sense—that is, while it can succeed in temporarily suspending power by creating a counter-reality, it all too often remains just that: a counter-reality that exists alongside the dominant reality, rarely interfering with it and often sanctified by it (such as in the coexistence of religious rituals with pagan festivities). For example, the popular Mexican clown Cantinflas certainly succeeds in making the agitated masses happy, but, as Ilan Stavans also points out, "his subversive spirit never quite upsets the status quo."[81] Invested with a purpose, however, a Cantinflas-inspired burlesque (just as John Gay's nineteenth-century operetta) can very well become a powerful form of modernist intervention.

Teatro Campesino presents such "slapstick with a purpose"; its burlesque comedies not only assert the farm workers' ethnic identity, but they also reveal the workings of capital and, in this manner, empower farm workers in their struggle for better working and living conditions. Most importantly, however, Teatro does not simply expropriate (the Brechtian term "Umfunktionierung," functional transformation, comes to mind here) the popular for an essentially modernist agenda, but in its lexicon and syntax (its language, images, gestures), it remains firmly embedded in the local vernacular of Chicano and Mexican working-class culture. In short, in the work of El Teatro Campesino, I see an effective amalgamation of Cantinflas and Brecht, collapsing the great divide between (a white) high modernism and (ethnic) popular culture.

In sum, like Schumann, Valdez links modernist and vernacular strategies of political theater. But in Teatro Campesino we encounter a new understanding of the vernacular. We have seen how both Bread and Puppet and Teatro seek to address their political agendas in a language commensurate with the cultural experience of their audiences. Similar to the vernacular political theater of the 1930s, Schumann sentimentalizes the political by translating conflict into archetypal moral and religious allegories that affect the audience's emotions (in contrast to his predecessors he, however, does not simply leave it at that but also infuses his collages with an excess of meaning that resists the easy culinary consumption). His is an approach geared toward a broad, heterogeneous (but predominantly white, middle-class, urban) audience, seeking to establish a basis for common action by preparing a visceral/emotional ground for communal thinking.

Valdez, by contrast, takes up the local syntax and lexicon of Chicano working-class culture. While he too seeks to tease out the moment of identificatory pleasure in the political, he locates that element, not in the shared moral or religious sentiment (the consolation of empathy and bread) but in the shared laughter. To him, political commitment is not a *sensibilité du cœur*; on the contrary, emotional identification is persistently undermined by satire.[82] Valdez does not seek to elicit moral consternation and emotional concern but the recognition of the self in the alienated image—recognition based on laughter, not empathy. In this manner, he also redefines the strategy of the vernacular from one that speaks the sentimental language of the middlebrow on behalf of a white middle-class consumer audience to one that speaks the carnivalesque language of the lowbrow on behalf of an ethnic working-class audience. Teatro Campesino then tackles the great divide in quite a different manner than Bread and Puppet. While the latter seeks to forge a marriage between vanguard and vernacular by infusing the modernist with the sentimental, Teatro collapses the divide entirely by showing that such rigorous segregation has never made much sense for a minority culture that exists on the margins of the sphere of influence of the dominant high culture.

New Vernaculars: Folk, Kitsch, and Counter-Culture

An analysis of the work of Bread and Puppet and Teatro Campesino not only shows the various ways in which the great divide of modernism and mass culture has increasingly come under attack in the 1960s but also how the two dominant paradigms of political theater resulting from this divide have begun to change in the process. The most obvious change is, of course, that by the 1960s, political modernism can no longer be described as a predominantly positivistic praxis anchored in the supposition of a direct correlation between mimesis and change (i.e., the rendition of a "workable picture of the world"). While the latter might still hold true for the work of Teatro Campesino, the semantic undecidability and excess in the imagery of Bread and Puppet already evinces some degree of skepticism toward language and reason as the primary means of social analysis. Furthermore, both theaters no longer define change entirely in economic and social terms but also in religious and ethnic ones. The predominant, Marxist category of "class" is now supplemented and increasingly replaced by alternative categories of identity such as race and ethnicity as well as community (later on, in the 1970s, also by gender and sexuality), all of which reflect the emergence of what Jameson has called "new subjects of history of a non-class type."[83]

With regard to the vernacular, this paradigmatic shift is even more drastic. Earlier on we defined the vernacular on the basis of three interrelated objectives: as the language of the common American man defining itself in opposition to colonial European culture (Leo Marx), as the language that seeks to tease out the pleasurable in the political (Farred), and as the language of the surrounding local, commercial culture (Jameson). In the American 1930s, these three objectives merged on behalf of the overall goal of breaking down class barriers between working and middle classes and strengthening a broad and heterogeneous Popular Front. The sentimental, consumerist language of the middlebrow seemed most conducive toward this end. By the 1960s, the three previous objectives are still evident, but they now combine to form a slightly different understanding of vernacularity—namely, as the rough, anti-elitist aesthetics of counter-cultural communities. This redefinition has to be read in the light of cultural transformations taking place in the 1940s and 1950s.

During the 1940s and 1950s, characteristics such as visceral pleasure, culinary consumption, accessibility, ease of interpretation, even realism and narrativity, which had previously been associated with middlebrow aesthetics, now became increasingly equated with the lowbrow. For Clement Greenberg, they were emblematic of the aesthetics of an urbanized industrial proletariat that, though clamoring for culture, lacked the education and training for its appreciation. "To fill the demand of the new market a new commodity was devised: ersatz culture, kitsch, destined for those, who insensible to the values of genuine culture, are hungry nevertheless for the diversion that only culture of some sort can provide," he maintained.[84] While other critics of the time, such as Oscar Handlin, still differentiated between an authentic, vital popular culture and an artificial, soulless mass culture,[85] Greenberg simply collapsed all such fine distinctions into an irreconcilable opposition between avant-garde (high art) and kitsch (everything else). Whereas the former kept culture moving and alive amid the violence of World War II and the ideological confusion of the cold war, kitsch not only impeded the advance of modern society but, what was more, evinced an odd propensity for propaganda and totalitarianism.[86]

Greenberg's aesthetic pronouncement was to mark a whole generation of cultural critics anxious about the proliferation of mass culture and the demarcation of clear social boundaries in the postwar era. His sharp distinction between avant-garde and kitsch was, in the end, an attempt to reinstate and secure a cultural gap between an educated, white middle class and an ethnic urban working class. In Greenberg's pronouncements about art, we thus also encounter the reassessment of the function of vernacular aesthetics. While in the 1930s, the sentimental, commercial, and popular aesthetics of mass culture was deemed to be effective in bridging class and ethnic differences, it now served to reinscribe them. Dissociating the vernacular aesthetics from the cultural interests of an aspiring middle class, it was relegated to the realm of working-class and ethnic culture.

Not surprisingly, the 1960s avant-garde was eager to dethrone cultural authorities like Greenberg, whom it considered emblematic of the mentality of the cold war. Turning toward the very culture that the arbiters of taste of the 1950s considered substandard, it appropriated mass culture as a source of energy, vitality, and renewal, one in which a youthful American culture could affirm itself independent of a, by now, institutionalized and hegemonic discourse of high modernism. It is important to note, that this radical turn to mass culture was directed not against modernism as such but against the domesticated modernism of the Greenberg generation. In other words, the renewed interest in mass culture went hand in hand with an attempt to "revitalize the heritage of the European avantgarde and to give it an American form along the Duchamp-Cage-Warhol axis," Huyssen writes.[87] For the avant-garde of the 1960s "kitsch" was no longer a question of brow, taste, class, or ethnicity but indicative of a stagnating and repressive hegemonic discourse of culture and society. It therefore drew the frontline no longer between high and low but between the establishment and the anti-establishment.

What Greenberg considered "kitsch" was now expropriated as the new folk art, as the authentic expression of a lively American culture rejecting the arcane symbolism of institutionalized high art. Theater critics, for example, detected in the experimental and iconoclastic language of Off-Off Broadway the latest expression of folk. "One need only be familiar with general American sociology to understand the new syntax: the movies on Saturday nights, popcorn, Cokes, the radio, TV, comic strips, drugs, etc.," Albert Poland and Bruce Mailman wrote.[88] They considered the "fashion illustrators, industrial designers, sign makers, photographers" the craftsmen of that new folk art.[89] In other words, folk became the new vernacular, and as such it was equated with popular entertainment as well as with mass media, with homespun craftsmanship as well as commercial art. It became synonymous for any production style that seemed deliberately crude and makeshift, unpolished and lively, playful and humorous and that offered a high degree of audience involvement, whether in Off-Off Broadway theaters, the new dance movement, underground films, pop art, Fluxus, or happenings. The one thing that united these very different uses of folk was their strong "anti-elitist punch."[90]

It is this insistence on the anti-elitist punch that joins the various endeavors of the American avant-garde to amalgamate the lowbrow virtues of mass and popular culture (accessibility, visceral gratification) with the highbrow virtues of modernism (rupture and renewal, experimentation), as evident in the work of Bread and Puppet and Teatro Campesino. Although we are not all too far from our previous definition of the vernacular, it is important to note that while in the 1930s the vernacular served as a means of creating social cohesion in support of Roosevelt's reform politics, the new folk vernacular of the 1960s was meant to radically undermine and unsettle the status quo of American society, particularly its definitions of class and taste. Moreover, it was to draw a sharp line between the dominant culture and the counter-culture.

Most importantly, 1960s folk stood for community. In evoking the traditional understanding of folk as art made by the community, about the community, and for the community, the folk vernacular helped to create counter-communities—that is, powerful models of collective work and communal living that could function as an alternative and corrective to the dominant society. This was the case not only with Bread and Puppet, as discussed earlier, but also with Teatro Campesino, which understood itself more and more along those lines, particularly after the foundation of El Centro Campesino Cultural in the Californian small town of San Juan Bautista in the late 1960s.[91] The distinctive homespun style of both groups' aesthetics was meant to evoke the moral and political values of egalitarianism and to suggest the successful integration of art and life. In short, folk, even in its new urban mass cultural definition, was thought to affirm and create communal bonds not just between the performers but also between the troupe and its audiences (Schumann's bread, Valdez's *actos* and, later on, *mitos*). The anti-elitist punch of the rough aesthetics of the folk vernacular was thus not only meant to affront the tastemakers of the parent generation and to upset the status quo of the 1960s but also to provide the spectators with an alternative social and cultural model.

Due to their various attempts of amalgamating and collapsing previous distinctions between high and low, the authentic and the mediatized, the auratic and the commercial, the artists of the 1960s have frequently been identified as the first generation of postmodernists. For Banes, for instance, it was precisely their inherently conflicted position with regard to mass culture that characterized the work of these young artists as postmodern. While they "used icons of popular culture to comment on bourgeois life," they "almost overnight found themselves written up in *Life*," she asserts.[92] This very tension between resistance and co-option heralded for her the end of the modernist avant-garde and the beginning of postmodernism. Yet, as Banes also asserts, in marked contrast to the next generation, artists of the 1960s still continued to entertain "a utopian dream of freeing themselves from the past."[93] For me, it is precisely this latter characteristic, the capacity to imagine a radically different function of art in society (as well as a radically different society) along with the ability to retain what Jameson has called "the luxury of the old-fashioned ideological critique, the indignant denunciation of the other,"[94] which ties Bread and Puppet and Teatro Campesino to the two older traditions of political theater—marking them, if anything, as late modernist rather than early postmodernist.

Huyssen too emphasizes the similarity and continuity between the American artists of the 1960s and the European avant-garde of the 1920s and 1930s, particularly with regard to the ways in which they combined formal experimentation with an attack of institution art (a domesticated modernism). But he also adds that precisely because the

American avant-garde of the 1960s encountered a culture industry that was no longer in its inception but one that could easily absorb, diffuse, and market the most subversive elements, this new avant-garde found it much harder to sustain an aesthetic iconoclasm and political agenda independent of the culture industry. He thus agrees with Banes when he insists that the avant-garde rebellion of the 1960s "was in danger of becoming affirmative culture right from the start."[95] Huyssen therefore reads the 1960s as both "an American avantgarde *and* the endgame of international avantgardism."[96] Although it opened up new frontiers in American culture, it also reflected the fragmentation and decline of what was once "a genuinely critical and adversary culture."[97]

Regardless of whether we describe the period as late modernist or early postmodernist, what matters most here for our discussion is that in tackling the great divide of modernism and mass culture by merging modernist and vernacular traditions, the political theaters of the 1960s brought about a new configuration of these two cultural forces—one that could no longer be described entirely in terms of the older paradigms and one that paved the way for new forms and a new understanding of political theater.

Postmodern Political Theater

I want to conclude this study with a few brief remarks about the possibilities for a postmodern praxis of political theater and the ways in which the earlier vernacular and the modernist praxes figure as important predecessors for it.

Critics generally agree that in Western culture postmodernism had fully arrived by the 1970s.[98] Yet, they also detect different tendencies within it. While a wholly affirmative strand seemed to abandon "any claims to critique, transgression and negation," an alternative postmodernism attempted to continue the 1930s and 1960s tradition of "resistance, critique, and negation of the status quo."[99] Both Huyssen and Jameson agree that this alternative postmodernism could, however, no longer be defined in modernist or avant-gardist terms. Given the new configurations of mass culture and art, the older terms of radical cultural critique simply proved useless for analyzing an art that, despite all attempts at critique and resistance more often than not tended to reinforce and reproduce the cultural logic of consumer capitalism. At the end of his seminal essay "Postmodernism and Consumer Society" (1981), Jameson is rather doubtful as to whether postmodernism could at all fulfill a similar cultural function as that of the older modernism. "We have seen that there is a way in which post-modernism replicates or reproduces—reinforces—the logic of con-sumer capitalism," he writes, "the more significant question is whether there is also a way in which it resists that logic. But that is a question we must leave open."[100]

Almost a decade later, Philip Auslander ventured an answer to Jameson's question and in doing so also suggested a new language for thinking of the political in postmodern art. Auslander too acknowl-edges the inability of the political art strategies of the 1930s and 1960s to address the postmodern condition along with the inability of criti-cism up to that date to think of the political in art in terms other than those of the previous decades. But he also insists that the so-called apolitical postmodernist performances have very well been capable of asserting a political critique—albeit, in terms different from those of their predecessors. Drawing on the work of Hal Foster, Auslander asserts that we have to move from understanding political theater as an aesthetics of transgression to understanding it as an aesthetics of resistance. Postmodern art might no longer be capable of placing itself outside the object of its critique, nor of articulating alternative social visions, as Jameson and other critics have argued. But even when posi-tioned *within* postmodern culture, even when subject to instant com-modification as well as to reproducing the hegemonic mimetic forms, it can nevertheless articulate its suspicion of those forms and their function in contemporary culture; it can challenge "representation through representation," as Auslander maintains.[101] According to him, this is postmodernism's most crucial strategy of resistance.

In his study of American performance art of the 1980s, Auslander shows how performers such as Laurie Anderson and Spalding Gray succeeded in mounting a critique of contemporary culture "even from within seemingly co-opted practices"[102] precisely by drawing attention to the constructedness and performativity of representation itself and, in this manner, also alerting spectators to the constructedness and performativity of the ideological structures behind it. Such shift in strategy and focus of critique does not make postmodern art any less political than its predecessors. It merely acknowledges the obvious, namely, that the terrain of contention has shifted from outright ideo-logical denunciation to a complex awareness of the artist's as well as the art work's embeddedness in the dominant culture.

Yet, even though the terms of cultural critique have changed, its overall goal nonetheless appears to be consistent with that of previous decades. As in the 1930s and 1960s, political theater still pledges to unveil what Tony Kushner has called "the great historical project of capitalist myth-making: the transformation of that which is social, cultural, and political, and hence changeable, into nature, which is immutable and eternal."[103] With this assertion, Kushner, like many other contemporary artists, affirms his place in a tradition of leftist political theater that spans the entire twentieth century, one that is committed to revealing the workings of power, whether it is in terms of class, race and ethnicity, gender, sexuality, language, commodity, and so on. There is no doubt that we still need such unveiling of dominant power structures. As Kushner points out, while we are trained to see the personal dimension of an event, we are often unable to detect its political meaning, particularly since the mass media are strongly invested in blurring it. Riots, wars, and epidemics are often transcribed as "human tragedies"—a term that in eliciting our empathy also prevents us from asking the more uncomfortable political questions about what motivated these events in the first place and in what social, economic, ethnic, gendered, and cultural contexts they occurred. The task of political theater thus remains essentially the same: to reveal the political at the heart of the seemingly personal, to unmask systems of oppression behind that what seems "eternally human" and "natural."

What is striking about the contemporary theater is its liberal use of a plethora of approaches to the dilemma of public and form that has haunted the political theater ever since its inception in the early twentieth century. In conclusion, I want to point to two of them, fully aware that each of them deserves a fuller study than can be provided within the framework of my argument.

Perhaps more than any other contemporary American playwright, Tony Kushner has shown that he is heir to both the modernist and the vernacular tradition in theater. As Kushner himself asserts, his work is "as much a part of trash culture as [of] high art."[104] Plays such as the epic drama *Angels in America* (1993) and the more recent musical *Caroline, or Change* (2004) reveal the influence of Brecht's epic theater, particularly with regard to their insistence on the historicization of social conflict, the distillation of fundamental social gests, and the frequent deployment of alienation effects. At the same time, Kushner's Theater of the Fabulous also abundantly draws on forms of mass culture (1960s R&B, Broadway musical, Hollywood film) as well as the vernaculars of camp and Charles Ludlam's Theater of the Ridiculous. It relies just as much on realistic modes of narration as on the "angelic" and the meta-theatrical, freely merging the everyday and the political with the stuff of dreams and fantasies. Bertolt Brecht and

Walter Benjamin are just as much a source of inspiration for Kushner as are Steven Spielberg and Judy Garland. The moment when the Angel crashes through the ceiling of AIDS patient Prior Walter's bedroom in *Angels in America: Millennium Approaches* is both utterly astonishing in the Brechtian sense and thoroughly camp in its playful imitation of the most obvious deus-ex-machina tricks of Hollywood. As we laugh and wonder about this spectacular act of theatricality, we also recognize its inherent historical gest: Kushner's Angel is a relative of Benjamin's Angel of History, pointing to the social wreckage that has been piling up from the McCarthy trials to the Reagan era. Such amalgamation of various traditions and techniques from modernism and mass culture enables Kushner to articulate incisive critiques of American capitalism, which are "workable" as well as "fabulous."[105]

We encounter a similarly playful and yet provocative mixing of genres, languages, and styles in the theater of Suzan-Lori Parks. Particularly in her plays *Imperceptible Mutabilities in the Third Kingdom* (1989), *America Play* (1994), and *Venus* (1995), Parks develops the dramaturgy of "Rep&Rev" (repetition and revision), a style that simultaneously replicates and deconstructs the very discourse it imitates. Rep&Rev might strike one as a new postmodern technique with regard to its poststructuralist approach to history and language. But a closer look reveals that Rep&Rev is firmly embedded in the vernacular tradition of African American oral culture, specifically in what Henry Louis Gates has called "signifying"—that is, the constant play with words and their meaning, their perpetual deconstruction and transformation.[106] Signifying is also in place in Parks's later, more "realistic," dramas *Topdog/Underdog* (1992) and *The Red Letter Plays* (2001), all of which partake in continuous intertextual cross-referencing and revisions. The essentially vernacular strategy of Rep&Rev thus also functions as an effective means of alienation and fragmentation—at times turning narrative into allegory and thus producing abstractions that demand the critical attention of the spectator and at other times mimicking and questioning the very notion of mimesis, as when the Lesser Known, Lucy, and Brazil in the *America Play* undermine and question the possibility of historiography by taking its myriad representations of history *ad absurdum*.[107] In this manner, such classic paradigms as modernist alienation and vernacular identification combine to produce a completely new mode of cultural critique that alerts us to the ideological purposes representation as such has been put in contemporary society.

Kushner and Parks are, of course, just two examples of a lively contemporary political theater scene in the United States that still startles and alerts us and makes us laugh and weep. In amalgamating the two older traditions of articulating cultural critique, the contemporary stage has moved well beyond the great divide of mass culture and high modernism. Yet, in bearing the aesthetic and political traces of these two fundamental approaches to the question of form and public, it also reveals the extent to which the modernist and the vernacular political theaters of the 1920s and 1930s have been crucial predecessors for postmodern political theater.

Notes

Prologue

1. Michael Gold. "Change the World." *Daily Worker* 5 December 1935.
2. Morgan Y. Himmelstein. "The Pioneers of Bertolt Brecht in America." *Modern Drama* 9:2 (1966):179. Himmelstein is also referring to an unsuccessful production of *The Threepenny Opera* at the Empire Theatre in New York in April 1933, in an adaptation by Gifford Cochran and Jerrold Krimsky.
3. Qtd. in Ben Blake. *The Awakening of the American Theatre.* New York: Tomorrow Publishers, 1935, 35.
4. Fredric Jameson. "Reification and Utopia in Mass Culture." *Social Text* 1 (Winter 1979):134.
5. For studies of modernist political theater see e.g., Michael Patterson. *The Revolution in German Theatre 1900–1933.* Boston: Routledge & Kegan Paul, 1981; Christopher Innes. *Erwin Piscator's Political Theatre: The Development of Modern German Drama.* Cambridge: Cambridge University Press, 1972; John Willett. *The Theatre of Erwin Piscator: Half a Century of Politics in Theatre.* London: Methuen, 1978; Lars Kleberg. *Theatre as Action: Soviet-Russian Avant-Garde Aesthetics.* London: Macmillan, 1993 (1980); Erika Fischer-Lichte. *Die Entdeckung des Zuschauers: Paradigmawechsel auf dem Theater des 20. Jahrhunderts.* Tübingen: Francke, 1997.
6. In 1936, the Group Theatre staged Erwin Piscator's epic drama *Case of Clyde Griffiths* (an adaptation of Dreiser's *American Tragedy*). The production flopped. See Gerhard F. Probst. *Erwin Piscator and the American Theatre.* New York: Peter Lang, 1991.
7. Daniel Aaron. *Writers on the Left: Episodes in American Literary Communism.* New York: Columbia University Press, 1961; Gerald Rabkin. *Drama and Commitment: Politics in the American Theatre of the Thirties.* Bloomington, IN: Indiana University Press, 1964; Malcolm Goldstein. *The Political Stage: American Drama and Theater of the Great Depression.* New York: Oxford University Press, 1974; Eberhard Brüning. *Das amerikanische Drama der dreißiger Jahre.* Berlin: Rütten & Loening, 1966; and Ira A. Levine. *Left-Wing Dramatic Theory in the American Theatre.* Ann Arbor, MI: University of Michigan Press, 1980.
8. Barbara Foley. *Radical Representations: Politics and Form in U.S. Proletarian Fiction, 1929–1941.* Durham, NC: Duke University Press, 1993; and Michael Denning. *The Cultural Front.* London: Verso, 1997.

Chapter One: Brecht on Broadway: Reconsidering Political Theater

1. *Die Mutter: Das Leben der Revolutionärin Pelagea Vlassova of Tver* was written in collaboration with Günther Weisenborn, Slatan Dudow, and Hanns Eisler. For the American production, Theatre Union slightly changed the title by shortening it and by dropping the initial definite article.

2. Bertolt Brecht. *Brecht on Theatre*, ed. and trans. John Willett. New York: Hill & Wang, 1964, 133.

3. Ibid., 39.

4. See Fredric Jameson. *Brecht and Method*. London: Verso, 1998, 39–40.

5. Fredric Jameson. *The Prison House of Language*. Princeton, NJ: Princeton University Press, 1972, 58.

6. Brecht, *Brecht on Theatre*, 185.

7. Bertolt Brecht. *Collected Plays*, vol. 3/2, ed. and trans. John Willett and Ralph Mannheim. London: Methuen, 1970, 240 and Walter Benjamin. *Understanding Brecht*, trans. Anna Bostock. London: Verso, 1998, 34.

8. The transformation of Gorky's novel into the classic of socialist realism is one of the famous anachronisms of literary history, since the novel predates the proclamation of socialist realism by twenty-eight years. See Thomas Lahusen. "Socialist Realism." In *The Encyclopedia of Literature and Politics*, ed. M. Keith Booker. Westport, CT: Greenwood Press, 2005.

9. Theater board members Albert Maltz and George Sklar, qtd. in Lee Baxandall. "Brecht in America, 1935." *TDR* 12:1 (Fall 1967):71 and 75.

10. George Sklar qtd. in Baxandall, "Brecht in America, 1935," 71.

11. Ibid.

12. Letter to V. J. Jerome, chief cultural officer of CPUSA in Bertolt Brecht. *Werke: Grosse kommentierte Berliner und Frankfurter Ausgabe*, vol. xxviii, ed. Werner Hecht, Jan Knopf, Werner Mittenzwei, and Klaus-Detelf Müller. Berlin, Weimar, and Frankfurt/M.: Aufbau and Suhrkamp, 1989–2000, 522–523, trans. mine.

13. Ibid.

14. This part of Peters's adaptation was included by Brecht in his annotations to *Die Mutter*. See Brecht, *Werke*, vol. xxiv, 164.

15. Brecht, *Collected Plays*, vol. 3/2, 95.

16. Ibid., 138.

17. From unpublished manuscript of Peters's adaptation at Brecht Archive, Akademie der Künste Berlin (no. 443, pp. 65–66).

18. See Jane Tompkins. *Sensational Designs: The Cultural Work of American Fiction 1790–1860*. New York: Oxford University Press, 1985. Ironically, this device later on also became the classic trope of socialist realist literature in the form of the death of the revolutionary. See Katerina Clark. *The Soviet Novel: History as Ritual*. Chicago, IL: University of Chicago Press, 1981.

19. Brecht, *Collected Plays*, vol. 3/2, 264.
20. See their letters published in Brecht, *Werke*, vol. xxviii, 531 and 535, trans. mine. Brecht and Eisler did, however, like and approve the set design by Mordecai Gorelik, probably because it so closely resembled the original Berlin set: a bare revolving stage, two pianos stage right, and a large screen for the projection of titles and photos upstage. See Baxandall, "Brecht in America, 1935," 78 and Mordecai Gorelik. *New Theatres for Old*. London: Denis Dobson, 1947 (1940). For extensive documentation of the conflict between Brecht and Theatre Union, see Baxandall, "Brecht in America, 1935," 69–87 and James K. Lyon. "Der Briefwechsel zwischen Bertolt Brecht und der New Yorker Theatre Union von 1935." In *Brecht-Jahrbuch 1975*, ed. John Fuegi, Reinhold Grimm, and Jost Hermand. Frankfurt/M.: Suhrkamp, 1975, 136–155.
21. Brecht, *Werke*, vol. xxviii, 535.
22. Qtd. in Baxandall, "Brecht in America, 1935," 75.
23. The first essay on epic theater "The German Drama: Pre-Hitler," written by Brecht, appeared in the *New York Times* on 24 November 1935. It was followed by a longer piece by Eva Goldbeck. "Principles of 'Educational' Theater." *New Masses* 31 December 1935. Mordecai Gorelik subsequently published "Epic Realism: Brecht's Notes on the *Threepenny Opera*." *Theatre Workshop* (April–July 1937):29–41 and included a lengthy discussion of epic theater in his book *New Theatres for Old* (1940).
24. Qtd. in Baxandall, "Brecht in America, 1935," 75.
25. Theatre Union's choice of Wolfson is a peculiar one. According to Baxandall, such eminent directors as Elia Kazan and Erwin Piscator had been suggested and turned down by the board. Wolfson was at this point still fairly inexperienced, his credentials consisting of stage managing Broadway shows and directing plays by striking miners at a theater festival in West Virginia (Ibid., 73).
26. Qtd. in Brecht, *Collected Plays*, vol. 3/2, 248.
27. Baxandall, "Brecht in America, 1935," 69.
28. J. M. Olgin. "Mother: The Theatre Union's New Play." *Daily Worker* 22 November 1935.
29. Qtd. in Morgan Himmelstein. "The Pioneers of Bertolt Brecht in America." *Modern Drama* 9:2 (1966): 186.
30. Burns Mantle. "'Mother': Soviet Primer in Action." *New York Daily News* 20 November 1935.
31. Wilella Waldorf. "'Mother': Opens Theatre Union's Third Season." *New York Post* 20 November 1935.
32. Arthur Pollock. "The Theater." *Brooklyn Daily Eagle* 20 November 1935.
33. Mantle, "'Mother': Soviet Primer in Action."
34. Olgin, "Mother: The Theatre Union's New Play."
35. John Gassner. "Mother." *New Theatre & Film* (November/December 1935).
36. Michael Gold. "Change the World." *Daily Worker* 5 December 1935.

37. Michael Gold. "Change the World." *Daily Worker* 6 December 1935.
38. James T. Farrell. "Theatre Chronicle." *Partisan Review* 3 (February 1936):29.
39. "Text of Platform." *Daily Worker* 29 June 1936.
40. Listen Oaks. "Theatre Union Replies." *New Theatre* (November 1934):12.
41. Gorelik, *New Theatres for Old*, 396.
42. Thomas R. Dash. "Mother." *Women's Wear Daily* 20 November 1935.
43. Ibid.
44. Lyon, "Der Briefwechsel zwischen Bertolt Brecht und der New Yorker Theatre Union von 1935," 154–155.
45. The advance booking of 50,000 tickets by workers' organizations guaranteed a run of only 36 performances. By comparison, Friedrich Wolf's *Sailors of Cattaro* ran for 95 performances, Peters's and Sklar's *Stevedore* for a total of 175, and Albert Maltz's *Black Pit* for 85. According to Maltz, Theatre Union could not recover from the financial blow dealt by the failure of Brecht's play. It closed after two more productions, Silone's *Fontamara* and Lawson's *Marching Song*, with an annual deficit of $15,000. See Baxandall, "Brecht in America, 1935," 74; Lyon, "Der Briefwechsel zwischen Bertolt Brecht und der New Yorker Theatre Union von 1935," 137; and John Willett's editorial notes in *Collected Plays*, vol. 3/2.
46. Brecht, *Werke*, vol. xxviii, 535, trans. mine.
47. See Brecht's diary entries of summer and fall 1942 in *Werke*, vol. xxxviii.
48. Brecht, *Werke*, vol. xxiv, 177, trans. mine.
49. Qtd. in Maria Ley-Piscator. *The Piscator Experiment*. Carbondale, IL: Southern Illinois University Press, 1967, 40. *Case of Clyde Griffiths*, an adaptation of Dreiser's *American Tragedy*, was originally written for production by the Piscator Kollektiv at the Lessing Theater in Berlin in April 1931. The American version was written in collaboration with Lena Goldschmidt. It opened on 13 March 1936 at the Ethel Barrymore Theatre in New York, where it ran for nineteen performances only.
50. Fredric Jameson. "Reification and Utopia in Mass Culture." *Social Text* 1 (Winter 1979):134.
51. Fredric Jameson. "Reflections in Conclusion." In Theodor Adorno, Walter Benjamin, Ernst Bloch, Bertolt Brecht, and Georg Lukács. *Aesthetics and Politics*. London: Verso, 1999 (1977), 198.
52. Brecht, *Brecht on Theatre*, 204.
53. Ibid., 82.
54. Georg Lukács. "Realism in the Balance" (1938). In Theodor Adorno, Walter Benjamin, Ernst Bloch, Bertolt Brecht, and Georg Lukács. *Aesthetics and Politics*. London: Verso, 1999 (1977), 33.
55. John Howard Lawson. "Technique and Drama." In *American Writers' Congress 1935*, ed. Henry Hart. London: Martin Lawrence, 1936, 128.
56. See Brecht's postulate of the "Nicht/Sondern" (not/but) method, according to which an actor had to act "in such a way that the alternative emerges

as clearly as possible, that his acting allows the other possibilities to be inferred and only represents one out of the possible variants" (Brecht, *Brecht on Theatre*, 137).

57. Lukács, "Realism in the Balance," 56–57.
58. Erika Fischer-Lichte. *Die Entdeckung des Zuschauers: Paradigmawechsel auf dem Theater des 20. Jahrhunderts.* Tübingen and Basel: Francke, 1997.
59. Stuart Hall. "Notes on Deconstructing the Popular." In *People's History of Socialist Theory*, ed. Raphael Samuel. London: Routledge, 1981, 233.
60. Michael Denning. *The Cultural Front.* London: Verso, 1997, xvi.
61. Hall, "Notes on Deconstructing the Popular," 233.

Chapter Two: Disjunctive Aesthetics: A Genealogy of Political Theater

1. Henri Stendhal. *The Charterhouse of Parma*, trans. Lowell Bair. New York: Bantam Books, 1960, 349.
2. Irving Howe. *Politics and the Novel.* New York: Columbia University Press, 1992, 24.
3. Qtd. in Gerald Rabkin. *Drama and Commitment: Politics in the American Theatre of the Thirties.* Bloomington, IN: Indiana University Press, 1964, 176.
4. Klaus Gleber. *Theater und Öffentlichkeit: Produktions- und Rezeptionsbedingungen politischen Theaters am Beispiel Piscators 1920–1966.* Frankfurt/M.: Peter Lang, 1979, iv, trans. mine.
5. Fredric Jameson. "Reification and Utopia in Mass Culture." *Social Text* 1 (Winter 1979):134.
6. Eric Bentley. "The Theatre of Commitment." In Eric Bentley. *The Theatre of Commitment and Other Essays on Drama in Our Society.* New York: Atheneum, 1967, 197.
7. Walter B. Rideout. *The Radical Novel in the United States 1900–1954.* Cambridge, MA: Harvard University Press, 1956, 12.
8. The terms modernism and avant-garde are often used interchangeably in reference to a highly experimental phase in modern Western theater, spanning, according to definition, anywhere between thirty to eighty years and combining such disparate practices as naturalism, art theater movement, historical avant-garde, and the post–World War II neo-avant-garde. Erika Fischer-Lichte defines it as the period between the transcendence of naturalist stage practices in the experiments of the art theater movement (1900s) and the forcing into line of all artistic movements by the totalitarian regimes in Germany, Italy, and the Soviet Union (Erika Fischer-Lichte. *Die Entdeckung des Zuschauers: Paradigmawechsel auf dem Theater des 20. Jahrhunderts.* Tübingen: Francke, 1997). Bert Cardullo and Robert Knopf likewise apply the terms modernism and avant-garde indiscriminately to

all non-naturalist theater forms from around 1890 to 1950 (Bert Cardullo and Robert Knopf, eds. *Theater of the Avant-Garde 1890–1950: A Critical Anthology*. New Haven, CT: Yale University Press, 2001). Joachim Fiebach, by contrast, also includes the naturalist practices of, e.g., Otto Brahm and Konstantin Stanislavsky in the avant-garde because of their vehement opposition to the shallow entertainment of the professional stages in the second half of the nineteenth century (Joachim Fiebach. *Von Craig bis Brecht: Studien zu Künstlertheorien in der ersten Hälfte des 20. Jahrhunderts*. Berlin: Henschel, 1975). Richard Schechner, again, reaches back to Ibsen's realism in his definition of the avant-garde ("The Five Avant Gardes or . . . Or None." In Richard Schechner. *The Future of Ritual: Writings on Culture and Performance*. London: Routledge 1993, 5–21)—a thesis corroborated by Kristine Sheperd-Barr, who evokes Ibsen's *Doll's House* (1879) as the first proto-modernist play (*Ibsen and the Early Modernist Theatre*. Westport, CT: Greenwood Press, 1997).

9. Peter Bürger. *Theory of the Avant-Garde*, trans. Michael Shaw. Minneapolis, MN: University of Minnesota Press, 1984.

10. Ibid., 22.

11. Ibid.

12. For Bürger, political art is possible only in individual works of art, which he considers at best of limited effectiveness. According to him, the autonomous status of art in bourgeois society is more or less secured unless a ruling class decides to employ the very institution of art toward political ends, as was the case under fascism. While Bürger acknowledges the emergence of the proletariat as the motivating force behind bourgeois self-criticism, he neglects to theorize the repeated attempts ventured by the European proletariat from 1917 onward to expropriate the very institution of bourgeois art toward a fundamental transformation of social totality under proletarian rule. Only in a footnote does Bürger address the issue at all. Here, he muses that it might be worthwhile investigating how far the changed social conditions after the October Revolution allowed the Russian avant-gardist at least partially to reintegrate art with life praxis (*Theorie der Avantgarde*. Frankfurt/M.: Suhrkamp, 1974, 75). Aside from the footnote and aside from individual art works, there is no place for political art in Bürger's theory.

13. Jochen Schulte-Sasse. "Foreword: Theory of Modernism versus Theory of the Avant-Garde." In Peter Bürger. *Theory of the Avant-Garde*, trans. Michael Shaw. Minneapolis, MN: University of Minnesota Press, 1984, xlvi.

14. Erwin Piscator. *The Political Theatre*, trans. Hugh Rorrison. New York: Avon Books, 1978, 23.

15. Brecht explicitly understands epic theater in the tradition of Schiller's concept of theater as a moral institution. See his essay "Theatre for Pleasure or Theatre for Instruction" (1935). In Bertolt Brecht. *Brecht on Theatre*, ed. and trans. John Willett. New York: Hill & Wang, 1964, 74–75. See also Friedrich Schiller. "Was kann eine gute stehende Schaubühne eigentlich wirken? (Die

Schaubühne als moralische Anstalt betrachtet)" (1784). In Friedrich Schiller. *Sämtliche Werke in fünf Bänden*, vol. 5, ed. Jost Perfahl. München: Winkler, 1968, 818–831.

16. George Brandes. "Inaugural Lecture 1871." In *The Theory of the Modern Stage*, ed. Eric Bentley. New York: Applause, 1997 (1968), 383. I put naturalism and not realism at the beginning of modern theater for I see the two as related movements. Particularly in the theater, a realist agenda (Brandes) was often combined with naturalist staging techniques (Zola). I am therefore applying the term naturalism to a phase in European theater ranging from about 1890 to 1910, which encompasses the works of Ibsen, Strindberg, Hauptmann, Chekhov, Gorky, and so on. I am aware that such periodization is somewhat simplified. The early Ibsen, for instance, was clearly influenced by romanticism, while the late Ibsen and Chekhov already anticipated the symbolist movement. Strindberg again became the precursor of expressionism. However, for the purposes of this argument, this rough periodization should suffice.

17. See Denis Diderot. "Conversations on the Natural Son" (1757). In Denis Diderot. *Selected Writings on Art and Literature*, trans. Geoffrey Brenner. London: Penguin, 1994, 1–80.

18. Both Brecht and Piscator pay tribute to the naturalist legacy of epic theater. See Erwin Piscator. *Schriften*, vol. 1, ed. Ludwig Hoffmann. Berlin: Henschel, 1968, 27 and Bertolt Brecht. *Werke: Grosse kommentierte Berliner und Frankfurter Ausgabe*, vol. xxi, ed. Werner Hecht, Jan Knopf, Werner Mittenzwei, and Klaus-Detelf Müller. Berlin, Weimar, and Frankfurt/M.: Aufbau and Suhrkamp, 1989–2000, 273.

19. Brecht, *Brecht on Theatre*, 219.

20. Brecht, *Werke*, vol. xxi, 232. Piscator similarly holds that while naturalism accurately renders the milieu of working-class life, it fails to analyze the causes of poverty and oppression (Piscator, *Schriften*, vol. 1, 31).

21. For extensive discussions of the role of distance in theater and art, see Michael Fried. *Absorption and Theatricality*. Chicago, IL: University of Chicago Press, 1980 and Daphna Ben Chaim. *Distance in the Theatre: The Aesthetics of Audience Response*. Ann Arbor, MI: University of Michigan Press, 1984.

22. Émile Zola. "Naturalism in the Theatre" (1881). In *Theory of the Modern Stage*, ed. Eric Bentely. New York: Applause, 1977, 351.

23. Vsevolod Meyerhold. "The Theater of Naturalism and the Theater of Mood" (1908) and "The Stylized Theatre" (1907). In Vsevolod Meyerhold. *Meyerhold on Theatre*, ed. and trans. Edward Braun. London: Methuen, 1969. Contemporary reception theory contests the modernist claim that the naturalist stage induced absolute passivity in the spectator. Anne Ubersfeld and Marco de Marinis, for instance, consider watching an activity entailing both emotional and intellectual work. See Anne Ubersfeld. "The Pleasure of the Spectator." *Modern Drama* 25:1 (March 1982):127–139 and Marco de Marinis. "Dramaturgy of the Spectator." *TDR* 31:2 (Summer 1987):100–114.

24. Meyerhold and Oskar Schlemmer, for example, shifted the focus of the mise-en-scène from the spoken text to the actor's body and its movement in space. Jacques Copeau, in dispensing with all props, stripped the theater to its essential minimum: a bare board. Others such as Adolphe Appia, Georg Fuchs, Max Reinhardt, and Vassily Kandinsky strove to synthesize all participating arts (choreography, light, music, design) into a synaesthetic *Gesamtkunstwerk*. Edward Gordon Craig, again, considered replacing the actor with an *Über-Marionette* in order to eliminate human contingencies and ensure formal perfection.

25. Reinhardt introduced the revolving stage, took down the curtain, and extended sets into the auditorium. He also experimented with intimate settings (*Kammerspiele*) and grand mass spectacles (e.g., his outdoor production of *Everyman* in Salzburg, 1920). Meyerhold similarly attempted to bridge stage and auditorium by lowering the stage to the level of the audience, abolishing the ramp and installing *hanamichi*-like footbridges.

26. Walter Gropius. "Introduction." In Oskar Schlemmer, Oskar László Moholy-Nagy, and Farkas Molnár. *The Theater of the Bauhaus*, ed. Walter Gropius and trans. Arthur Wensinger. Baltimore, MD: John Hopkins University Press, 1996 (1961), 12.

27. Walter Gropius. "Vom modernen Theaterbau, unter Berücksichtigung des Piscatortheaterneubaus in Berlin" (1934). In *Erwin Piscator: Eine Arbeitsbiographie in 2 Bänden*, vol. 1, ed. Knut Boeser and Renata Vatková. Berlin: Frölich & Kaufmann, 1986, 149, trans. mine. Due to enormous costs, the *Totaltheater* was never built. But its concept inspired the mise-en-scène of many of Piscator's production at his theater in Berlin. It also left its trace on contemporary theater architecture, as evident in the design of Berlin's Schaubühne. See Stefan Woll. *Das Totaltheater: Ein Projekt von Walter Gropius und Erwin Piscator*. Berlin: Gesellschaft für Theatergeschichte e. V., 1984.

28. The art theaters undermined Stanley Cavell's postulate of separateness as the fundamental condition of theater, precisely by acknowledging it. They realized that it was the very fear of theatricality and of separateness that had involuntarily widened the gulf between stage and spectator. It is for this reason that they chose to assert themselves precisely as theater (and not as life), for it is in the moment of utter theatricality that the stage is able to acknowledge the spectator in an affirmative way. See Stanley Cavell. "The Avoidance of Love." In Stanley Cavell. *Must We Mean What We Say?* Cambridge: Cambridge University Press, 1967.

29. Fischer-Lichte, *Die Entdeckung des Zuschauers*, 9–41.

30. See Vladimir Mayakovsky, David Burlyuk, Alexander Kruchenykh, and Viktor Khlebnikov. "A Slap in the Face of Public Taste" (1912). In *Russian Futurism through Its Manifestoes*, ed. Anna Lawton. Ithaca, NY: Cornell University Press, 1988 and Vassily Kandinsky. "On Stage Composition" (1912). In Vassily Kandinsky. *Complete Writings*, vol. 1, ed. Kenneth C. Lindsay and Peter Vergo. Boston, MA: G. K. Hall & Co., 1982, 257.

31. Renato Poggioli. *Theory of the Avant-Garde*. Cambridge, MA: Harvard University Press, 1968, 214.
32. Schechner, "The Five Avant Gardes or . . . Or None," 8.
33. See F. T. Marinetti. "The Variety Theater" (1913). In *Theater im 20. Jahrhundert: Programmschriften, Stilperioden, Reformmodelle*, ed. Manfred Brauneck. Reinbeck: Rowohlt, 1995, 85–92 and Sergey Eisenstein. "Montage of Attractions" (1923), trans. Daniel Gerould. *TDR* 18:1 (March 1974):78–79.
34. Piscator, *The Political Theatre*, 23.
35. Ibid.
36. Brecht, *Werke*, vol. xxi, 237.
37. Qtd. in Lee Baxandall. "Brecht in America, 1935." *TDR* 12:1 (Fall 1967):75.
38. Fredric Jameson. *Postmodernism, or the Cultural Logic of Late Capitalism*. Durham, NC: Duke University Press, 1991, 39.
39. Sieglinde Lemke. "Theories of American Culture in the Name of the Vernacular." In *Theories of American Culture, Theories of American Studies*, ed. Winfried Fluck and Thomas Claviez. Tübingen: Narr, 2003, 155–174.
40. Here the etymological root of "vernacular" is particularly important. "Verna" is the Latin word for "a slave born in his master's house, a native" (see ibid., 163).
41. Grant Farred. *What's My Name? Black Vernacular Intellectuals*. Minneapolis, MN: University of Minnesota Press, 2003, 1.
42. Ibid.
43. Stuart Hall. "Notes on Deconstructing the Popular." In *People's History of Socialist Theory*, ed. Raphael Samuel. London: Routledge, 1981, 227–240.
44. Farred, *What's My Name*, 1.
45. Ibid., 20.
46. See Michael Denning. *The Cultural Front*. London: Verso, 1997 and Lizabeth Cohen. *Making a New Deal: Industrial Workers in Chicago 1919–1939*. Cambridge: Cambridge University Press, 1990.
47. Leo Marx. "The Vernacular Tradition in American Literature." In *Amerikanische Dichtung in der höheren Schule der Interpretation*, ed. H. Galinsky, Leo Marx, and Calvin Rus. Frankfurt/M.: Verlag Moritz Diesterweg, 1958, 46–57. Constance Rourke similarly asserts that American culture is an expression of communal experience, of an indigenous common life praxis and that it can hence not be evaluated according to European standards. Its most distinctive trait is its pragmatic synthesis of fine and useful arts. See Constance Rourke. *The Roots of American Culture and Other Essays*. New York: Harcourt, Brace & Co, 1942.
48. Marx, "The Vernacular Tradition in American Literature" (1958), 50.
49. Ibid., 52.

50. Leo Marx. "The Vernacular Tradition in American Literature." In *Studies in American Culture*, ed. Joseph J. Kwiat and Mary C. Turpie. Minneapolis, MN: Minnesota Press, 1960, 113.

51. Marx, "The Vernacular Tradition in American Literature" (1958), 52.

52. Ibid. According to Marx, this fervent egalitarianism of the vernacular, which found its peak in Whitman and Twain, has become increasingly fragmented ever since. For a discussion of the further evolution of the vernacular trope of the common man, see Thomas Claviez. "'Muted Fanfares': The Topos of the Common Man in the Works of Walt Whitman, William Carlos Williams, and James Agee." In *Aesthetic Transgressions: Modernity, Liberalism, and the Function of Literature*, ed. Thomas Claviez, Ulla Haselstein, and Sieglinde Lemke. Heidelberg: Winter 2005.

53. Marx's essay has to be read in that very context. It too evinces a vernacular political strategy—the concerted effort of a newly emerging discipline of American Studies to break with the hegemony of British literature in English departments.

54. Kenneth Burke. "Revolutionary Symbolism in America." In *American Writers' Congress 1935*, ed. Henry Hart. New York: International Publishers, 1935, 87–94.

55. The question of whether or not America produced the equivalent of a historical avant-garde continues to occupy scholars of American Studies and theater history. The conclusion largely depends on one's definition of the avant-garde. Scholars of the Little Theaters, such as J. Ellen Gainor and Drew Eisenhauer, insist that Provincetown Players like Glaspell and Kreymborg constitute an indigenous avant-garde precisely because of their vehement anti-commercial, bohemian stance and their commitment to experimental forms. These scholars, however, also emphasize that Provincetown avant-gardism differs decisively from its European counterpart due to its fundamental hybridity (combining the modernist impulse for innovation with the commercial impulse for narrative). In my view, it is this very hybridity that fostered an accommodation with the culture industry rather than a fervent rebellion against it. See J. Ellen Gainor. "How High Was Susan Glaspell's Brow?: Avant-Garde Drama, Popular Culture, and Twentieth-Century American Taste," unpublished seminar essay presented at American Society for Theater Research 2004 and Drew Eisenhauer. "Alfred Kreymborg and the Two Modernisms: Modernism, Avant-Garde, and the Provincetown Players," unpublished paper presented at II International Conference on American Theatre & Drama, 18–20 May 2004.

56. Andreas Huyssen. *After the Great Divide: Modernism, Mass Culture, Postmodernism*. Bloomington, IN: Indiana University Press, 1986, 6.

57. Cardullo and Knopf, *Theater of the Avant-Garde 1890–1950* and Arnold Aronson. *American Avant-Garde Theatre*. New York: Routledge, 2000.

58. Aronson, *American Avant-Garde Theatre,* 2. Aronson argues that something comparable to the historical avant-garde did not emerge in the United States until the 1960s, when under the influence of abstract expressionism a theater evolved that "radically altered both the aesthetic and organizational basis upon which performance was created" (Ibid.).

59. Friedrich Wolf. "New York—Theaterfront 1935." In Friedrich Wolf, *Aufsätze über das Theater.* Berlin: Aufbau, 1957, 300, trans. mine. Erwin Piscator likewise wrote about the American theater: "On the one hand, theater as an activity has grown deeper roots in the people; on the other, however, it lacks the hundred stages subsidized by the state or the municipality that we have in Germany. With the exception of four or five stages sponsored with public means, the American theater is an object of individual, i.e. private capitalist enterprise." See Erwin Piscator. "The Dramatic Workshop in New York" (1948). In Erwin Piscator. *Schriften,* vol. 2, ed. Ludwig Hoffmann. Berlin: Henschel, 1968, 155, trans. mine.

60. Kenneth Tynan. "A Bouquet for the British." *Observer* 29 May 1960.

61. Robert Forsythe. "Wanted a Theater." *New Masses* 18 October 1938.

62. Theatre Union prices ranged from 30 cents to $1.50, with more than half the seats under $1. See Ben Blake. *The Awakening of the American Theatre.* New York: Tomorrow Publishers, 1935, 35. The Federal Theatre price scale offered tickets at 10–25 cents, always under $1, often free of charge. See Hallie Flanagan. *Arena.* New York: Duell, Sloan and Pearce, 1940, 30.

63. See Lizabeth Cohen. "The Class Experience of Mass Consumption." In *The Power of Culture,* ed. Richard Wightman Fox and T. J. Jackson Lears. Chicago, IL: University of Chicago Press, 1993, 135–160 and Joan Shelley Rubin. *The Making of Middle/Brow Culture.* Chapel Hill, NC: University of North Carolina Press, 1992.

64. Blake, *The Awakening of the American Theatre,* 6.

65. Janice Radway. *A Feeling for Books.* Chapel Hill, NC: UNC Press, 1997, 152.

66. Janice Radway. "The Scandal of the Middlebrow: The Book-of-the-Month Club, Class Fracture and Cultural Authority." *SAQ* 89:4 (Fall 1991):708.

67. Ibid., 732.

68. Ibid., 708.

69. David Savran. "Middlebrow Anxiety." In David Savran. *A Queer Sort of Materialism: Recontextualizing American Theater.* Ann Arbor, MI: University of Michigan Press, 2003, 15.

70. John Howard Lawson. *With a Reckless Preface.* New York: Farrar & Rhinehart, 1934, vii.

71. Werner Sombart. *Why Is There No Socialism in the United States?* trans. Patricia M. Hocking and C. T. Husbands. White Plains, NY: International Arts and Sciences Press, 1976 (1906).

72. V. F. Calverton. "Proletarianitis." *Saturday Review of Literature* 9 January 1937, 4.

73. Ibid.

74. David Roediger. *The Wages of Whiteness: Race and the Making of the American Working Class*. London: Verso, 1991, 118.

75. Lewis Corey. *The Crisis of the Middle Class*. New York: Coivici Friede Publishers, 1935.

76. "The Pulps and Shinies." *Pen & Hammer Bulletin* 2 (5 April 1934):118.

77. Erin Smith. *Hard-Boiled: Working Class Readers and Pulp Magazines*. Philadelphia, PA: Temple University Press, 2000.

78. See Janice Radway. *Reading the Romance: Woman, Patriarchy, and Popular Literature*. Chapel Hill, NC: University of North Carolina Press, 1991. That workers were also avid readers of canonical novels is shown in Jonathan Rose's *The Intellectual Life of the British Working*. New Haven, CT: Yale University Press, 2001.

79. Henry Hart. "Contemporary Publishing and the Revolutionary Writer." In Henry Hart, ed. *American Writers' Congress*. New York: International Publishers, 1935, 159–162.

80. Louis Adamic. "What the Proletarian Reads." *Saturday Review of Literature* 11:20 (1 December 1934):1. Critics have pointed to some flaws in Adamic's study. According to Barbara Foley, he did not carry out his study in any systematic way and failed to take the role of the publishing industry as well as of public libraries into account. While Foley substantially revised Adamic's argument, rendering a much more differentiated picture of the reception of the proletarian/political novel in her influential study *Radical Representations: Politics and Form in U.S. Proletarian Fiction, 1929–1941* (Durham, NC: Duke University Press, 1993), she too concluded that it did not, by any stretch of the imagination, reach a large number of workers: "Still, even if we take into account the prohibitive prices for hard-cover novels and the likelihood that library copies of proletarian novels routinely reached sizable numbers of working-class readers, the fact remains that the proletarian novel can hardly be said to have attracted a mass audience" (Ibid., 107). See also Walter B. Rideout's *The Radical Novel*, which among other things discusses a study of reading habits in public libraries (Ibid., 237).

81. Adamic, "What the Proletarian Reads," 1.

82. Ibid. The question of what qualified as "well written" was examined in a study by William Gray and Bernice Leary. *What Makes a Book Readable* (Chicago, IL: University of Chicago Press, 1935). The authors came to the conclusion that two-thirds of American readers had limited reading abilities, ranging between elementary and high school proficiency. To accommodate such limitations, a book had to fulfill the following criteria: the content had to be of interest; the style was to be pleasing, neither vexing with overt complexity or simplicity but fitted to the reader's needs; the format was to be attractive; and readers needed to be able to get what they wanted quickly. In general, readability was defined as "easy to understand" and "no big words in it." Moreover, certain structural elements were considered to promote readability, such as simple sentences, personal pronouns, monosyllables and familiar words, and a straightforward narrative instead of complex figures of speech.

83. Adamic, "What the Proletarian Reads," 1.
84. Cohen, "The Class Experience of Mass Consumption," 152. In her case study of consumer behavior among Chicago workers, Cohen demonstrates how workers, while sharing certain modes of consumption with the middle classes, nevertheless made distinct choices that reflected and asserted their distinct ethnic and class origins. Throughout the 1920s, workers would prefer their local stores to chain stores for financial (giving credit) as well as cultural reasons ("shared foodways"). The Depression, however, forced workers to change their consumption behaviors and switch to chain stores. This resulted in a more homogenized working class, increasingly losing its ethnic traces and becoming more and more "Americanized." And yet, while working-class culture became increasingly more grounded in mass culture, it nonetheless remained distinct from the mass culture the middle class participated in (Ibid., 138).
85. Cohen, *Making a New Deal*, 365.
86. Ibid., 366.
87. Daniel Aaron. *Writers on the Left: Episodes in American Literary Communism*. New York: Columbia University Press, 1992 (1961), 2.

Chapter Three: Strike Songs: Working- and Middle-Class Revolutionaries

1. Mordecai Gorelik. *New Theatres for Old*. London: Denis Dobson, 1947 (1940), 271.
2. While two-thirds of all Broadway theaters shut down in 1931, the movie industry boomed (prompting a massive exodus of theater workers to Hollywood). By 1932, 14,000 cinemas had been equipped with sound, attracting 70,000,000 admissions per week in North America. Movie tickets cost a democratic $0.25, in contrast to Broadway tickets starting at $3.50.
3. Ben Blake. *The Awakening of the American Theatre*. New York: Tomorrow Publishers, 1935, 7.
4. The "new" audience was, in fact, not entirely new to the professional theater but had once even determined its repertory, the making and unmaking of actors' careers. During the second half of the nineteenth century, it had, however, been subjected to a series of disciplinary measures by cultural authorities, which had eventually resulted in its relegation from the "highbrow" art of drama to the "lowbrow" entertainment of vaudeville and musical theaters. See Lawrence W. Levine. *Highbrow/Lowbrow: The Emergence of Cultural Hierarchy in America*. Cambridge, MA: Harvard University Press, 1988.
5. Brooks Atkinson. "The Play." *New York Times* 11 December 1931.

6. Percy Hammond. "The Theaters." *New York Herald Tribune* 11 December 1931.
7. Unemployment peaked in 1933 with 17.5 million; in 1940, it was still at 8 million.
8. See Manuel Gomez. "A Proletarian Play on Broadway." *New Masses* January 1932 and Harold Clurman. *The Fervent Years*. New York: Da Capo Press, 1983 (1975), 72.
9. Hallie Flanagan. "A Theater Is Born." *Theatre Arts Monthly* 15 (1931):908.
10. On the role of immigrant workers' theaters, see Bruce McConachie and Daniel Friedman, eds. *Theatre for Working Class Audiences in the United States, 1830–1980*. Westport, CT: Greenwood Press, 1985 and Maxine S. Seller, ed. *Ethnic Theatre in the United States*. Westport, CT: Greenwood Press, 1983.
11. See Daniel Friedman. "A Brief Description of the Workers' Theatre Movement of the Thirties." In *Theatre for Working Class Audiences in the United States, 1830–1980*, ed. Bruce McConachie and Daniel Friedman. Westport, CT: Greenwood Press, 1985, 111–120 and Stuart Cosgrove. "From Shock Troupe to Group Theatre." In *Theatres of the Left 1880–1935: Workers' Theatre Movements in Britain and America*, ed. Raphael Samuel, Ewan MacColl, and Stuart Cosgrove. London: Routledge & Kegan Paul, 1985, 259–279.
12. See John Howard Lawson. "The Crisis in Theater." *New Masses* 15 December 1936.
13. Proletbühne was founded in 1925 as a drama circle of the German ethnic community. It became politicized with the arrival of John Bonn (Hans Bohn) from Germany in 1928. See Stuart Cosgrove. "Prolet Buehne: Agitprop in America." In *Performance and Politics in Popular Drama*, ed. David Brady, Louis James, and Bernard Sharratt. Cambridge: Cambridge University Press, 1980, 201–212.
14. Hallie Flanagan. "Federal Theatre Project." *Theatre Arts* 19 (November 1935):860.
15. Hallie Flanagan. "Report of the Director." *New York Times* 17 May 1936.
16. See, for instance, Elmer Rice. *The Living Theatre*. New York: Harper, 1959.
17. "American Writers Look Left." *Times Literary Supplement* 22 February 1936.
18. Bosley Crowther. "Theatre on the Left." *New York Times* 14 April 1935.
19. Michael Blankfort and Nathaniel Buchwald. "Social Trends in Modern Drama." In *American Writers' Congress 1935*, ed. Henry Hart. New York: International Publishers, 1935, 132.
20. Ira A. Levine. *Left-Wing Dramatic Theory in the American Theatre*. Ann Arbor, MI: University of Michigan Press, 1980, xiv.
21. Blake, *The Awakening of the American Theatre*, 15.
22. Ibid.
23. Ibid., 16.
24. Ibid.

25. Flanagan, "A Theatre Is Born," 914.
26. Michael Gold in foreword to his mass chant *Strike!* published in *New Masses* (July 1926).
27. Blake, *The Awakening of the American Theatre*, 49.
28. Albert Prentis. "Basic Principles." *Workers Theatre* 1 (May 1931):2.
29. Jake Shapiro. "On Breaking Thro' the Proscenium." *Workers Theatre* 1:3 (June 1931):7.
30. Ibid.
31. Ibid.
32. Levine, *Left-Wing Dramatic Theory in the American Theatre*, 108.
33. John Bonn. "Dram Buro Report." *Workers Theatre* (May 1932):8.
34. John Bonn. "Situation and Tasks of the Workers Theatre in the U.S.A." *Workers Theatre* 2:3 (June–July 1932):8. See also his "Constitution of the League of Workers Theatres of U.S.A." *Workers Theatre* (May 1932):14.
35. "Send Us Scripts." *New Theatre* (September 1934):26.
36. Ibid.
37. Ibid.
38. Margaret Larkin. "Building an Audience." *New Theatre* (October 1934), italics hers.
39. Ibid.
40. Conrad Seiler. "Workers Theatre: A Criticism." *New Theatre* (June 1934):17.
41. Larkin reports that Theatre Union managed to secure a 16-week run for its first play *Peace on Earth* with the help of some 158 benefit parties. For its second play *Stevedore*, it managed to arrange 44 benefit parties, thus securing two-thirds of the play's running expenses for a period of 6 weeks. For *Stevedore*, it moreover started a subscription service, which signed up some 1,400 during the first two months of the show alone ("Building an Audience").
42. See John Bonn. "Constitution of the League of Workers Theatres of the U.S.A." *Workers Theatre* (May 1932):14 and "Editorial." *New Theatre* (February 1935):3.
43. Qtd. in Lee Baxandall. "Brecht in America, 1935." *TDR* 12:1 (Fall 1967):75.
44. Clurman, *The Fervent Years*, 148.
45. For more information on the taxi strike and the genesis of Odets's play, see Gerald Weales. "Waiting for Lefty." In *Critical Essays on Clifford Odets*, ed. Gabriel Miller. Boston, MA: G. K. Hall & Co., 1991, 147–152.
46. Clurman, *The Fervent Years*, 148.
47. Ibid.
48. Once *Waiting for Lefty* secured a reputation as the most successful proletarian show in town at the Civic Repertory, it was moved uptown to the Longacre Theatre, where it opened on 26 March 1935. Here, it ran for 136 performances in a double bill with Odets's anti-fascist one-act *Till the Day I Die*. It was then moved to the Belasco, where it ran together with *Awake and Sing!* for another four weeks.

49. Clifford Odets. "How a Playwright Triumphs." *Harper's Magazine* (September 1966), reprinted in *Critical Essays on Clifford Odets*, ed. Gabriel Miller. Boston, MA: G. K. Hall & Co., 1991, 83.
50. Qtd. in David Barbour and Lori Seward. "Waiting for Lefty." *TDR* 28:4 (Winter 1984):40.
51. Odets lists the minstrel show as his immediate point of reference. But the structural similarities of his play to the minstrel show (the use of chorus, end men, specialty men, and interlocutor) are rather tenuous. Odets certainly derives the emotional drive of the play from the agitprop form, which he was familiar with, if not from the street theaters then from the Group's production of the agitprop play *Dimitroff*. See Clifford Odets. "Notes on Production." In Clifford Odets. *Three Plays*. New York: Random House, 1935."
52. Odets, *Three Plays*, 4.
53. Ibid., 48.
54. Odets, "How a Playwright Triumphs," 83.
55. A term used by Sergey Eisenstein. See his essay "Film Form: New Problems." In Sergey Eisenstein. *Film Form: Essays In Film Theory*, ed. Jay Leyda. New York: Harcourt, 1949, 127.
56. Odets, *Three Plays*, 3.
57. Ibid., 53.
58. Ibid.
59. Ibid., 36. The stereotyping of the bad guy is further underlined by the fact that Fatt, Fayette, and Grady were all played by the same actor: Morris Carnovsky at the Civic Repertory and Russell Collins at the Longacre.
60. Joseph Wood Krutch. "Waiting for Lefty and Till the Day I Die." *Nation* 10 April 1935.
61. Odets, *Three Plays*, 22.
62. Ibid., 42.
63. Ibid.
64. Ibid., 48.
65. Ibid., 51.
66. Ibid., 52.
67. Erwin Piscator. *The Political Theatre*, trans. Hugh Rorrison. New York: Avon Books, 1978, 82.
68. Richard Watts. "Sight and Sound." *New York Herald Tribune* 31 March 1935. John Mason Brown agrees that "Mr. Odets seems to have employed a machine gun rather than a pen" ("The Play." *New York Evening Post* 27 March 1935).
69. Eisenstein, "Film Form," 166.
70. See Tom Gunning. "The Cinema of Attraction: Early Film, Its Spectator and the Avant-Garde." *Wide Angle* 8:3–4 (1986):64.
71. Odets, "How a Playwright Triumphs," 83.
72. John Mason Brown. "The Play." *New York Evening Post* 27 March 1935.

73. Robert Garland. "Two Plays by Odets at Longacre Theater." *New York World Telegram* 27 March 1935.

74. Odets, *Three Plays*, 51.

75. Ibid., 16.

76. John Anderson. "Till the Day I Die: 2 Plays by Odets Picture Nazi Terror in Reich, Taxi Strike Here." *New York Evening Journal* 27 March 1935.

77. Brooks Atkinson. "The Play." *New York Times* 27 March 1935.

78. Stanley Burnshaw. "The Theater." *New Masses* 29 January 1935.

79. Krutch, "Waiting for Lefty and Till the Day I Die."

80. Richard Lockridge. "The New Play." *New York Sun* 27 March 1935.

81. Atkinson, "The Play."

82. John Gassner. "American Social Theatre in the Thirties." In *Theatre and Drama in the Making*, vol. 2, ed. John Gassner and Ralph G. Allen. Boston, MA: Houghton Mifflin, 1964, 1003.

83. John Howard Lawson. "History Making Plays." *New Masses* 2 July 1935.

84. Cosgrove, "Prolet Buehne," 211.

85. Arthur Pollock. "The Theater." *Brooklyn Daily Eagle* 27 March 1935.

86. Atkinson, "The Play."

87. See Barbour and Seward, "Waiting for Lefty," 42 and Stuart Cosgrove, Raphael Samuel, and Ewan MacColl, eds. *Theatres of the Left 1880–1935: Workers' Theatre Movements in Britain and America*. New York and London: Routledge & Kegan Paul, 1985.

88. Odets, *Three Plays*, 52.

89. Weales, "Waiting for Lefty," 147.

90. Ibid.

91. Eberhard Brüning. *Das amerikanische Drama der dreißiger Jahre*. Berlin: Rütten & Loening, 1966, 139.

92. Krutch, "Waiting for Lefty and Till the Day I Die."

93. Lawson, "History Making Plays."

94. Ibid.

95. John McCarten. "Revolution's Number One Boy." *New Yorker* 22 January 1938.

96. Lewis Corey. *The Crisis of the Middle Class*. New York: Coivici Friede Publishers, 1935. Corey points out that out of 17.5 million unemployed during the height of the depression, about 45% were workers and 35% were salaried employees.

97. Ibid., 31.

98. See Weales, "Waiting for Lefty," 151. Without doubt, this episode was influenced by Odets's short-lived affiliation with the Communist Party, which lasted a mere eight months (from late 1934 to mid-1935). It quickly disappeared from the script after Odets's separation from CPUSA— already deleted in the 1939 edition of his play. For more details about Odets's CPUSA membership and his later HUAC hearings, see Gerald Rabkin. *Drama and Commitment: Politics in the American Theatre of the Thirties*. Bloomington, IN: Indiana University Press, 1964, 179.

99. Clurman, *The Fervent Years*, 151.
100. John Gassner. "Politics and Theatre." In Morgan Himmelstein. *Drama Was a Weapon: The Left-Wing Theatre in New York, 1929–1941*. New Brunswick: Rutgers University Press, 1963, xv.
101. Clurman, *The Fervent Years*, 124.
102. William Kozlenko. "Introduction." In *The Best Short Plays of the Social Theatre*, ed. W. Kozlenko. New York: Random House, 1939, x.
103. Harold Clurman. "Introduction." In Clifford Odets. *Waiting for Lefty and Other Plays*. New York: Grove Press, 1979, ix.

Chapter Four: Plays of Cash and Cabbages: From Proletarian Melodrama to Revolutionary Realism

1. "Send Us Scripts." *New Theatre* (September 1934):26.
2. Michael Blankfort. "Facing the New Audience." *New Theatre* (November 1934):25.
3. Peter Brooks. *The Melodramatic Imagination*. New Haven, CT: Yale University Press, 1995 (1976), 32.
4. Sergey Dmitrievich Balukhatyi. "Poetika melodramy" (1927). In Sergey Dmitrievich Balukhatyi. *Voprosy Poetiki*. Leningrad: Isdatel'stvo Leningradskogo Universiteta, 1990. Parts of this essay have been translated and published by Daniel Gerould in "Russian Formalist Theories of Melodrama." In *Imitations of Life*, ed. Maria Landy. Detroit, MI: Wayne State Press, 1991, 118–134.
5. Eric Bentley. "Melodrama." In Eric Bentley. *The Life of the Drama*. New York: Atheneum, 1964, 195–218.
6. Brooks, *The Melodramatic Imagination*, 41, italics his.
7. Ibid.
8. Ibid., 20.
9. Henry Schoenmakers and Ed Tan. "'Good Guy Bad Guy' Effects in Political Theater." In *Semiotics of Drama and Theater*, ed. Herta Schmid and Aloysius van Kesteren. Amsterdam: J. Benjamins, 1984, 467–508.
10. Christof Decker. *Hollywoods kritischer Blick: Das soziale Melodrama in der amerikanischen Kultur 1840–1950*. Frankfurt/M.: Campus, 2003, 41.
11. Qtd. in Gerould, "Russian Formalist Theories of Melodrama," 128.
12. Brooks, *The Melodramatic Imagination*, 15.
13. Daniel Gerould. "Gorky, Melodrama, and the Development of Early Soviet Theatre." *Yale/Theatre* 7:2 (Winter 1976):41. Gorky and Lunacharsky initiated a melodrama playwriting contest for Petrograd workers in 1919. Although this particular contest remained unsuccessful, melodrama still prospered as the dominant genre of the revolutionary

and post-revolutionary period from about 1917 to 1928. See also Daniel Gerould and Julia Przyboś. "Melodrama in the Soviet Theater 1917–1928: An Annotated Chronology." *New York Literary Forum* 7 (1980): 75–92.

14. It needs to be stressed that while melodrama for a while also strongly influenced the radical modernist stages of Meyerhold, Eisenstein, Sergey Radlov, and Nikolay Forreger, these directors used the genre toward very different ends. It was above all the sheer theatricality of melodrama, its inherent tendency toward the grand spectacle, which they found exciting and useful for their goal of shocking, astonishing, and stimulating the spectator. See Gerould and Przyboś, "Melodrama in the Soviet Theater 1917–1928."

15. Qtd. in Gerould, "Gorky, Melodrama, and the Development of Early Soviet Theatre," 35, italics mine.

16. Ibid.

17. Ibid., 40.

18. Ibid.

19. Balukhatyi, "Poetika melodramy," 40, trans. mine.

20. Jane Gaines. "The Melos in Marxist Theory." In *The Hidden Foundation: Cinema and the Question of Class*, ed. D. James and R. Berg. Minneapolis, MN: University of Minnesota Press, 1996, 60.

21. Thomas Elsaesser. "Tales of Sound and Fury: Observations on the Family Melodrama" (1972). In *Imitations of Life*, ed. Marcia Landy. Detroit, MI: Wayne State University Press, 1991 and John Cawelti. "The Evolution of Social Melodrama" (1976). In *Imitations of Life*, ed. Marcia Landy. Detroit, MI: Wayne State University Press, 1976, 33–49.

22. Elsaesser, "Tales of Sound and Fury," 72.

23. Ibid.

24. Lothar Fietz. "On the Origins of English Melodrama in the Tradition of Bourgeois Tragedy and Sentimental Drama." In *Melodrama: The Cultural Emergence of a Genre*, ed. Michael Hays and Anastasia Nikolopoulou. New York: St. Martin's Press, 1996, 83–101.

25. Jack Conroy. "The Worker as Writer." In *American Writers' Congress 1935*, ed. Henry Hart. New York: International Publishers, 1935, 84.

26. Albert Maltz, qtd. in Michael Gold. "Change the World." *Daily Worker* 31 December 1935.

27. Qtd. in Ben Blake. *The Awakening of the American Theatre*. New York: Tomorrow Publishers, 1935, 35. Theatre Union managed to organize over 100,000 spectators through various working- and middle-class organizations.

28. Listen Oak. "Theatre Union Replies." *New Theatre* (November 1934):12.

29. Ibid.

30. Blankfort, "Facing the New Audience," 25.

31. Ibid.

32. Albert Maltz and George Sklar. *Peace on Earth: An Anti-War Play in 3 Acts*. New York: Samuel French, 1934, 14.

33. Ibid., 18.

34. Ibid., 66.
35. Ibid., 81.
36. Ibid., 199.
37. Ibid.
38. Ibid., 2.
39. Ibid.
40. Ibid., 18–19.
41. Blankfort, "Facing the New Audience," 25.
42. Elmer Rice. *Seven Plays*. New York: Viking, 1950, 253.
43. Qtd. in Blake, *The Awakening of the American Theater*, 36.
44. John Anderson. "Authors of 'Merry-Go-Round' Retain Their Carbolic Mood in Thrust against War." *New York Evening Journal* 1 December 1933. For more reviews, see Percy Hammond. "The Theaters." *New York Herald Tribune* 30 November 1933; Burns Mantle. "'Peace on Earth' Is Against War." *New York Daily News* 30 November 1930; Richard Lockridge. "The New Play." *New York Sun* 1 December 1933; Robert Garland. "Propaganda Is Polite in Peace on Earth." *New York World Telegram* 1 December 1933; Gilbert Gabriel. "Peace on Earth." *New York American* 30 November 1933; John Mason Brown. "The Play." *New York Evening Post* 1 December 1933; Arthur Pollock. "The Theaters." *Brooklyn Daily Eagle* 1 December 1933; and Bernard Sobel. "'Peace on Earth' Has Premiere at Civic Repertory." *New York Daily Mirror* 30 November 1933.
45. "Peace on Earth." *Nation* 27 December 1933.
46. William Gardener. "The Theatre." *New Masses* 16 January 1934. See also Sherwood Anderson. "Foreword." In *Peace on Earth*. New York: Samuel French, 1934.
47. Further productions of the play were subsequently mounted by the Contemporary Theatre in Los Angeles, the Civic Players of Milwaukee, and the San Francisco Theatre Union. See Albert Maltz. "The Left-Wing Theatre in America." *New Republic* 24 July 1935.
48. Michael Gold. "Stevedore." *New Masses* 1 May 1934 and Gilbert Gabriel. "Stevedore." *New York American* 19 April 1934.
49. Gold, "Stevedore."
50. Gabriel, "Stevedore."
51. John Howard Lawson. "Straight from the Shoulder." *New Theatre* (November 1934):11.
52. John Mason Brown. "The Play." *New York Evening Post* 19 April 1934.
53. Gold, "Stevedore."
54. Paul Peters and George Sklar. *Stevedore*. New York: Covici Friede, 1934, 45, 24.
55. Ibid., 138.
56. Gold, "Stevedore."
57. Peters and Sklar, *Stevedore*, 137.
58. Oak, "Theatre Union Replies," 12.
59. Lawson, "Straight from the Shoulder," 11.
60. Ibid.

61. See Arthur Pollock. "The Theaters." *Brooklyn Daily Eagle* 19 April 1934; Brooks Atkinson. "The Play." *New York Times* 19 April 1934; and Richard Lockridge. "The New Play." *New York Sun* 19 April 1934.

62. Gabriel, "Stevedore."

63. Bernard Sobel. "'Stevedore' Gives Thrilling Session of Able Acting." *New York Daily Mirror* 20 April 1934.

64. Pollock, "The Theaters."

65. Robert Garland. "'Stevedore' Exciting, Full of Violent Vitality." *New York World Telegram* 24 April 1934.

66. Burns Mantle. "Colored Boys Go Rioting in Stevedore." *New York Daily News* 19 April 1934.

67. Gold, "Stevedore."

68. Ibid.

69. Atkinson, "The Play."

70. *Stevedore* ran for 111 performances in the spring and another 64 performances in the fall 1934. It went on the road to Philadelphia, Washington, DC, Detroit, and Chicago. It also played in London, starring Paul Robeson. See Malcolm Goldstein. *The Political Stage: American Drama and Theater of the Great Depression.* New York: Oxford University Press, 1974, 67. Immediately following *Stevedore* was *Sailors of Cattaro* by German playwright Friedrich Wolf.

71. Joseph North. "The Theatre." *New Masses* 2 April 1935.

72. Albert Maltz. *Black Pit.* New York: Putnam's Sons, 1935, 45.

73. Ibid., 108.

74. Ibid., 65.

75. In preparation of the play, Maltz went on a field trip to West Virginia. To prove the accuracy of his play, he included extensive footnotes in the script explaining the customs and habits of the miners.

76. Maltz, *Black Pit*, 105.

77. John Anderson. "'Black Pit': Theatre Union Hits Mark with Play Revealing Life in Coal Fields." *New York Evening Journal* 21 March 1935.

78. Maltz, *Black Pit*, 98.

79. Robert Garland. "'Black Pit' Offering of the Theater Union." *New York World Telegram* 21 March 1935.

80. Arthur Pollock. "The Theaters." *Brooklyn Daily Eagle* 21 March 1935.

81. M. B. "'Black Pit' Opens at Civic Repertory, Is Stirring Drama." *New York American* 21 March 1935.

82. Garland, "'Black Pit' Offering of the Theater Union."

83. Ibid.

84. Richard Lockridge. "The New Play." *New York Sun* 21 March 1935.

85. Margaret Larkin. "How One Type of Worker Is Corrupted by Capitalism Is Theme of 'Black Pit.'" *Daily Worker* 19 March 1935.

86. Carl Reeve. "Despicable Role of a Scab Portrayed in Play 'Black Pit.'" *Daily Worker* 23 March 1935.

87. North, "The Theatre."

88. Jack Stachel. "On the Theatre Union's Play 'Black Pit.'" *Daily Worker* 29 April 1935.

89. Joseph North. "Joseph North Answers Stachel on 'Black Pit.'" *Daily Worker* 30 April 1935.

90. Ibid.

91. See Thomas Postlewait. "From Melodrama to Realism: The Suspect History of American Drama." In *Melodrama: The Cultural Experience of a Literary Genre*, ed. Michael Hays and Anastasia Nikolopoulou. New York: St. Martin's Press, 1996, 39–60.

92. "American Writers Look Left." *Times Literary Supplement* 22 February 1936.

93. "The Coming Writers' Congress." *Partisan Review* (January–February 1935):94–95.

94. Earl Browder. "Communism and Literature." In *American Writers' Congress*, ed. Henry Hart. New York: International Publishers, 1935, 66.

95. In the American context, it was Michael Gold who originally defined proletarian literature in his seminal essay "Go, Left Young Writer!" (1929): "When I say 'go leftward,' I don't mean the temperamental bohemian left, the stale old Paris posing, the professional poetizing etc. No the real thing; a knowledge of working class life in America gained from first hand contacts, and a hard precise philosophy of 1929 based on economics, not verbalism." *New Masses* 4 (January 1929):3–4. See also his essay "Proletarian Realism." *New Masses* (September 1930):4–5.

96. Waldo Frank. "Values of Revolutionary Writers." In *American Writers' Congress*, ed. Henry Hart. New York: International Publishers, 1935, 76.

97. Joseph Freeman. "The Tradition of American Revolutionary Literature." In *American Writers' Congress*, ed. Henry Hart. New York: International Publishers, 1935, 58.

98. Frank, "Values of Revolutionary Writers," 76.

99. Malcolm Cowley. "What the Revolutionary Movement Can Do for a Writer." In *American Writers' Congress*, ed. Henry Hart. New York: International Publishers, 1935, 65.

100. Granville Hicks. "The Dialectics of the Development of Marxist Criticism." In *American Writers' Congress*, ed. Henry Hart. New York: International Publishers, 1935.

101. See, for instance, the debate "What Is Americanism?: A Symposium on Marxism and the American Tradition." *Partisan Review & Anvil* (April 1936):3–16.

102. William Phillips and Phillip Rahv. "Recent Problems of Revolutionary Literature." In *Proletarian Literature in the United States*, ed. Granville Hicks, Michael Gold, Isidor Schneider, Joseph North, Paul Peters and Alan Calmer. New York: International Publishers, 1935, 372.

103. Ibid., 373.

104. Frank, "Values of Revolutionary Writers," 69.

105. Blankfort, "Facing the New Audience," 25.

106. Ibid.
107. John Howard Lawson. "Technique and the Drama." In *American Writers' Congress 1935*, ed. Henry Hart. New York: International Publishers, 1935, 128.
108. Conroy, "The Worker as Writer," 84.
109. Blankfort, "Facing the New Audience," 26.
110. Nathaniel Buchwald and Michael Blankfort. "Social Trends in Modern Drama." In *American Writers' Congress 1935*, ed. Henry Hart. New York: International Publishers, 1935, 133.
111. Ibid., 134.
112. Ira A. Levine. *Left-Wing Dramatic Theory in the American Theatre.* Ann Arbor, MI: University of Michigan Press, 1980, 109.
113. J. M. Olgin. "A Pageant to Soviet Literature." *New Masses* (October 1934):17–18. See also Edwin Seaver. "Review and Comment." *New Masses* 22 October 1935.
114. Olgin, "A Pageant to Soviet Literature," 18.
115. Mordecai Gorelik. *New Theatres for Old.* London: Denis Dobson, 1947 (1940), 357.
116. William Kozlenko. "Introduction." In *The Best Short Plays of the Social Theatre*, ed. William Kozlenko. New York: Random House, 1939, ix.
117. Phillips and Rahv, "Recent Problems of Revolutionary Literature," 372, italics mine.
118. Conroy, "The Worker as Writer," 86.
119. Kenneth Burke. "Revolutionary Symbolism in America." In *American Writers' Congress 1935*, ed. Henry Hart. New York: International Publishers, 1935, 90–92. Burke was vehemently attacked for his proposition since it seemed reminiscent of fascist demagoguery to some and of bourgeois revolutions to others. But he found himself completely vindicated only a couple of months later, when in August 1935 CPUSA officially adapted the Popular Front platform at the Seventh Congress of the Comintern. See Philip Rahv. "Two Years of Progress—From Waldo Frank to Donald Ogden Stewart." *Partisan Review* (February 1938):22–30.
120. "Text of Platform." *Daily Worker* 29 June 1936.
121. Ibid.
122. Granville Hicks. *The Great Tradition: An Interpretation of American Literature since the Civil War.* New York: Macmillan, 1933. Here Hicks postulates that the great tradition in American letters is that of social conflict and revolutionary struggle.
123. Raphael Samuel. "Introduction." In *Theatres of the Left 1880–1935*, ed. Raphael Samuel and Ewan MacColl. New York and London: Routledge, 1985, xx.
124. Rahv, "Two Years of Progress," 25.
125. Ibid.
126. See Sam Smiley. "Friends of the Party: The American Writers' Congresses." *Southwest Review* 54 (Summer 1969):298.
127. According to Mark Naison, party membership rose from 26,000 to 85,000 between 1934 and 1939. See Mark Naison. "Remaking

America: Communists and Liberals in the Popular Front." In *New Studies in the Politics and Culture of U.S. Communism*, ed. Michael Brown et al. New York: Monthly Review Press, 1993, 45.

128. Rahv, "Two Years of Progress," 22.

129. Joseph Freeman. "Towards the Forties." In *The Writer in a Changing World*, ed. Henry Hart. New York: Equinox Cooperative Press, 1937, 10.

130. Malcolm Cowley. "The Seven Years of Crisis." In *The Writer in a Changing World*, ed. Henry Hart. New York: Equinox Cooperative Press, 1937, 45.

131. John Howard Lawson. "The Crisis in the Theatre." *New Masses* 15 December 1936: 35–36.

132. John Gassner. "The Diluted Theatre." *New Theatre & Film* (March 1937): 30.

133. Robert Forsythe. "Wanted a Theatre." *New Masses* 18 October 1938.

134. Although Hemingway was scheduled to give the keynote address in 1937, it was actually opened by Archibald MacLeish since Hemingway had been delayed at the airport (Smiley, "Friends of the Party," 290). The third congress (August 1939) convened more delegates than any of the two previous ones but overall had a much smaller public. Formerly revolutionary writers such as Louis Aragon and Albert Maltz now insisted that literary craftsmanship ought to supersede political considerations. See Joseph Hilton Smyth. "The Third Writers' Congress." *Saturday Review of Literature* 10 June 1937. A fourth congress took place in June 1941, bringing together the largest number of delegates (500) but drawing few writers of influence. With the crumbling of the Popular Front after the Hitler-Stalin Non-Aggression Pact on 22 August 1939, public interest in revolutionary literature was on the wane.

135. Jeffrey D. Mason. *Melodrama and the Myth of America*. Bloomington, IN: Indiana University Press, 1993; Linda Williams. "Melodrama Revised." In *Refiguring American Film Genre: History and Theory*, ed. Nick Browne. Berkeley, CA: University of California Press, 1998, 42–88.

Chapter Five: Why Sing of Skies Above?: Labor Musicals and Living Newspapers

1. Ira A. Levine. *Left-Wing Dramatic Theory in the American Theatre.* Ann Arbor, MI: University of Michigan Press, 1980, 150.

2. Marc Blitzstein. *The Cradle Will Rock: A Play in Music.* New York: Random House, 1938, 41.

3. Ibid., 150.

4. Threatened with deferral and the possibility of complete cancellation, Welles and Houseman invited New York's cultural elite to an unofficial

preview on June 15—the only time Blitzstein's musical was performed as planned, i.e., with full sets, cast, and orchestra.

5. In early 1937, General Motors succumbed to a general strike and extended recognition to the United Auto Workers. U.S. Steel followed suit and agreed to a union contract. Another major corporation, Little Steel, however, remained adamant—only one of its companies, Jones & Laughlin, gave in after a two-day general strike at Aliquippa, Pennsylvania. The conflict between Little Steel and the CIO finally escalated on Memorial Day 1937 in Chicago, when police killed ten strikers and injured eighty. For more background, see John O. Hunter. "Marc Blitzstein's 'The Cradle Will Rock' as a Document of America, 1937." *American Quarterly* 18:2/1 (Summer 1966):227–233 and Michael Denning. *The Cultural Front.* London: Verso, 1997, 287.

6. Hallie Flanagan. *Arena.* New York: Duell, Sloan and Pearce, 1940, 201–205.

7. Washington had already approved a 30% budget cut of FTP funds, resulting in the dismissal of 1,700 theater workers and the discontinuation of the *Federal Theatre Magazine* but also sparking vivid protests in the form of numerous sit-down strikes against WPA's new art policies.

8. See John Houseman. *Run Through: A Memoir.* New York: Simon & Schuster, 1972; Marc Blitzstein. "Out of the Cradle." *Opera News* 13 February 1960, 10–11; Marc Blitzstein. "As He Remembered It." *New York Times* 12 April 1964; and J. E. Vacha. "The Case of the Runaway Opera: The Federal Theatre and Marc Blitzstein's *The Cradle Will Rock*." *New York History* 62:2 (April 1981):133–152.

9. *Cradle Will Rock*, dir. Tim Robbins, Buena Vista Pictures, 1999.

10. Barry B. Witham. "Backstage at *The Cradle Will Rock*." *Theatre History Studies* 12 (1992):213–219.

11. Houseman, *Run Through*, 248.

12. Actors' Equity barred its members from performing in venues other than those rehearsed in if they wanted to retain their WPA status. The Musicians' Union demanded that if the orchestra was to be moved to a private stage, then the number of members had to be increased as well and each had to be paid Broadway salary.

13. Blitzstein, "Out of the Cradle," 11.

14. Houseman, *Run Through*, 270.

15. Blitzstein, "Out of the Cradle," 29.

16. Ibid.

17. Eric Englander. "'Cradle' Rocks at Mercury." *Daily Worker* 7 December 1937.

18. Ibid.

19. Brooks Atkinson. "The Play." *New York Times* 6 December 1937.

20. MacLeish rendered a version of this speech in his "Foreword" to Blitzstein, *The Cradle Will Rock*.

21. "'Cradle Will Rock' Will Continue Run." *New York Times* 20 June 1937, 24.

22. In 1947, Leonard Bernstein staged a concert revival of the play in a similar fashion but for the first time using the original orchestration. In 1964, after Blitzstein's death, he revived it once more in the minimalist Venice style with himself at the piano. The full-scale lavish production that Blitzstein had originally envisioned was not put on till 1960, when it opened at the New York City Opera under the sponsorship of the Ford Foundation.

23. Thomas R. Dash used this comment in his review of Theatre Union's production of *Mother* ("Mother." *Women's Wear Daily* 20 November 1935).

24. Marc Blitzstein. "The Case for Modern Music, Part II." *New Masses* 21 July 1936. See also the sequel "The Case for Modern Music, Part III." *New Masses* 28 July 1936. Blitzstein was a member of the leftist Composers Collective (founded in 1929), which aimed to produce proletarian music in the United States without, however, restricting itself to one particular concept, instead drawing on European modernism, American folklore, *Gebrauchsmusik*, and other sources.

25. Marc Blitzstein. "Author of 'The Cradle' Discusses Broadway Hit." *Daily Worker* 3 January 1938.

26. Qtd. in Houseman, *Run Through*, 245.

27. Blitzstein, "Out of the Cradle," 10.

28. Qtd. in Houseman, *Run Through*, 248.

29. For detailed discussion of score, see Wilfrid Howard Meller. *Music in a New Found Land*. New York: Knopf, 1965.

30. R. D. Darrell. "Blitzstein Brings New Tunes to Music." *New Masses* 28 December 1937.

31. Blitzstein, "As He Remembered It."

32. Blitzstein, *The Cradle Will Rock*, 40.

33. Ibid., 44.

34. Ibid., 51.

35. Ibid., 132–133.

36. Ibid., 114.

37. Ibid., 150.

38. Ibid., 140.

39. Blitzstein, "Author of 'The Cradle' Discusses Broadway Hit."

40. Ibid.

41. Blitzstein, *The Cradle Will Rock*, 107.

42. See Darrell, "Blitzstein Brings New Tunes to Music."

43. Denning, *The Cultural Front*, 292.

44. Virgil Thomson. "In the Theatre." *Modern Music* (January–February 1938):113.

45. Virgil Thomson. "Lively Revival." In Virgil Thomson. *A Virgil Thomson Reader*. Boston, MA: Houghton Mifflin, 1981, 301.

46. Denning, *The Cultural Front*, 292.

47. Burns Mantle. "Cradle Will Rock Given Stage Room by New Mercury Theater." *New York Daily News* 6 December 1937.

48. "Steel Strike Opera Is Put Off by WPA." *New York Times* 17 June 1937.

49. Blitzstein, "Author of 'The Cradle' Discusses Broadway Hit."

50. Denning, *The Cultural Front*, 290.

51. Blitzstein, *The Cradle Will Rock*, 23.
52. Ibid., 97–98.
53. Ibid., 98.
54. Brecht stated this lesson quite bluntly in *The Threepenny Opera* (1928): "Erst kommt das Fressen, dann kommt die Moral" (Food comes first, morals follow). See Bertolt Brecht. *Werke: Große kommentierte Berliner und Frankfurter Ausgabe*, ed. Werner Hecht, Jan Knopf, Werner Mittenzwei and Klaus-Detlef Müller, vol. ii. Frankfurt and Berlin: Suhrkamp and Aufbau, 1989–2000.
55. Denning, *The Cultural Front*, 284.
56. Philip Barr. "Opera in the Vernacular." *American Magazine of Art* 32 (June 1939):356.
57. Ibid.
58. Denning, *The Cultural Front*, 285.
59. Darrell, "Blitzstein Brings New Tunes to Music."
60. Thomson, "In the Theatre," 114.
61. Flanagan, *Arena*, 201.
62. John Mason Brown. "Two on the Aisle." *New York Post* 6 December 1937.
63. Mantle, "Cradle Will Rock Given Stage Room by New Mercury Theater."
64. Richard Lockridge. "The New Play." *New York Sun* 6 December 1937.
65. Atkinson, "The Play."
66. Richard Watts. "The Theaters." *New York Herald Tribune* 6 December 1937.
67. Sidney Whipple. "'Cradle Will Rock' at Mercury Theater." *New York World Telegram* 6 December 1937.
68. Thomson, "In the Theatre," 113.
69. Ibid.
70. Houseman, *Run Through*, 257.
71. On the night of *Cradle*'s unofficial opening, two sit-down strikes took place at federal theaters in New York in protest of WPA cuts: 300 members of the staff of the African American unit of the FTP sat down after the close of a performance at the Lafayette Theatre; at the Federal Theatre of Music, 350 spectators sat down together with the performers of a Brahms concert. See "Steel Strike Opera Is Put Off by WPA." *New York Times* 17 June 1937.
72. "Scenery or No Scenery?: A Symposium." *Theatre Workshop* 2:1 (April–June 1938):12.
73. Englander, "Cradle Rocks at Mercury."
74. "Scenery or No Scenery?" 14.
75. Hallie Flanagan. "Report of the Director." *New York Times* 17 May 1936. See also Hallie Flanagan. "Federal Theatre Project." *Theatre Arts* 19 (November 1935): 865–68.
76. Qtd. in Flanagan, *Arena*, 20.
77. Flanagan, *Arena*, 45. Hopkins stipulated that theater prices were not to exceed $1 (Flanagan, *Arena*, 30). Compare this with Broadway tickets starting at $3.50.

78. Flanagan, "Report of the Director." For more details on background, organization, and scope of FTP, see Willson Whitman. *Bread and Circuses: A Study of the Federal Theatre.* Freeport, NY: Books for Libraries Press, 1937.
79. Flanagan, *Arena*, 20.
80. *Triple-A Plowed Under* apparently employed a total of 243 people (Richard Lockridge. "The New Play." *New York Sun* 16 March 1936), while in *One Third of a Nation* the cast alone consisted of some eighty actors. See Brooks Atkinson. "The Play." *New York Times* 18 January 1938. At its height, FTP employed a total of 13,163 workers (Whitman, *Bread and Circuses*, 31).
81. Flanagan, *Arena*, 183.
82. Douglas McDermott counts a total of thirty-eight Living Newspaper manuscripts in the United States. See his "The Living Newspaper as a Dramatic Form." *Modern Drama* 8:1 (May 1965):82–94. The 1938 Random House edition of all New York Living Newspapers greatly contributed to their popularity. See *Federal Theatre Plays*, vol. 2, ed. Pierre de Rohan. New York: Random House, 1938.
83. See Bosley Crowther. "Once over the WPA." *New York Times* 15 March 1936.
84. Flanagan, *Arena*, 45.
85. See Stuart Cosgrove. "From Shock Troupe to Group Theatre." In *Theatres of the Left 1880–1935: Workers' Theatre Movements in Britain and America*, ed. Stuart Cosgrove, Raphael Samuel, and Ewan MacColl. New York and London: Routledge, 1985, 269.
86. McDermott, "The Living Newspaper as a Dramatic Form," 85.
87. Arthur Arent. *One Third of a Nation.* In *Federal Theatre Plays*, vol. 1, ed. Pierre de Rohan. New York: Random House, 1938, 13.
88. Ibid., 23.
89. Ibid., 40.
90. Ibid., 104.
91. Ibid., 120.
92. Ibid.
93. Ibid., 121.
94. Ibid., 35.
95. McDermott, "The Living Newspaper as a Dramatic Form," 88.
96. Arent, *One Third of a Nation*, 39.
97. Arthur Arent. "The Technique of the Living Newspaper." *Theatre Arts* 22 (November 1938):825.
98. See McDermott, "The Living Newspaper as a Dramatic Form," 86–87.
99. John Dewey. *How We Think.* Boston: Heath, 1933.
100. Arent, *One Third of a Nation*, 41.
101. Arent, "The Technique of the Living Newspaper," 820–821.
102. Hallie Flanagan. "Introduction." In *Federal Theatre Plays*, vol. 2, ed. Pierre de Rohan. New York: Random House, 1938. xi.
103. Levine, *Left-Wing Dramatic Theory in the American Theatre*, 150.

104. "Scenery or No Scenery?" 6.

105. Barbara Foley. *Radical Representations: Politics and Form in U.S. Proletarian Fiction, 1929–1941*. Durham, NC: Duke University Press, 1993, 144.

106. Ibid., 155.

107. Harnett T. Kane. "'One Third of Nation' Packs Dramatic Punch; Well Done." *New Orleans Item* 28 June 1938.

108. John Mullen. "A Worker Looks at Broadway." *New Theatre* (March 1936):26–27.

109. *One Third of a Nation* was developed in a collaborative summer workshop at Vassar College, to which Flanagan had invited directors, designers, and technicians from all over the country. It was then adapted to local conditions before opening simultaneously in various U.S. cities in the beginning of 1938 (Flanagan, *Arena*, 217).

110. See, for instance, Brooks Atkinson. "The Play." *New York Times* 18 January 1938.

111. Sidney Whipple. "Problem of Slums Presented in Play." *New York World Telegram* 18 January 1938.

112. Richard Watts. "The Theaters." *New York Herald Tribune* 18 January 1938.

113. According to newspaper reports, the opening of *Triple-A Plowed Under* was accompanied by heavy police presence at the theater. See, e.g., Brooks Atkinson. "The Play." *New York Times* 16 March 1936 and John Mason Brown. "Two on the Aisle." *New York Evening Post* 16 March 1936.

114. Gilbert Gabriel. "Power." *New York American* 24 February 1937.

115. John Mason Brown. "Two on the Aisle." *New York Post* 18 January 1937.

116. Douglas Gilbert. "Power at the Ritz as Living Newspaper." *New York World Telegram* 24 February 1937.

117. See Stark Young's review of *The Case of Clyde Griffiths* and *Triple-A Plowed Under* in "Expressionistic." *New Republic* 1 April 1936.

118. Ulrich Halfmann. "Formen und Tendenzen des sozialkritischen Dramas der zwanziger und dreißiger Jahre." In *Das amerikanische Drama*, ed. Gerhard Hoffmann. Bern and München: Francke, 1984, 180.

119. Qtd. in Flanagan, *Arena*, 185.

120. Sacvan Bercovitch. *The American Jeremiad*. WI: University of Wisconsin Press, 1978.

121. Arent, *One Third of a Nation*, 117.

122. Ibid., 120.

123. *Triple-A Plowed Under*, 15.

124. John Gassner. "The Theatre: In Praise of New York." *One Act Play Magazine* (February 1938):948.

125. Flanagan, *Arena*, 338.

126. Qtd. in ibid., 347. One committee was headed by Martin Dies in December 1938, the other by Clifton A. Woodrum in spring 1939. The

committees questioned a total of eighty-one plays, out of which only twenty-nine originated with the Federal Theatre. See ibid., 432 for account of allegations.

127. At the hearings as well as in her book *Arena* of 1940, Flanagan repeatedly emphasized that FTP was not a political theater. If it appeared political, she insisted, then only "because life in our country is mixed up with politics" (*Arena*, 78). Her statements certainly have to be read in the context of the hearings and the onset of a rightist backlash against New Deal liberalism. Federal One might not have presented a radical cultural critique, but it was left enough of the center to be considered subversive by its foes. Naturally, its closing for budgetary reasons was only a pretext. Out of a total budget of $4.8 billion, WPA appropriated $27 million for five culture projects (visual arts, music, drama, writing, historical records), less than 0.75% of the total appropriations. None of the other art projects was closed down (until four years later), nor was the money saved on FTP redistributed among them. Already in 1937, the project's magazine *Federal Theatre* had been discontinued and 8,000 employees suspended.

128. See Barry Witham's excellent study of the FTP in Seattle, in which he shows to what extent the various productions influenced public debates and political decisions. Barry Witham. *The Federal Theatre Project: A Case Study*. Cambridge: Cambridge University Press, 2003.

129. Founded in 1900, ILGWU was initially part of the American Federation of Labor (AFL). Its membership consisted mostly of immigrant workers. In 1935, ILGWU formed, together with seven other AFL unions, the Congress of Industrial Organizations (CIO), which attempted to organize the workers in mass-production industries. ILGWU returned to the AFL in the late 1930s in protest against the growing communist influence within the CIO. Under the leadership of David Dubinsky (1932–1966), the membership of the ILGWU grew from 45,000 in 1932 to 450,000 in the 1960s. The union offered a variety of recreational and educational courses such as sports, writing, dance, and theater. In 1936, it founded Labor Stage, which, in addition to various smaller pieces, staged two major productions: John Wexley's *Steel* (January 1937) and *Pins and Needles*.

130. Qtd. in Harry Goldman. "When Social Significance Hit Broadway." *Theatre Quarterly* 7:28 (Winter 1977–1978):26.

131. Pins and Needles: Souvenir Program (1938), unpublished document at New York Public Library Theater Collection.

132. All lyrics are taken from the unpublished song sheets at the Music Archive of the New York Public Library of the Performing Arts at Lincoln Center. Some of them have been reprinted in Goldman, "When Social Significance Hit Broadway."

133. Richard Watts. "The Theaters." *New York Herald Tribune* 13 December 1937.

134. From unpublished song sheets, New York Public Library of the Performing Arts at Lincoln Center.

135. Ibid.

136. Ibid.
137. John Mason Brown. "In Praise of 'Pins and Needles.'" *New York Post* 6 December 1937.
138. E. D. B. "The Theater." *Brooklyn Daily Eagle* 7 January 1938.
139. Watts, "The Theaters."
140. Brown, "In Praise of 'Pins and Needles.'"
141. Watts, "The Theaters."
142. Sidney Whipple. "The Rich Cleverly Satirized." *New York World Telegram* 30 December 1937.
143. Eleanor Roosevelt. "My Day." *Raleigh News Observer* 17 February 1938.
144. From unpublished song sheets, New York Public Library of the Performing Arts at Lincoln Center.
145. Ibid.
146. Qtd. in Goldman, "When Social Significance Hit Broadway," 39.
147. Watts, "The Theaters."
148. Brown, "In Praise of 'Pins and Needles.'"
149. Ben Irwin. "The AFL Theatre Presents." *Daily Worker* 17 June 1936.
150. Pins and Needles: Souvenir Program (1938).
151. Robert Coleman. "Pins and Needles." *New York Daily Mirror* 8 January 1938.
152. From unpublished song sheets, New York Public Library of the Performing Arts at Lincoln Center.
153. Qtd. in Harry Goldman. "Pins and Needles: A White House Command Performance." *Educational Theatre Journal* 30:1 (1978):96.
154. "President in Stitches or Sew It Seams." *New York Time* 13 March 1938. See also "Theatre." *Time Magazine* 14 March 1938.
155. Qtd. in Goldman, "When Social Significance Hit Broadway," 36.
156. Ibid.
157. During the troupe's national tour, Pearman and other black actors again and again encountered segregation. The city of Cleveland refused to let her go on stage unless she played a maid. Pearman had the week off with pay. See Goldman, "When Social Significance Hit Broadway," 32.
158. Ibid.
159. Nettie Harary qtd in ibid., 29.
160. Whipple, "The Rich Cleverly Satirized."
161. "The Theater," *Brooklyn Daily Eagle* 7 January 1938.
162. J. G. "The Play." *New York Times* 29 November 1937.
163. Qtd. in Goldman, "When Social Significance Hit Broadway," 32.
164. Mary McCarthy. "Theater Chronicle." *Partisan Review* (April 1938):52.
165. N. C. "Somebody Has Given the Revised 'Pins' the Needles." *Daily Worker* 30 November 1939. *Daily Worker* had at first endorsed the show as "a most zestful, buoyant musical revue [. . .] which no one should miss." See Eric Englander. "Sparkling Revue on Labor Stage." *Daily Worker* 29 November 1937.

166. N. C. "Somebody Has Given the Revised 'Pins' the Needles."

167. Pins and Needles: Souvenir Program (1938).

168. From unpublished song sheets, New York Public Library of the Performing Arts at Lincoln Center.

169. Ibid.

170. Ibid.

171. Of the four songs that were kept through the entire run of the revue, three were working-class romances: "Song with Social Significance," "Nobody Makes a Pass at Me," and "Sunday in the Park" (the fourth was "Four Little Angels of Peace"). Of the seven original songs published as sheet music, six were songs of love and everyday life, the three above plus "Chain Store Daisy," "What Good Is Love?" and "One Big Union for Two" (the seventh was "Doing the Reactionary"). See Denning, *The Cultural Front*, 301.

172. Denning also claims that it was thanks to these songs that *Pins and Needles* survived the crisis brought on by the conflict between AFL and CIO and the Hitler-Stalin Pact (Denning, *The Cultural Front*, 299). It needs to be added that Dubinsky and Schaffer deliberately shied away from any radical political stance. As Dubinsky, who had at first helped to establish the CIO, returned the ILGWU to the AFL, Schaffer fired director Charles Friedman and actress Millie Weitz from the show for their communist sympathies.

173. Vice President Rose Pesotta (1934–1944) was the only female official in the ILGWU.

174. Denning, *The Cultural Front*, 306.

175. Grant Farred. *What's My Name? Black Vernacular Intellectuals.* Minneapolis, MN: University of Minnesota, 2003, 1.

176. Denning, *The Cultural Front*, 309.

177. Denning remarks on this process only in passing, seeing in the erasure of ethnic markers above all an expression of the "backstage struggles and controversies" that marked the second generation's attempt to create a culture that was distinct from their parents' enclave immigrant culture (Ibid., 307–308).

178. Arguably, the show remained public property due to the broadcasting of some of its most popular songs on the radio. Yet, even here cosmetic changes took place before their release, illustrating the deliberate attempt of depoliticizing its lyrics. "Sing Me a Song of Social Significance" was banned by NBC as "not suitable" for public broadcast. The NBC censor department likewise demanded that Rome change the lyrics in "One Big Union for Two" from "Fifty million union members can't be wrong" to "fifty thousand happy couples can't be wrong" (Manngreen. "Left on Broadway." *Daily Worker* 26 January 1938).

179. See Fredric Jameson. "Reification and Utopia in Mass Culture." *Social Text* 1 (Winter 1979):130–148 and Richard Dyer. "Entertainment and

Utopia." In *Genre: The Musical*, ed. Rick Altman. London: Routledge, 1981.
180. Jameson, "Reification and Utopia in Mass Culture," 144.
181. See Dyer, "Entertainment and Utopia," 177.
182. Hans Magnus Enzensberger. "Constituents of a Theory of the Media." In *Sociology of Mass Communication: Selected Readings*, ed. Dennis McQuail. Harmdonsworth: Penguin Books, 1972, 114. Rick Altman likewise asserts that "in leaving normal day-to-day causality behind, the music creates a utopian space in which the singers and dancers achieve a unity unimaginable in the now superseded world of temporal, psychological causality" (Rick Altman. *The American Film Musical*. Bloomington, IN: Indiana University Press, 1987, 68).
183. Dyer, "Entertainment and Utopia," 185, italics his.
184. From unpublished song sheets, New York Public Library of the Performing Arts at Lincoln Center.
185. Ibid.
186. Jameson, "Reification and Utopia in Mass Culture," 141.
187. Roosevelt, "My Day."
188. Qtd. in Goldman, "When Social Significance Hit Broadway," 39.
189. McCarthy, "Theater Chronicle," 52.
190. Theodor W. Adorno and Max Horkheimer. "Kulturindustrie: Aufklärung als Massenbetrug." In Theodor W. Adorno and Max Horkheimer. *Dialektik der Aufklärung*. Frankfurt/M.: Fischer, 1998, 128–176.
191. Theodor W. Adorno. *Gesammelte Schriften*, vol. 10/1, ed. Rolf Tiedeman. Frankfurt/M.: Suhrkamp, 1970–1986, 338, italics and trans. mine.
192. This claim might seem like a sweeping generalization itself to students of the Frankfurt School. After all, Adorno and Horkheimer briefly beckon to the housewife at the movies seeking refuge and rest from the routines of her work life for a couple of hours. The "Hausfrau," however, is not central to their thesis on the culture industry as a form of anti-enlightenment. Walter Benjamin, also affiliated with the Frankfurt School, offers a more complex and differentiated analysis of the interaction of the masses with mass cultural products. In his seminal essay "The Work of Art in the Age of Mechanical Reproduction" (1936–1939), he convincingly argues with the example of film that as a mass medium its aesthetics might be entirely subordinated to the laws of capital but that precisely this commodity aesthetic also trains new modes of perception in the recipient, which might be appropriated for revolutionary purposes. "Das Kunstwerk im Zeitalter seiner technischen Reproduzierbarkeit." In Walter Benjamin. *Gesammelte Schriften*, vol. vii/2, ed. Rolf Tiedemann and Hermann Schweppenhäuser. Frankfurt/M.: Suhrkamp, 1989, 350–384.
193. From unpublished song sheets, New York Public Library of the Performing Arts at Lincoln Center.
194. Ibid.

Chapter Six: Toward Postmodernism: The Political Theater of the 1960s

1. Sohnya Sayres, Anders Stephanson, Stanley Aronowitz, and Fredric Jameson. "Introduction." In *The 60s without Apology*, ed. Sohnya Sayres, Anders Stephanson, Stanley Aronowitz, and Fredric Jameson. Minneapolis, MN: University of Minnesota Press, 1984, 1.

2. Howard Stein. "The Uncomfortable Theater." *Dialogue* 8:2 (1975): 36.

3. O. L. Guernsey, Jr. "The Season in New York." In *The Best Plays of 1970–1971: The Burns Mantle Yearbook of the Theatre*, ed. O. L. Guernsey, Jr. New York: Mead Dodd, 1971, 9.

4. Ron Davis. "Introductory Note." *Radical Theatre Festival*. San Francisco Mime Troupe, San Francisco, 1969, 7.

5. See Theodore Shank. "Political Theater, Actors and Audiences: Some Principles and Techniques." *Theater* 10:2 (1979):94–103. Arthur Sainer makes a similar claim about the need for an inherently non-illusionist approach to political theater in *The Radical Theatre Notebook*. New York: Avon Books, 1975, 15.

6. Arnold Aronson. *American Avant-Garde Theatre: A History*. New York: Routledge, 2000, 3.

7. Ibid.

8. Recently, critics such as J. Ellen Gainor and Drew Eisenhauer have shown how a similar kind of work had already been accomplished by the Provincetown Players in the 1910s and 1920s. However, as argued in greater detail in chapter two, I agree with Robert Knopf, Bert Cardullo, Aronson, and Andreas Huyssen that these earlier iconoclastic experiments did not amount to a full-blown historical avant-garde in Bürger's sense. See note 55, chapter 2.

9. See, e.g., Mordecai Gorelik. *New Theatres for Old*. London: Dobson, 1940; Bertolt Brecht. *Brecht on Theatre*, ed. and trans. John Willett. New York: Hill & Wang, 1964; and Eric Bentley's *Theory of the Modern Stage*. Hamondsworth: Penguin, 1968. Charles Laughton's brilliant *Galilei* interpretation in Beverly Hill, Los Angeles in 1947, Marc Blitzstein's triumphant revival of *Threepenny Opera* in 1954 at the Theater de Lys in Greenwich Village, and finally the international success of *Mother Courage* in Paris in 1954 had further paved the way for Brecht in the United States.

10. See Frank Anderson Trapp. "The Armory Show: A Review." *Art Journal* 23:1 (Autumn 1963):2–9. The revival of the Armory Show was organized by the Munson-William-Proctor Institute in Utica, New York, and was shown there at first before being moved to New York City. The opening of the show was also shown on network television. Frank Trapp organized an earlier exhibition based on the original show at Amherst College in Amherst, Massachussetts in 1958.

11. Andreas Huyssen. *After the Great Divide: Modernism, Mass Culture, Postmodernism.* Bloomington, IN: Indiana University Press, 1986, 167.
12. Sally Banes. *Greenwich Village 1963.* Durham, NC: Duke University Press, 1993, 6, italics hers.
13. Qtd. in Françoise Kourilsky. "Dada and Circus: Peter Schumann's Bread and Puppet Theatre." *TDR* 18:1 (March 1974):108.
14. Peter Brook. *The Empty Stage.* New York: Simon & Schuster, 1968, 65.
15. Davis, "Introductory Note," 10.
16. Qtd. in Kourilsky, "Dada and Circus," 105.
17. Davis, "Introductory Note," 16.
18. Helen Brown and Jane Seitz. "With the Bread and Puppet Theatre: An Interview with Peter Schumann." *TDR* 12:2 (Winter 1968):70.
19. Peter Schumann. "Bread and Puppets." *TDR* 14:3 (1970):35.
20. Qtd. in Brown and Seitz, "With the Bread and Puppet Theatre," 66.
21. See Stefan Brecht. *The Bread and Puppet Theatre*, vol. 1. London and New York: Methuen and Routledge, 1988, 519–522 for various accounts of the parade as well as of similar parades.
22. Qtd. in Erika Munk. "TDR Comment." *TDR* 14:3 (1970):34.
23. Roland Barthes. "Diderot, Brecht, Eisenstein." In *Image-Music-Text*, ed. Stephen Heath. New York: Hill and Wang, 1977, 73–74. Brecht defines the *Gestus* (which John Willett translates as "gest") as "the mimetic and gestural expression of the social relationships prevailing between people of a given period." See Bertolt Brecht. *Brecht on Theatre*, ed. and trans. John Willett. New York: Hill and Wang, 1964, 139.
24. Qtd. in Brown and Seitz, "With the Bread and Puppet Theatre," 69.
25. Qtd. in S. Brecht, *The Bread and Puppet Theatre,* 580.
26. Qtd. in Kourilsky, "Dada and Circus," 106.
27. S. Brecht, *The Bread and Puppet Theatre,* 45.
28. Ibid.
29. John Bell. "Beyond the Cold War: Bread and Puppet Theater and the New World Order." In *Staging Resistance: Essays on Political Theater*, ed. Jeanne Colleran and Jenny Spencer. Ann Arbor, MI: University of Michigan Press, 1998, 47.
30. Brecht, *Brecht on Theatre,* 133.
31. Qtd. in S. Brecht, *The Bread and Puppet Theatre,* 682.
32. Nicole Zand. *Le Monde* 26 April 1968, qtd. in Christian Dupavillon and Etienne George. *Bread and Puppet Theatre: Spectacles en Noir et Blanc.* Paris: Les Loges, 1978, 9.
33. George Dennison. "Fire." *TDR* 14:3 (1970):42.
34. Schumann, "Bread and Puppets," 35.
35. Roland Barthes. "On Bunraku." *TDR* 15:2 (1971):81.
36. Gerd Burger. *Agitation und Argumentation im politischen Theater.* Berlin: Verlag für Wissenschaft und Bildung, 1993, 13.
37. Beth Cleary. "Negation Strategies: The Bread and Puppet Theatre and Performance Practice." *New England Theatre Journal* 9 (1998):27.

38. Ibid., 29.
39. Ernst Bloch. *The Principle of Hope*, trans. N. Plaice, 3 vols. Cambridge, MA: MIT Press, 1986, 98.
40. Qtd. in Brown and Seitz, "With the Bread and Puppet Theatre," 64.
41. Greg Cuma, ed. *Bread and Puppet: Stories of Struggles & Faith from Central America.* Burlington, VT: Green Valley Film and Art Inc., 1985, 14.
42. Qtd. in Brown and Seitz, "With the Bread and Puppet Theatre," 64.
43. Qtd. in Burger, *Agitation und Argumentation im politischen Theater,* 53.
44. See Theodore Shank. *Beyond the Boundaries: American Alternative Theatre,* rev. ed. Ann Arbor, MI: University of Michigan Press, 2002, 5.
45. Barry Goldensohn. "Peter Schumann's Bread and Puppet Theater." *Iowa Review* (Spring 1977):73.
46. The role of redemption and regeneration is most emblematically embodied in *Our Domestic Resurrection Circus*, in which a giant puppet gets burned and resurrected every year. Bread and Puppet performed the *Resurrection Circus* annually from 1970 to 1998 in Vermont (once also in France).
47. Schumann, "Bread and Puppet," 35.
48. Whether Bread and Puppet offers "a viable model for political theater of the future," as John Bell claims, is debatable ("Beyond the Cold War: Bread and Puppet Theater and the New World Order," 52). To be sure, Schumann has practiced his form of political theater for more than forty years. But as he himself admits, while Bread and Puppet has found a strong following (attracting between 20,000 and 40,000 spectators each year at *Our Domestic Resurrection Circus* in Vermont), it has hardly effected profound cultural change. Moreover, the counter-cultural spirit of Bread and Puppet, which has been so essential to its politics, has become more and more reified, as evident in the history of *Our Domestic Resurrection Circus*. See John Bell. "The End of Our Domestic Resurrection Circus: Bread and Puppet Theater and Counterculture Performance in the 1990s." *TDR* 43:3 (Fall 1999):62–80.
49. Peter Schumann. *The Old Art of Puppetry in the New World Order: A Lecture with Fiddle by P. Schumann.* St. Johnsbury, VT: Troll Press, 1993, 7.
50. "Ce que nous voulons, c'est ouvrir quelque chose. Non pas inventer un problème et essayer de le résoudre, mais inventer un problème et le laisser là. Cette ouverture me paraît essentielle. [...] J'ai l'impression que ce que nous faisons se situe avant la prise de conscience, ... il s'agit de quelque chose qui se trouve plus bas, qui est plus simple et plus facile d'accès que conscience." ("What we would like to achieve, is to open up something. Not to invent a problem and try to solve it, but to invent a problem and to leave it there. This aperture seems essential to me. I am under the impression that what we are doing is situated prior to consciousness. [...] It is about something lower/more profound, something that is more simply and more easily accessible than consciousness.) Qtd. in S. Brecht, *The Bread and Puppet Theatre,* 580, trans. mine.

51. Qtd. in Beth Agby. "El Teatro Campesino: Interview with Luis Valdez." *Tulane Drama Review* 11:4 (Summer 1967):78.
52. Luis Valdez. "El Teatro Campesino." *Ramparts* (July 1966):55. See also Luis Valdez. "The Actos." In El Teatro Campesino. *Actos*. San Juan Bautista, CA: Menyah Productions, 1971.
53. Luis Valdez. "Notes on Chicano Theater." In El Teatro Campesino. *Actos*. San Juan Bautista, CA: Menyah Productions, 1971, 2.
54. Ibid.
55. Valdez, "El Teatro Campesino," 55.
56. Jorge Huerta. "Chicano Agit-Prop: The Early Actos of El Teatro Campesino." *Latin American Theatre Review* 10:2 (1977):48. Brecht himself translated *Lehrstück* as "learning play." See his "The German Drama: Pre-Hitler." In Brecht, *Brecht on Theatre*, 79.
57. El Teatro Campesino. *Actos*. San Juan Bautista, CA: Menyah Productions, 1971, 16.
58. Ibid.
59. Ibid., 19.
60. Ibid.
61. Ibid., 28.
62. Ibid., 30.
63. Ibid., 34.
64. Ibid.
65. Brook, *The Empty Stage*, 65.
66. The term *rascuache* or *rascuachismo* refers to Mexican/Chicano lowbrow proletarian culture, which in being pitched against the dominant Europeanized culture of Mexico, asserts the pride of the dispossessed. Moreno was widely considered the Mexican counterpart to Chaplin. For more information on Moreno's *rascuachismo*, see Ilan Stavans. "The Riddle of Cantinflas: On Laughter and Revolution." *Transition* 67 (1995):22–46.
67. El Teatro Campesino, *Actos*, 31.
68. Carlos Morton. "La Serpiente Sheds Its Skin: The Teatro Campesino." *TDR* 18:4 (December 1974):75.
69. Jorge Huerta. *Chicano Theater: Themes and Forms*. Ypsilanti, MI: Bilingual Press, 1982, 15.
70. Qtd. in Agby, "El Teatro Campesino," 78.
71. Ibid.
72. Ibid.
73. Valdez, "The Actos," 5.
74. Valdez, "El Teatro Campesino," 55.
75. Huerta, *Chicano Theater*, 27.
76. Yolanda Broyles-González. *El Teatro Campesino: Theater in the Chicano Movement*. Austin, TX: University of Texas Press, 1994, 6.
77. Ibid., 7.
78. See, for instance, the work of Gloria Anzaldua. *Borderlands/La Frontera: The New Mestiza*. San Francisco, CA: Aunt Lute Foundation, 1987 and

Trinh T. Minh-ha. "Not You/Like You: Post-Colonial Women and the Interlocking Questions of Identity and Difference." In *Making Face, Making Soul*, ed. Gloria Anzaldua. San Francisco, CA: Aunt Lute Foundation, 1990.

79. Brecht, *Brecht on Theatre*, 108.
80. For more information on Karl Valentin's influence on Brecht, see Denis Clandra. "Karl Valentin and Bertolt Brecht." *TDR* 18:1 (March 1974):86–98.
81. Stavans. "The Riddle of Cantinflas." 36.
82. At least not in the early *actos*. Toward the late 1960s, Teatro Campesino developed a new form of theater, the *mitos*, a kind of religious theater inspired by Mayan philosophy. If the *acto* is the perfect tool for explaining the external (economic) struggle of the Chicano, then the *mitos* is created for expressing the internal (cultural) struggle of La Raza (Valdez, "The Actos," 3). In this regard, we perceive a rapprochement in the aesthetics of Teatro Campesino and Bread and Puppet, whose performances of the late 1960s also went into an increasingly religious and mythological direction.
83. Fredric Jameson. "Periodizing the Sixites." In *The 60s without Apology*, Ed. Sohnya Sayres, Anders Stephanson, Stanley Aronowitz, and Fredric Jameson. Minneapolis, MN: University of Minnesota Press, 1984, 207.
84. Clement Greenberg. "Avant-Garde and Kitsch." *Partisan Review* 6:5 (Fall 1939):39. See also Dwight Macdonald. "Masscult and Midcult." *Partisan Review* 27:2 (1960):203–233.
85. Oscar Handlin. "Comments on Mass and Popular Culture." In *Culture for the Millions?: Mass Media in Modern Society*, ed. Norman Jacobs. Princeton, NJ: D. Van Nostrand, 1961.
86. Greenberg, "Avant-Garde and Kitsch," 36.
87. Huyssen, *After the Great Divide*, 188.
88. Albert Poland and Bruce Mailman, eds. *The Off Off Broadway Book: The Plays, People, Theatre*. IN : Bobbs-Merrill, 1972, xii.
89. Ibid.
90. Banes, *Greenwich Village 1963*, 86.
91. See Morton, "La Serpiente Sheds Its Skin," 71–76. Numerous other examples of theater groups working and often living together could be mentioned; foremost among them are the Living Theatre, the Open Theatre, the Judson Poets' Theatre. See also Banes, *Greenwich Village 1963*, 33–81.
92. Banes, *Greenwich Village 1963*, 6.
93. Ibid., 8.
94. Fredric Jameson. *Postmodernism, or the Cultural Logic of Late Capitalism*. Durham, NC: Duke University Press, 1991, 46.
95. Huyssen, *After the Great Divide*, 170.
96. Ibid., 195.
97. Ibid., 170.

98. See Huyssen, *After the Great Divide;* Jameson, *Postmodernism, or the Cultural Logic of Late Capitalism;* and Linda Hutcheon. *A Poetics of Postmodernism: History, Theory, Fiction.* New York: Routledge, 1988.

99. Huyssen, *After the Great Divide;* Jameson, *Postmodernism, or the Cultural Logic of Late Capitalism;* and Linda Hutcheon. *A Poetics of Postmodernism: History, Theory, Fiction.* New York: Routledge, 1988.

100. Fredric Jameson. "Postmodernism and Consumer Society." In *The Anti-Aesthetic: Essays on Postmodern Culture,* ed. Hal Foster. Seattle, WA: Bay Press, 1983, 125.

101. Philip Auslander. *Presence and Resistance: Postmodernism and Cultural Politics in Contemporary American Performance.* Ann Arbor, MI: University of Michigan Press, 1992, 31.

102. Ibid., 29.

103. Tony Kushner. "Notes about Political Theater." *Kenyon Review* 19:3–4 (Summer/Fall 1997):21.

104. Michael Cunningham. "Thinking about Fabulousness." In *Tony Kushner in Conversation,* ed. Robert Vorlicky. Ann Arbor, MI: University of Michigan Press, 1998, 63.

105. See Tony Kushner. "The Theatre of the Fabulous." In *Out on Stage: An Anthology of Contemporary Gay Male Drama,* ed. John Clum. Boulder, CO: Westview-Harper Collins, 1996.

106. See Henry Louis Gates. *The Signifying Monkey: A Theory of African American Literary Criticism.* New York: Oxford University Press, 1988.

107. For an in-depth discussion of Parks's work, see Ilka Saal "The Politics of Mimicry: The Minor Theater of Suzan-Lori Parks." *South Atlantic Review* 7:2 (Spring 2005):57–71.

Index

Ubersfeld, Anne, 189
Uj Elöre, 54
Ukrainian Dramatic Circle, 54

Valdez, Luis, *see also* El Teatro
    Campesino, 164–170, 172, 176,
    219, 220
Valentin, Karl, 171, 220
vaudeville, 27, 115, 121, 137, 154,
    195
Venice Theatre, 112, 114, 122
Verfremdung, see also alienation, 10,
    13, 20, 38, 158, 165–166
vernacular/vernacularity/vernaculari
    ze, 2–5, 7–8, 19–20, **37–42**, 45,
    51, 60, 62, 68, 81, 101, 106,
    108, 120–123, 128–132, 144,
    154–156, 159–161, 164,
    169–172, **173–181**, 192
    vernacular theater, *see also*
        vernacular political theater,
        4–5, 44, 136, 155
Vietnam War, 157, 160
Volksbühne, 111, 125, 129

Waiting for Lefty (1935), 5–6, 26,
    62–75, 101, 104, 112, 118–121,
    129–130, 197–198, 199, 200
Waldorf, Wilella, 17, 185
Wallace, Henry, 42
Watts, Richard, 67, 122, 131, 138,
    198, 209, 211
We, the People (1933), 88, 96
Weales, Gerald, 71–72, 197
Weill, Kurt, 111, 115
Weitz, Millie, 140, 142–143, 214
Welles, Orson, 112–114, 122, 206
West, Nathanael, 102
Wexley, John, 19, 212

Whipple, Sidney, 122, 131, 138,
    141, 209, 211, 213
Whitman, Walt, 40
Wilder, Thornton, 130
Willett, John, 183, 184, 186, 217
Williams, Linda, 109, 206
Williams, Raymond, 148
Willis, Paul, 148
Windsor Theatre, 140, 142
Wise Man (1923), 155
Witham, Barry, 113, 212
WLT, *see under* Workers Laboratory
    Theatre
Wolf, Friedrich, 43, 83, 186, 203
Wolfson, Victor, 16, 83, 185
Women's Wear Daily, 208
Workers' Drama League, 55
Workers Laboratory Theatre (WLT),
    55, 59, 61–62
Workers Theatre, 55, 61, 62, 197
Works Progress Administration
    (WPA), 56, 122, 123, 131, 207,
    209, 210, 212
Wounds of Vietnam (1967), 160
WPA, *see under* Works Progress
    Administration
Wright, Richard, 102
Writers' Congress
    American Writers' Congress, 6,
        18, 21, 57, 77, **101–109**,
        204, 205
    Soviet Writers' Congress, 60

Yiddish Art Theatre, 54

Zach, Benjamin, 136
Ziegfeld Follies (1907–1916), 137
Zola, Émile, 32, 189
Zoo Story (1959), 151